The Jekyll Island Club

The Jekyll Island Club

Southern Haven
for America's Millionaires

William Barton McCash
and June Hall McCash

The University of Georgia Press

Athens and London

Designed by Sandra Strother Hudson
and Madelaine Cooke
Set in Cheltenham by the Composing Room
of Michigan, Inc.
Printed and bound by Thomson-Shore

The paper in this book meets the guidelines for
permanence and durability of the Committee on
Production Guidelines for Book Longevity of the
Council on Library Resources.

Printed in the United States of America
93 92 91 90 89   5 4 3 2 1

Library of Congress Cataloging in Publication Data

McCash, William Barton, 1931–
    The Jekyll Island Club: Southern haven for
America's millionaires / William Barton McCash
and June Hall McCash.
        p.   cm.
    Bibliography: p.
    Includes index.
    ISBN 0-8203-1070-0 (alk. paper)
    1. Jekyl Island Club (Jekyll Island, Ga.)—
History. I. McCash, June Hall. II. Title.
HS2725.J45J456 1989
366′.9758742—dc19   88-17520
                                         CIP

British Library Cataloging in Publication Data
available

To the memory of Richard A. Everett

and to our children,

Pam, Vicki, Michael, Rodney, and Bren

Contents

Preface

A casual trip to Jekyll Island, Georgia, in the summer of 1983 and a tour of its historic district provided the impetus for this book. As we sought to learn more about the famous club that once flourished there but which had faded away in the wake of the Great Depression and World War II, we were astonished to discover how little had been written on the subject. There were, to be sure, a few pamphlets and guidebooks, some promotional literature, here and there a chapter in a longer monograph, and a series of brief but penetrating articles penned by the late Richard A. Everett under the pseudonym of "Porcupine" for *Georgia's Coastal Illustrated*, but little more.

The reason for this paucity of information quickly became apparent. Extant club records were meager, having been for the most part destroyed or lost after the state of Georgia assumed control of the island. The correspondence of club officers, members, and employees, to the extent that it was available at all, was widely scattered and difficult to find. And surprisingly few modern biographies of the businessmen who belonged to the organization had been written and those that had been published shed sparse light on Jekyll activities. To reconstruct the history of the Jekyll Island Club from its inception to its close, therefore, it became necessary to travel extensively, visiting repositories from Saint Paul to New York and from Boston to Brunswick in search of primary sources. Four years of research in both public and private holdings, coupled with occasional serendipitous discoveries, allowed us finally to piece together and to document the captivating story of the Jekyll Island Club, stripped of myth and enhanced by hundreds of historic photographs.

In the process we inevitably incurred a debt to many individuals and institutions for their generous assistance. In the early stages of our research Liesel Boettcher, the widow of Richard A. Everett, kindly permitted us unlimited access to his collection of photographs and files that contained a wealth of biographical, genealogical, and statistical data pertaining to the club and that have since been donated to the Coastal Georgia Historical Society, Saint Simons Island.

We are also indebted to Dr. Thomas A. Rhodes, director of the Museums and Historic Preservation Division of the Jekyll Island Authority and to his staff, past and present, for their courteous treatment and for opening their archives and the historic houses to our inspection. Many of the photographs appearing in this book were supplied by the Jekyll Island Museum, and a number of others, provided by the Georgia Department of Archives and History from the Vanishing Georgia Collection, were taken from originals owned by the Jekyll Island Museum. A very special word of thanks is due to Ellen Rogers, then chief curator of the Jekyll Island Museums Division, who not only rendered constant help from the outset of our work but acted as a cheerleader for the project at every turn.

Our gratitude goes as well to the many relatives of Jekyll Island Club members and employees who shared their recollections, photographs, memorabilia, and personal papers, among whom we must mention John J. Albright, Nancy Albright Hurd Schluter, Henry H. Anderson, Jr., Nathalie Bell Brown, Lady Helen de Freitas, Howard E. Etter, George F. Goodyear, R. Campbell James, Doris F.

Liebrecht, Katherine G. Owens, Frederick Shrady, Anita B. Souter, and Jeurdine B. Wood. Others who have been most cooperative in providing us with valuable information on various aspects of the club's history include Alfred W. Jones, Jr., T. Miesse Baumgardner, B. W. Caples, Walter Matthews, Edie Lewellyn, Faye Boddiford, Doris M. Cort, Anne Gallion, Carole L. Perrault, Sherrill Redmon, Lee and Elsie Schwartz, and Melvin Crandell.

We also wish to express our appreciation to the following repositories for permission to use their sources: AT&T Company Historical Archive, New York; Baker Library, Harvard University Graduate School of Business Administration, Boston; Rare Book and Manuscripts Library, Columbia University, New York; Manuscripts Division, Library of Congress; Diocesan Library and Archives, Episcopal Diocese of Massachusetts, Boston; Georgia Department of Archives and History, Atlanta; James Jerome Hill Reference Library, Saint Paul, Minnesota; Kornhauser Health Sciences Library, University of Louisville, Louisville, Kentucky; National Trust for Historical Preservation, Lyndhurst, Tarrytown, New York; Museum and Library of Maryland History, Baltimore; Pierpont Morgan Library, New York; New York Historical Society; Rockefeller Archive Center, North Tarrytown, New York; State Historical Society of Wisconsin, Madison, Wisconsin; Society for the Preservation of Long Island Antiquities, Setauket, Long Island; Minnesota Historical Society, Saint Paul, Minnesota; Southern Historical Collection, the Library of the University of North Carolina, Chapel Hill; Glynn County Regional Library, Brunswick, Georgia; Personal Services Division, Department of the Army, U.S. Army Reserve Personnel Center, St. Louis, Missouri; United States Military Academy Library, Department of the Army, West Point, New York.

We are no less indebted to our friends and colleagues at Middle Tennessee State University who contributed in a variety of significant ways to the making of this book. Our thanks go to Betty McFall and Almyra Medlen for their efficient handling of our interlibrary loan and reference requests; Jack Ross, Photographic Services, and Suma Clark, Judy Hall, Hugh Shelton, and Mitzi Brandon, Publications and Graphics, for their help with illustrations and prints; and Jennifer Vecchio-Conn who cheerfully performed myriad secretarial chores and whose efforts made our task infinitely lighter.

We are equally grateful to Selby McCash who read our manuscript with a keen critical eye and made many valuable suggestions. To all of these people we extend our warm thanks. They deserve credit for much that may be meritorious in this book but, of course, should not be held accountable for its faults.

Although our work on this project has often been painstaking, it has been intensely satisfying and has afforded us the joy of working as a team in uncovering the fascinating history of the Jekyll Island Club. If the reader derives half as much pleasure from perusing these pages as we have shared in writing them, our efforts will have been well rewarded.

JUNE HALL McCASH
WILLIAM BARTON McCASH

The Jekyll Island Club

1. Formation of the Club

The Jekyl* Island Club was described in the February 1904 issue of *Munsey's Magazine* as "the richest, the most exclusive, the most inaccessible" club in the world. It boasted an impressive membership, including such men as J. P. Morgan, William Rockefeller, Vincent Astor, Joseph Pulitzer, James J. Hill, and William K. Vanderbilt. Throughout its sixty-two year history, however, it was shrouded in mystery for most Americans. Gleaming like a bright jewel just two miles off the coast near Brunswick, Georgia, the island might as well have been a million miles away. It is little wonder that such a tantalizing unknown engendered myth and that so much of what has been published about the island has been fed, for lack of accurate information, by the fertile imaginations of curious outsiders. Even the most common accounts of the club's origins are pure fantasy. According to an often-repeated story published in the *Saturday Evening Post* in 1941, a group of millionaires gave two Johns Hopkins doctors the task of seeking the world over for the perfect spot for a club like Jekyl, a tale which is impossible in view of the fact that Johns Hopkins Hospital did not open its doors until 1889, and the medical school did not begin until 1893, well after the founding of the club.[1]

The true beginning of the club, although less fanciful perhaps, has, nonetheless, a romance of its own. It all started with a little-known but extraordinary man named Newton Sobieski Finney.

The future seemed full of promise for seventeen-year-old Newton Finney of Fond du Lac, Wisconsin. For three years he had been doggedly petitioning Secretary of War Jefferson Davis for an appointment to the United States Military Academy. Approval had finally come through in early April 1854.

Like many of the academy's applicants at the time, Finney was not so much interested in a career in the army as he was in acquiring the engineering skills highly valued in that age of rapidly advancing technology. He was in an optimistic frame of mind when he arrived at West Point, seeing it as "one of the most beautiful places in the world." By early winter, however, his enthusiasm had been tempered by a realization that the academy was "a very hard school; no one could like the stern iron discipline under which we are constantly kept and very few would bear it were it not for a bright future which is before them." Although he vowed to stick it out "if it busts me," his hopes were dashed when he was forced to resign in January 1855 for academic deficiencies.

As his application papers had suggested, he was a "young man of extraordinary talents, industry, and energy," and, unfailingly resilient, he bounced back quickly. By 1856 he had landed a promising job with the United States Coast Survey, which provided a good salary and an opportunity to travel. As fate would have it, one of his first assignments was to help chart the topography of Saint Simons Sound and Brunswick harbor. He headed for the coast of Georgia aboard the schooner *Meredith* in April. It was during this trip that he met his bride-to-be, Josephine du Bignon.[2]

History has not recorded Finney's meeting with the fetching Josephine, nor how he came to be drawn into the circle of her prominent and colorful family. Most likely the introduction came through Colonel Charles L. Schlatter, chief engineer of the

---

*Jekyll was spelled with only one "l" until 1929.

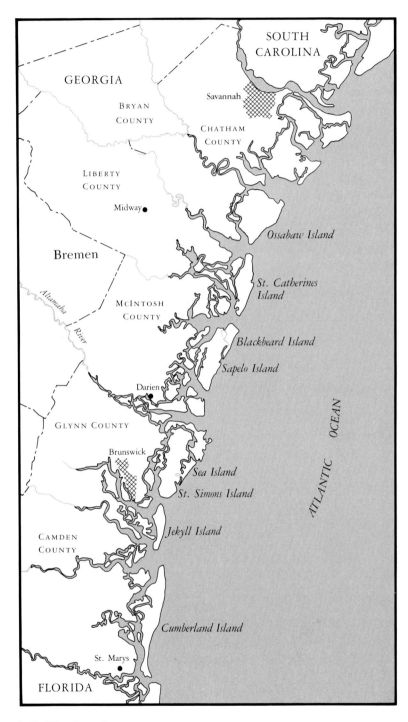

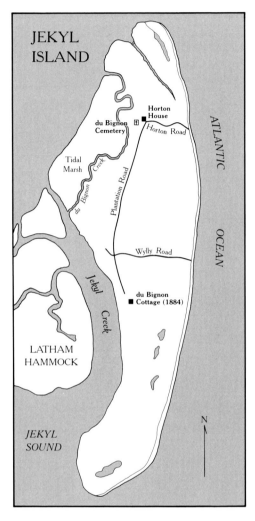

Left: The Georgia coast.

**Right: The island as it was
at the time the Jekyl
Island Club was founded.**

Newton Sobieski Finney, founder of the Jekyl Island Club. (Courtesy of Mrs. L. C. Liebrecht)

Josephine du Bignon Finney. (Courtesy of Mrs. L. C. Liebrecht)

Brunswick and Florida Railroad, who gave Finney courteous and valuable assistance during his surveying duties. Schlatter was well acquainted with the du Bignons, and some years later his daughter would marry Josephine's brother, John Eugene.

The du Bignons, a family of French royalists, had come to America to escape the turmoil of the French Revolution. In 1792 Christophe Poulain du Bignon, the family's patriarch, had purchased Jekyl Island and settled there to raise sea island cotton, a prosperous enterprise until the Civil War. Josephine's grandfather, Henri Charles du Bignon, inherited the island from his father and would, in turn, deed it prior to his death in 1866 to his three surviving sons, Charles, John, and Henry, with thirty acres set aside for his eldest daughter, Eliza. Josephine's father, Joseph, however, had died in 1850 and his family would not share in the division of Jekyl. Although Josephine may have spent her childhood on the island, she was living with her widowed mother, Félicité Riffault, and her five brothers and sisters, on property the family owned in Brunswick when she met Newton Finney in 1856.

Romance blossomed between Newton and Josephine, but his work with the coast survey carried him away from Brunswick. Between 1857 and 1860, he took part in surveying the seacoasts of Florida and Virginia as well as New York's Hudson River. By 1860, however, Finney was back in the South, surveying the west coast of Florida. Georgia was evidently never far from his thoughts during this period, for he found a way to make the trip back to Brunswick, where on April 17 he and eighteen-year-old Josephine were wed.

On the very brink of the Civil War, Finney had married into an ardent fire-eating family, some of whom had been indicted for their participation in the activities of the slave ship *Wanderer*, the last vessel to bring a major shipment of slaves to the United States. It had landed on the shores of Jekyl Island just before dawn on November 29, 1858, to disgorge its cargo of 409 slaves, survivors of a forty-day journey under agonizing conditions.[3]

Despite his marriage and the secession of Georgia from the Union in January 1861, Finney continued to cling to his job with the coast survey until the actual outbreak of fighting would compel him to resign. In February 1861, while Southern delegates were meeting in Montgomery, Alabama, to write the constitution for the Confederate States of America, Newton Finney, still surveying Florida's west coast for the Union, was confronted by a band of armed secessionists from Bayport, who unceremoniously brought his work to a halt on February 11. Finney proceeded to Brunswick and filed his report on April 3. Nine days later South Carolina troops fired on Fort Sumter, and his employment with the United States government was forever ended.

Only twenty-four years old, high-spirited, and no doubt pressured by Josephine's family, Finney did not hesitate to take part in the war. His own family was still in the North, and both his brother and his brother-in-law fought for the Union, as he would learn only after peace was restored. Finney, on the other hand, accepted a commission in the Confederate army. Rising to the rank of captain of engineers, he served briefly on Robert E. Lee's staff and in April 1862 was assigned to duty in Augusta, where for several years he was in charge of manufacturing torpedoes and mines. During the last three months of the conflict, he was dispatched to build an arsenal at Savannah.

Finney did not let the war interfere with his entrepreneurial spirit, however. He speculated freely during those years and, by his own estimate, accumulated a fortune of more than $200,000. But the defeat of the South left him virtually empty-handed. His entire investment in Confederate bonds was worthless, and much of his property and that of his wife was confiscated. He wrote to his brother that General Sherman had captured not only rice, sugar, steel, and rope from his storehouses in Savannah but also the English hemp "that I had just got from Liverpool by Blockade vessels to sell." All of the furniture from his "four story brick house full and elegantly furnished from cellar to garrett" had been seized, along with a "fine Library," a "span of horses," and "a good carriage."

"I found myself worse off than when the war commenced for then I had a fine position with two thousand dollars a year and my wife was well off," he wrote. "But now she has lost all but her land, and that we won't get back for a long time yet, for her family were well known, and very bitter secessionists at the start."

But he was already looking ahead with optimism. "I don't mind the loss of property at all. If I have good luck and the South improves, I can easily make a living and perhaps another fortune. For I have a good many influential friends North and South who will throw business in my way."[4]

Finney was right. In December 1865 he formed a partnership with General John Brown Gordon, a powerful political figure and later governor of Georgia, and New York businessman J. W. Neeley, in a commission and shipping business. During one of his periodic trips to New York, Finney met Oliver Kane King, with whom he

John Eugene du Bignon, Brunswick entrepreneur who sold Jekyl Island to the club. (Everett Collection, Coastal Georgia Historical Society)

would establish a new partnership in the early 1870s under the name of King, Finney & Company, brokers and railroad suppliers.

King was both financially successful and very popular in New York social circles. He had served as governor of the prestigious Union Club, the so-called "mother of clubs," and had been recently elected secretary, a post he would hold for more than a decade. In 1873 he sponsored his new partner, Finney, who had by then moved his growing family to New York, for membership in the organization. Soon Finney could be found rubbing elbows with such wealthy and important figures as J. P. Morgan, William K. Vanderbilt, and Pierre Lorillard, and his contacts with them gave him fresh ideas for making money.

One of the things that had struck Finney most sharply on his first return trip to the North after the Civil War was the bitter cold. He had commented to his brother at the time, "I thought I should freeze, for I have not seen cold weather before in 11 years, for you know I always was South in the winter while on the Coast Survey." It was probably Finney, always on the lookout for a good opportunity, who saw Jekyl Island as a perfect lure to his rich friends yearning to escape from the bone-chilling northern winters and who suggested to his brother-in-law, John Eugene du Bignon, the possibility of selling the island to a northern businessman.

Du Bignon, Josephine's younger brother by almost eight years, shared Finney's enthusiasm for the main chance and had also noticed the tendency of the wealthy to gravitate to the South in the winter. He had already bought the southern third of the island from the estate of his deceased uncle, Charles du Bignon, in 1879, apparently intending to live there. In 1884 he built a house on Jekyl and began raising "some fine blooded and graded Devon stock." The family had lost the rest of the island after the Civil War, except for the thirty acres belonging to his Aunt Eliza. A man named Martin Tufts had obtained the northern portion in 1876, and Gustav Friedlander and Company had acquired the middle third in 1883.[5]

The plan Finney and du Bignon hatched appears to have been to entice New York backers to advance the money to buy out Tufts and Friedlander, using the island as security, then to sell the whole thing for a price sufficient to repay the loan and enjoy a tidy profit to boot. Their success must have exceeded anything they imagined, for within a year du Bignon would manage to purchase the remainder of Jekyl for less than $8,000 and resell it for the princely sum of $125,000.

John Claflin was a part of the history of the Jekyl Island Club from 1885 until his death on June 11, 1938. He was the last surviving original member. (Brooklyn Historical Society)

In mid-March 1885 the first group of prospective buyers arrived on Jekyl Island. The *Brunswick Advertiser and Appeal* took note of the visit, reporting that "The party who went to Jekyl yesterday on a hunting expedition, the guests of Mr. J. E. Du-Bignon, returned delighted with their sport. Mr. Anderson of New York, brought down the only deer killed." Nothing came of this trip, but the next one was to prove more productive.

The second contingent, arriving a month later, included John Claflin and his cousin and business partner, Edward E. Eames. Thirty-five-year-old Claflin was a highly successful partner with his father in the firm of H. B. Claflin & Company, which had been the largest wholesale dry goods business in New York following the Civil War, rivaling for a time even Marshall Field in Chicago and John Wanamaker in Philadelphia.

Claflin, a short, slender fellow with gentle manners and a reputation for energy and diligence, was also something of an adventurer. In the summer of 1877, he had made a dangerous trek with a single companion across the South American continent "by a route seldom or never traversed by a white man . . . journeying afoot, on muleback, or by canoe, through the countries of savage tribes."

The *Advertiser and Appeal* took an unusual interest in the visit, at first saying Eames and Claflin had returned from a hunt "up about Jamaica." The following week the newspaper made a correction, saying "we were in error last week as to the section of our county in which Messrs. Eames and Claflin, of New York, got those fine wild turkeys. They were bagged on Jekyl Island, and not Jamaica. These gentlemen were on the Island, the special guests of Mr. J. E. DuBignon." The earlier story had been right about one thing, however. It had reported without further explanation that "the visit, though under the guise of pleasure, means business for Brunswick, as further developments will show."

The editor obviously knew something of the transactions which had been taking place. Exercising superb salesmanship, du Bignon not only persuaded Claflin to advance him money enough to buy out Tufts and Friedlander but also to purchase the island himself once du Bignon had gained control of it. Despite his appreciation for the island, Claflin was dubious about becoming the sole owner of such a large piece of property and would pounce on the first opportunity to unburden himself of the obligation.

Du Bignon cottage. This "farm house" was built in 1884, according to the club prospectus, "to replace the old manor house burned down during the [Civil] war. . . ." It served variously as the superintendent's cottage and as a residence for guests, called "club cottage." (Georgia Department of Archives and History)

An agreement was recorded on June 16, 1885, in the Glynn County Superior Court minutes whereby du Bignon secured, with Jekyl Island as collateral, three separate promissory notes to Claflin, one for $350, payable in six months, and two others, one for $350 and the other for $10,000, both payable in one year. With these funds du Bignon was able to pay for three tracts of Jekyl land, with $3,500 going to Tufts for his northern parcel, $4,000 to Friedlander for his middle portion, and a token $100 to his aunt, Eliza du Bignon, for her thirty acres; $3,100 remained for any necessary improvements.

In the June 20 issue, the *Advertiser and Appeal* extended its congratulations:

Mr. John DuBignon is now the happy owner of the entire island of Jekyl, having purchased recently the middle and north end. His residence is on steamboat channel, where he has been residing for the past few years. The island is one of the most valuable on the entire coast. The lands are rich, the [climate] excellent, and as for game no island in this section can equal it. We congratulate Mr. DuBignon on the consumation of his cherished plans, viz:—the ownership of the entire island.

At this juncture, du Bignon learned from Finney and King that his profits would be enhanced considerably if the island could be sold to a club rather than an individual. When du Bignon explained the situation, Claflin readily agreed to release him from the sale and even expressed a willingness to take a share in such an organization.

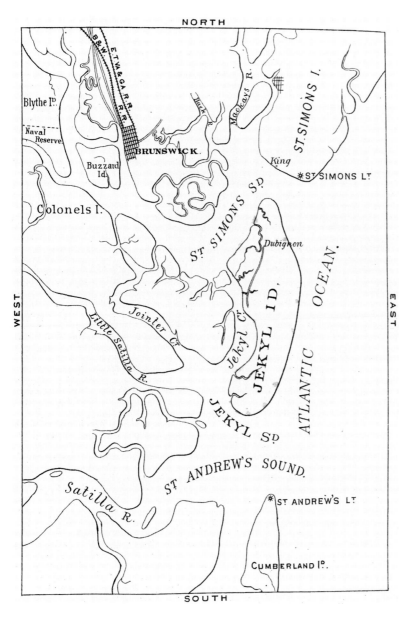

The neighboring port city of Brunswick was vital to the Jekyl Island Club for its transportation facilities and the services the community could provide. (Southern Historical Collection, University of North Carolina)

Du Bignon now set to work stocking the island with game and seeking good publicity for Jekyl. The growing awareness among citizens of Brunswick's potential as a resort area made his job easier. A pamphlet published that year by the *Advertiser and Appeal* stated that "Brunswick, as a winter resort and sanitarium, and as a summer resort, possesses advantages certain, with reasonable hotel facilities, to bring ample compensation to hotel proprietors." The pamphlet touted the one thing that would appeal to wealthy northerners, a climate "as pleasant . . . as can be found. The winters are never severe, snow being almost unknown and ice a rarity, and our summers are rendered . . . quite pleasant by constant refreshing breezes."[6]

Finney, at his end, was equally busy. There is no doubt that he was from the outset the prime mover and animating spirit behind the establishment of the Jekyl Island Club. An 1896 publication on "select organizations" in the United States acknowledged his role quite succinctly in stating that "This club was originated and organized by N. S. Finney of the Union Club, New York."[7] But his friend and partner, Oliver K. King, provided invaluable help in the planning and recruitment phase of the project and would be counted among the founding members of the club.

By December 1885, the two men were prepared to incorporate under the name "The Jekyl Island Club." The corporate petition expressed the club's intent to raise livestock, birds, and game; to hunt, fish, and yacht; to maintain a race course; to erect a club house and other necessary buildings; to own and operate tramways or trains as needed; to install telephone and telegraph lines; to purchase or lease real estate, water rights, and docking privileges; to create debts or issue bonds; or to do anything else that was deemed essential.

The petition was filed on December 9, 1885, in Glynn County Superior Court by du Bignon and his two brothers-in-law, Alfred J. Crovatt and Charles L. Schlatter, Jr. Crovatt had just completed his second term as Brunswick's mayor. He would go on to serve as the club's legal counsel for decades. Both Crovatt and Schlatter appear to have signed the petition primarily as a favor to their kinsman. Crovatt never considered membership in the club, and Schlatter, although his name appears on Finney's subscription list of members, gave up his place to Edward E. Eames before the roster of original shareholders was finalized.

The next day the petition was signed and witnessed before the commissioner of the state of Georgia in New York by Finney, King, Thomas C. Clarke, William B. D'Wolf, and Richard L. Ogden. All were men whose lives had been deeply affected by the rising tide of industrialism in the United States. D'Wolf was a member of the New York Stock Exchange and a partner in the brokerage firm of D'Wolf and Parsons. He was well acquainted with Finney and King because of his membership in the Union Club, and he was also the brother-in-law of Lloyd Aspinwall, a popular New Yorker who would become the Jekyl Island Club's first president. Clarke, also a member of the Union Club, was a man of impeccable social credentials, a descendent of the Thomas Clarke who had been mate on the *Mayflower*, an 1848 graduate of Harvard, and a prominent civil engineer.

Ogden, listed on the petition as being from California, had moved from New York to San Francisco in 1850 and served in the Union army during the Civil War, attaining the rank of major. After the war he had risen rapidly in the social world and the business community, but the depression of the 1870s had brought him to a low ebb financially. He was, nevertheless, a popular man with a genial disposition and a wry sense of humor. His contribution to the Jekyl Island Club would be considerable.

Plans were to issue one hundred shares of Jekyl Island Club stock to be sold to fifty individuals each owning two shares at a par value of $600 a share. On February 17, 1886, Finney, representing the newly chartered club, signed an agreement with du Bignon to purchase the island for $125,000, with all improvements, fixtures, and livestock, including "400 head of cattle, 100 horses, 600 hogs, and all fowls [sic] and game of every kind." The agreement included a clause that it should be "of no effect, unless the one hundred shares of said stock be subscribed for by April 1st, 1886." This would give du Bignon time to raise the money to repay Claflin's loan, which fell due on June 16.[8]

Finney must have been fairly certain that he would have no difficulty in finding fifty interested parties. In fact, he already had agreement from a number of people. Six of the first seven names on his original subscription list, which fortunately has survived, were those who had signed the charter petition: du Bignon, Finney, Ogden, King, Schlatter, and D'Wolf. Additional members were invited to join, for the most part, by virtue of family relationships with another member or by strong business and social connections. The former gave birth to the myth that the only way to attain membership in the exclusive Jekyl Island Club was to inherit it. While inheritance was never the only method of gaining entry, it would be the surest way, especially in later years. In the beginning, however, business and social ties and an acquaintance with Newton Finney and Oliver Kane King were equally valuable. Finney and King moved easily through the Union Club finding potential members, all of whom shared several characteristics: they were eager to escape the New York winters, they were interested in hunting and yachting, and they were anxious to find respite from the hectic pace of their busy lives in the North.

Of the original members of the Jekyl Island Club, almost half belonged to the Union Club. An impressive list to anyone familiar with New York society, it included among its number such luminaries as John Pierpont Morgan, at the peak of his powers at forty-nine, who was making his fortune at the time primarily in banking and railroads; Pierre Lorillard, then fifty-three, who made his millions in tobacco and was himself in the process of organizing a hunting club and residential park on his family's 7,000-acre tract in Orange County, New York, to be known as Tuxedo Park; and William Kissam Vanderbilt, who, upon the death in 1885 of his father, William H. Vanderbilt, had been catapulted into control of the family's railroad fortune and through the efforts of his wife, Alva, had risen to the apex of New York society following a struggle with Caroline Schermerhorn Astor for recognition as the reigning queen of society.

The eagerness of so many well-known New Yorkers to become a part of this society on a distant island in Georgia that most of them had never seen is striking. It is best reflected in a letter to King from Henry Hyde, another of the Union Club recruits, whose forceful personality had made his firm, The Equitable Life Assurance Society, into the largest life insurance company in the world. Hyde wrote, "It seems like a fairy tale. . . . I will be happy to join."[9]

Finney was delighted with the response not only in numbers but also in the quality of the people who were showing enthusiasm for his club. These were not just rich and successful businessmen. They were at the very top of the social ladder—prominent men at the height of their careers. He could not help being elated to find himself in their company, for their very names on his list guaranteed the club's success. A profile of these members reveals that almost all were native-born Americans with ancestral origins in the British Isles; derived from old colonial families; were Episcopalians or Presbyterians (recognized as the "elite" religions of the nineteenth century); preferred the Republican Party; and had been born to wealth.

Before the April deadline, Finney had obtained not just fifty subscriptions for club membership, but fifty-three, as several members had agreed to split their two shares with a friend. Finney, for example, gave up his two shares to the newspaper magnate Joseph Pulitzer, but to avoid forfeiting membership, he bought one of the shares belonging to du Bignon. Thirty-nine-year-old Pulitzer was something of an anomaly among the original members. He had been born to a Jewish father and a Catholic mother in Budapest, spoke little English when he first came to the United States in 1864, and was an ardent Democrat openly opposed, despite his own increasing fortune, to the "aristocracy of money." Pulitzer's prominence and wealth, along with his personal charm and that of his wife, overcame any concerns Finney may have had, and he was welcomed with the other New York elite.

Next to New York, the largest number of original members came from Chicago. The Chicagoans were tightly knit by civic, social, and commercial activities. They had been at the forefront of relief and recovery efforts after the great fire of 1871, belonged to the prestigious Chicago Club, and were key figures on the Chicago Board of Trade. This important Jekyl element consisted of such men as dry goods merchant Marshall Field, his lawyer and friend Wirt Dexter, and Ezra McCagg, also a successful lawyer who had made a fortune in real estate and had served as the first president of the Chicago Club. Clearly the small Chicago clique of only six members was, like the New York group, composed of select men of substance, representing the most elite society in their city. They would form a harmonious and influential circle significantly affecting the development of the Jekyl Island Club.

Other members were accepted from Philadelphia, Albany, Boston, Buffalo, San Francisco, and Athens, Pennsylvania. John E. du Bignon would remain the lone original member from the South. Of the original fifty-three, only one, Dunbar Price, defaulted on payment for his shares and, in spite of the fact that his name appears on the first official membership list published in New York in 1886, he was never an active member of the Jekyl Island Club.[10]

Final payment was made to du Bignon on April 1, 1886, with $50,000 coming out of club coffers and $75,000 raised by the issue of 150 first mortgage bonds at $500 each, bearing 4½ percent interest and maturing in twenty years. The Mercantile Trust Company of New York served as trustee and held the deed to the island.[11]

On the same day, a meeting was held in New York to adopt the club's constitution and by-laws and to choose officers, directors, and the executive committee. The distinction of being chosen the first president went to Lloyd Aspinwall, known commonly as "General" Aspinwall since his election to the rank of brigadier general of the Fourth New York Brigade after the Civil War. He had succeeded his father in the shipping firm of Howland and Aspinwall and had been a director of the Mexican National Railroad and of the Brooklyn Bridge Company. He was a genial and highly respected man with a wide circle of friends.[12]

Unfortunately, his son, Lloyd, Jr., who would join the Jekyl Island Club later that same year and would be elected treasurer for only one season in 1888, was not stamped from the same mold but would squander his wealth and end his life in poverty and disgrace. General Aspinwall served but five months as club president, for he died unexpectedly, at only fifty-one years of age, on September 4, 1886.

The club's vice president and the man who would succeed Aspinwall as president was Judge Henry Elias Howland, a distinguished jurist who would the following year rise to the position of justice of the New York Supreme Court. He was a noted wit, a composer of epigrams, and a highly popular after-dinner speaker. The

Left: Marshall Field, a pioneer in the department store business and one of the six original club members from Chicago. He belonged from 1886 until his death in 1906. (Library of Congress)

Right: Wirt Dexter of Chicago, club member 1886–90 and wealthy corporation lawyer. Among his clients were Marshall Field and George Pullman, who was elected to join the Jekyl Island Club but declined. (Chicago Historical Society)

Lower right: Ezra B. McCagg of Chicago, club member 1886–1902. At sixty-one he was one of the oldest and most respected of the original members. (Chicago Historical Society)

treasurer was Franklin M. Ketchum, the son of Morris Ketchum of Ketchum, Son, & Company, which had during the Civil War been one of the largest and most successful banking houses in New York. Richard L. Ogden was chosen secretary.[13]

With the completion of the organizational details, the Jekyl Island Club was officially in business. It would become over the years a veritable retreat for the wealthy. Cut off from the busy workaday world of New York and the nation's other urban centers, it would be the one place where they could set a tranquil pace and tenor for their lives. The island location, the family orientation, the residential community, and the simple joys of its natural setting would make the Jekyl Island Club unique among the nation's social clubs.

That is what it would become. All that existed at the moment, however, was a mostly undeveloped and overgrown plot of land. Ground would be broken the following August for an imposing club house to overlook the legendary Marshes of Glynn. In the meantime, a great deal of difficult work lay ahead.

Above: Lloyd Aspinwall, first president of the Jekyl Island Club, during the 1860s as an officer in the Twenty-second New York State Militia. (Library of Congress)

Right: Judge Henry Elias Howland, second president of the Jekyl Island Club, 1886–97. He remained a member of the club until 1901. (Library of Congress)

2. The Early Seasons

The new "association of wealthy gentlemen" was publicly announced on April 4, 1886, for the first time, by the *New York Times:* "It is predicted that the Jekyl Island Club is going to be the 'swell' club, the *crème de la crème* [sic] of all, inasmuch as many of the members are intending to erect cottages and make it their Winter Newport." That the club would have a family orientation was clear from the outset. As the *Times* article indicated, it was not intended to be "a selfish and exclusive 'man's' club. On the contrary, ladies will constitute an attractive element and will be freely admitted to all the privileges to which their husbands, fathers, and brothers are entitled. They can fish, shoot, ride on horseback, bathe, camp out, and enjoy themselves. This new feature of the club will, of course, be popular."

But there was a great deal of work to be done before the island was suitable for club activities. In May, members of an investigative committee traveling south to inspect Jekyl Island were delighted with what they found. They pronounced the island quite satisfactory and abundant in game. Future plans, they recommended, should include a club house, building lots for members, various outbuildings, and gardens. Among their proposals was one calling for "the immediate employment of a competent landscape architect" to furnish a comprehensive design. The property, they concluded, was "far too valuable to make . . . irremediable mistakes."[1]

The next step was to select committees to make arrangements for constructing and furnishing the club house, landscaping the island, purchasing a steam launch, and providing a variety of other things pertaining to the opening and operation of the club. To coordinate these activities and to keep members informed of the progress, Finney resigned from the executive committee at its meeting on December 6 to assume the post of permanent secretary. His friend, Oliver K. King, who was suffering from ill health and would die the following year at age forty-nine, surrendered his club membership at the same meeting. Before resigning, however, King offered a final resolution that Finney, who had voluntarily given up a $2,000 commission due him for acting as broker in transferring the island to the club, should receive "fair compensation" for his "unremitting services during the past year." The executive committee approved $2,500 in compensation to Finney, who would continue to work indefatigably during the coming year to assure the club a good beginning. But he was not required to shoulder the burdens alone.[2]

A number of other members took on time-consuming tasks in an effort to launch the Jekyl Island Club successfully. The Chicago group was particularly active during the formative stages. Ezra McCagg, who had served on the Lincoln Park Commission in Chicago, was elected chairman of the committee on landscape engineering, and Wirt Dexter was named chairman of the building committee. Dexter's committee selected Charles A. Alexander, a noted, though aging, Chicago architect, to design the club house, while McCagg's committee chose to lay out the grounds Horace William Shaler Cleveland, who, along with Frederick Law Olmsted, was one of the two best-known landscape architects in the country. Cleveland most recently had been in charge of planning and directing the parks and parkways in Minneapolis, but he had previously been entrusted with the supervision of Chicago's South Park and had

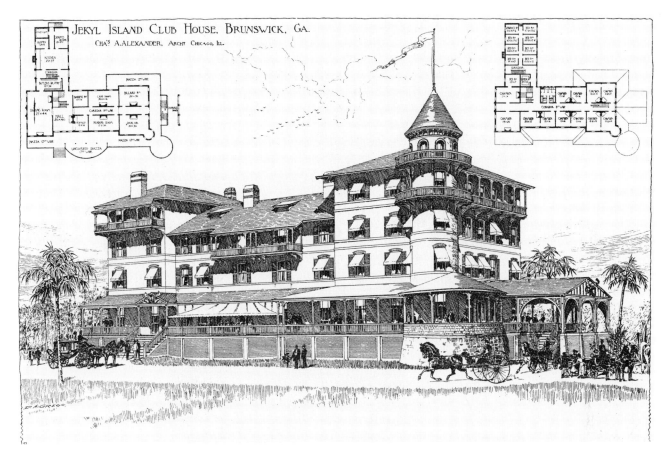

JEKYL ISLAND CLUB HOUSE, BRUNSWICK, GA.
CHA'S A. ALEXANDER, ARCH'T CHICAGO, ILL.

Charles A. Alexander's drawing of the proposed club house was reproduced in the January 1887 issue of *American Architect and Building News.* (Jekyll Island Museum)

influenced the development of the Boston Common. He had also submitted a plan for the design of Central Park in New York, losing in the competition only to Olmsted, who had nonetheless adopted Cleveland's fundamental idea of what landscape architecture should be: "the art of arranging land so as to adapt it most conveniently, economically and gracefully to any of the varied wants of civilization." In 1873 he had published an influential book, *Landscape Architecture as Applied to the Wants of the West,* which had gained for him even greater recognition.[3]

The design of the Jekyl Island Club property must have been an arduous undertaking for seventy-three-year-old Cleveland. In a letter to his friend Olmsted, he described his initial survey of the island and the difficulties it involved: "It took all the resolution I could muster to traverse on foot or on horseback the areas of forest I had to explore, and in spite of every possible precaution, I was bitten and stung from head to foot by red bugs, wood ticks and other 'benevolent machines' and thought myself fortunate in seeing only one rattlesnake. However, I accomplished my object and felt no little satisfaction in doing so."[4]

He set about the task with enthusiasm, taking into consideration the special environment of Jekyl Island and the views expressed to him by McCagg's committee. Unlike Newport, with its ornate mansions

Club house under con-
struction, 1887. (Jekyll Island Museum)

One of the earliest
photographs of the Jekyl
Island club house, taken
before its completion,
1887. The porches and
porte-cochère have yet to
be added. The house at far
right is the club cottage
formerly owned by John
du Bignon. (Everett
Collection, Coastal
Georgia Historical
Society).

and nabob manners, the Jekyl Island Club sought to stress simplicity of style and social harmony, which Cleveland fully understood. He also took into consideration members' desires to escape both the harried business world and the social conventions of "ordinary fashionable resorts." His plan sought rather to enhance the island's beauties "which nature here affords in such rich profusion." The Jekyl of his creation would be a "natural paradise" without the "artificial decoration . . . in common use by landscape gardeners." It would have a "style of severe simplicity," eschewing everything "which even in appearance involves the idea of continuous care and labor."

His design included building lots and roadways "no wider than is absolutely necessary" to remote points on the island and carefully routed "to avoid disturbing the favored haunts of deer or wild fowl." On August 10, 1886, Cleveland submitted his plans to McCagg, who accepted them with only minor modifications.[5]

To complement the landscaper's plan, the architect, Alexander, set to work on a suitably large Queen Anne club house. It was to be a magnificent though not ostentatious building of four stories, complete with dining facilities; sixty guest rooms; rooms for reading, card playing, and billiards; a barber shop; and a pavilion.

From the beginning, the construction was fraught with pitfalls. Alexander's report to Wirt Dexter on May 1, 1887, outlined his progress and his problems in some detail. "Ground was broken for the Club House about the middle of August; and there being no stone available, the foundations were put in in a very solid manner with Rosendale Cement mixed with oyster shells, forming a very solid concrete." So far, so good. But it did not take Alexander long to realize that he had a serious problem. The Georgia contractor who had been hired to oversee the job could not even read the plans. And the black workmen he had brought with him seemed no more skilled than he at their jobs. Frantically the architect scoured Jacksonville and Savannah for experienced construction workers, but, finding only a handful, he was finally compelled to import "ten good New York bricklayers."

The inept contractor was relegated to running the boarding house for workers while the architect took over supervision of the labor. He found himself "for the first time in his practice of thirty years, architect, master mason and master carpenter, and purchasing agent and paymaster." When sickness broke out among the workers, the blame fell to the unsanitary conditions in the boarding house. Alexander made up his mind at this point to get rid of the contractor altogether. But not wanting to fire him outright and "incur for the Club a possible law suit in Georgia," he persuaded him that the project was a losing proposition. On February 22, 1887, the man abandoned the project, received whatever wages were owed him at that point, and "gave the Club full release from all demands." Alexander then hired a foreman from Brunswick ("a very able man, and I regret that I did not know of his ability from the first") and made do with northern workers returning from Saint Augustine and Jacksonville.

Labor problems, unfortunately, were not the only difficulties Alexander faced in building the Jekyl Island club house. He found the pier "unfit for landing materials" and was forced to modify it; transport from the mainland was inadequate, with all

available barges being "old and leaky."
Although the club was in the process of
constructing a lighter and a new yacht, the
Howland, to be named for the club's second president, neither was ready for immediate use; hence Alexander was compelled
to make do with hired barges from
Brunswick. Nevertheless, the architect believed his progress "to be very creditable."
He pointed out to the building committee
that Thomas C. Clarke, who had visited
the island in January and was himself an
engineer, had "examined the construction
of the house from top to bottom [and] pronounced it very thorough and perfect."
Alexander projected as his completion date
August 1, 1887.[6] But it would be
November 1 before he finally proclaimed
the club house finished. It would prove to
be the final completed project of the aging
architect, who died the following May at
his hotel in Chicago.

The house now stood ready for the
opening of the club's first season. On December 1, a journalist from the *Advertiser
and Appeal* was invited to the island to see
the new improvements. Having been transported to Jekyl aboard the steam yacht
Howland, he reported his delighted reactions at seeing the new club house, which
he found to be

> an elegant structure . . . unlike anything else
> in this section. . . . From a distance it looks
> like some English castle with its square
> shaped windows and its lofty tower. The
> building is constructed for comfort—the ceil-
> ings low, but each room is well ventilated,
> and the entire building can be heated from
> cellar to garret by means of a heater in the
> basement, and besides each room is fur-
> nished with a great fireplace with plain man-
> tle—in fact there is no attempt at display,
> and there is nothing gaudy about the build-
> ing—everything is substantial.

Furniture which had arrived only the day
before was pronounced "elegant and mas-
sive" and, like the club house, "not gaudy."
The shell road that led from the club compound and "by a sudden turn" brought the
ocean into full and unexpected view was
judged "a thing of beauty." In short, the
journalist was impressed, as he anticipated
the arrival of the Jekyl families, "all of
whom are looking forward with interest to
the coming winter's pleasures."

The man appointed to prepare for and
oversee the club's initial season was one of
the original members—Richard Livingston
Ogden—who, elected as the club's first
secretary prior to Finney, had agreed also
to serve as club superintendent for a salary
of $2,500 per annum plus room and board
while on the island. He had been appointed to the post at the first called meeting of the executive committee on June 16,
1886, and had probably accepted the
position because he needed the money. He
had been manager of the Kimball Manufacturing Company, the largest industrial
concern in San Francisco until the depression of the 1870s had forced the Bank of
California, which backed the Kimball
Company, to close its doors. Ogden's fortune, heavily invested in his firm, was seriously undermined. In personality, he
seemed the perfect man for the job. His
reputation as a sportsman and the "best
known yachtsman on San Francisco Bay"
had led to his election as commodore of the
San Francisco Yacht Club in 1875. His
greatest pleasure in his more prosperous
days had been "in filling his yacht [the
Peerless] chock-a-block with the pleasan-
test people he could find and filling those
people with the 'best the market af-

Club house soon after it was completed at a cost of $45,000. (Jekyll Island Museum)

forded.'" He was, thus, not unfamiliar with the desires of wealthy bons vivants. To top it off, he had the genial and energetic personality, as well as the tact and courtesy, to do the job well. It would have been difficult to find a more suitable club member to undertake the task than "Captain Dick" or "Podgers," as he was fondly known to his friends.[7]

Ogden had worked for more than a year to prepare Jekyl for its first club season, scheduled to open officially in January 1888. To assist Ogden, the executive committee had hired a staff consisting of a clerk, Ernest Gilbert Grob; an assistant

superintendent, William Turner; a housekeeper, Kate Graf; and a yacht captain, James A. Clark. Together they set about their tasks, which included everything from seeing that the wild horses were removed from the island to supervising the drilling of an artesian well.

The board of directors and the game committee had decided that, if game were to be propagated adequately, the number of cattle and horses had to be reduced. Du Bignon, a member of both groups and familiar with the area, was requested to dispose of the animals for a profit if he could. He had been able to sell some of the cattle and the mares to the Thomas Carnegie family on neighboring Cumberland Island,

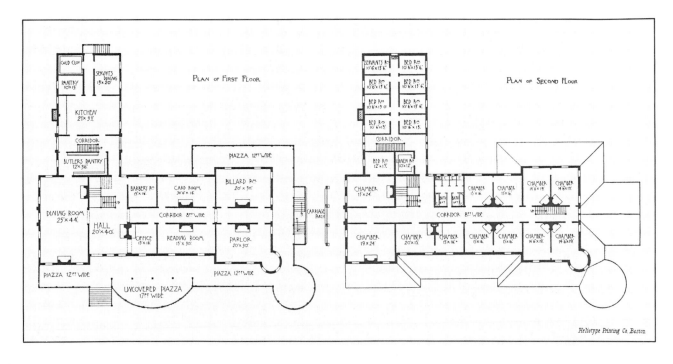

Club house floor plan.
(Baker Library, Harvard
Business School)

but the stallions were a more difficult problem. They were finally purchased by a C. W. Lamb, whose roundup of the animals was achieved only at the expenditure of much time and energy.

More serious than the dilemma of stallions, however, was that of the wild hogs which threatened to overpopulate Jekyl. The same Mr. Lamb was contracted to rid the island of them, but, as Ogden reported, "after a whole day spent utilizing his whole force of men and dogs, he frequently failed to get one animal, while his pack of dogs was almost annihilated by the tusks of the boars when attacked, and he had to retire defeated and very short of dogs." In the summer of 1899 another professional hunter, Captain W. R. Townsend, was employed to deplete their numbers, and members were given open season on the beasts. But, as Ogden had

reported in 1888, they were wily creatures that "seem to possess almost human intelligence and cunning, and the fleetness of the wind." Consequently, although the fights between Townsend's dogs and the hogs were declared "thrilling" by the *Brunswick Call*, they were at best inconclusive. The wild pigs would remain, in Ogden's words, "a vexatious problem" for many decades.[8]

The *Saturday Evening Post* reported in 1941 that the hogs on Jekyl were "descendants of a herd presented to . . . J. P. Morgan by King Humbert of Italy." In fact, the gift came from King Victor Emmanuel III of Italy, who in 1909 sent a pair of wild boar not to Morgan but to American diplomat Lloyd C. Griscom. As Griscom would later tell it: "I completely forgot about the King's wild boar until one day I received a telegram from a frantic shipping agent, saying that they were at the New York docks. Would I have them removed at once?" Griscom, perplexed as to

Club house entrance hall. The draped opening led to the dining room. (Georgia Department of Archives and History)

First page of the club register, January 21, 1888. The first signature is that of club president, Henry Howland. (Everett Collection, Coastal Georgia Historical Society)

what to do with the animals, persuaded Morgan to find a place for them on his property in the Adirondacks, but local residents were horrified. Morgan finally "found sanctuary for the beasts" on Jekyl Island, where they were allowed to mingle with the indigenous wild pigs.[9]

Unwanted livestock and game were only two of the many problems that confronted Superintendent Ogden, who was doing his best to stave off crisis. He had had to deal with grading roads, draining ponds, cutting a canal, stocking the island with quail and pheasants, selling surplus hunting dogs, constructing henhouses, stables, and a cottage for the gamekeeper's assistant, clearing and planting the land with useful crops (such as buckwheat, oats, corn, peas, rice, and sorghum), checking the condition of the boats and wharf, and overseeing the club house. It was, however, the complex operation of the latter that during the club's first season would prove to be most difficult and most frustrating.

The club house opened its doors officially with the arrival of the executive committee on the island on January 21, 1888. The first name in the club register was that of its president, Henry Howland, who had been elected upon the death of Lloyd Aspinwall and whose visit lasted only nine days. Most of the subsequent guests were members and their families, although under club rules they were entitled to bring guests for as long as two weeks. And by March in excess of two hundred members and guests plus their maids, valets, and children had poured into the Jekyl Island club house with great expectations and high spirits, anticipating a relaxed vacation of carriage driving, riding, hunting, bathing, and yachting.

The island was rich in history and legend, having been occupied by Indians,

Kate Graf, Jekyl Island housekeeper, and her future husband, Henry Clay Butler, of New York, standing with unidentified people on the porch of the du Bignon house. Both were working on Jekyl by the time of the first club season in 1888. They were married in 1891 and returned to New York to work for the Union Club. Kate was replaced as housekeeper by Minnie Schuppan. (Georgia Department of Archives and History)

Spanish missionaries, English settlers, and, most recently, French planters (the du Bignons). Remnants of the past such as the du Bignon cemetery and the "old tabby," ruins of a house built by Major William Horton, aide to Georgia's founder, General James Edward Oglethorpe, still recalled those bygone eras. But above all the natural beauty of Jekyl, combined of course with the club's improvements, made it, as the prospectus had promised, a veritable "paradise" for people of means, where they could lead a life of "unalloyed pleasure."

The island was, as reported in the club prospectus, extraordinarily beautiful. Its varied pleasures included not only superb ocean views and a magnificent beach 150 feet wide at high tide but also an opportunity to experience the incomparable

Marshes of Glynn, the likes of which club guests had never seen in the North and which had been made famous only a few years before in a popular poem, "The Marshes of Glynn" by Sidney Lanier. Spanish moss hung mysteriously from immense live oak trees and seemed to bespeak the many legends of Indians, pirates, and buried treasure that enchanted the island's past. Game was abundant and hunting always an adventure, for visitors never knew when they might encounter, along with the deer, doves, and wild turkeys, a ferocious wild boar or a rattlesnake. Giant sea turtles, crabs, and a vast array of seashells could be found on the beach. Above all, the island provided a warm and salubrious refuge from the bitter northern winter they had left behind.

Almost half the members were on the island during some portion of the first season. Among them were those responsible

The ruins of the second plantation house of William Horton, known to Jekyl Islanders as "old tabby." (Jekyll Island Museum)

The *Alva,* steam yacht of William Kissam Vanderbilt, came for the club's opening season in 1888. (Peabody Museum of Salem)

The Oglethorpe Hotel in Brunswick shared its maiden season with the Jekyl Island Club. Architectural similarities between the two are striking. (Courtesy of B. W. Caples)

for the very existence of the club: Claflin, du Bignon, and Finney. Others added splendor and excitement to the season. Mr. and Mrs. William Rockefeller and the Marshall Fields arrived on March 2, and "fashionably late," on March 31 came what can only be described as Alva Vanderbilt's party, for she was the undisputed queen of New York society. The Vanderbilt yacht, the *Alva*, had sailed regally into Brunswick harbor the day before and had

anchored off the southern tip of Jekyl Island. Its party of seven, plus the crew members and servants, included not only Alva and her husband, club member William K. Vanderbilt, but also O. H. P. Belmont, who would a few years later, to the raised eyebrows of the Jekyl Islanders, become her second husband a little too soon after her divorce from Vanderbilt.[10]

William Rockefeller, brother of John D., and his wife, the former Almira Geraldine Goodsell, arrived for Jekyl's first season on March 2, 1888. (Rockefeller Archive Center)

The people of Brunswick observed the comings and goings of the wealthy Jekyl guests with more than casual interest. Their arrivals and departures were regularly reported in the local newspaper as they passed through the city or paused briefly to spend the night in the new Oglethorpe Hotel, as the Rockfellers did on March 16. Never had the growing city of Brunswick seen such a dazzling panoply of wealthy people debarking from the club launch at the port, riding through the streets in handsome carriages, and nonchalantly boarding their private train cars at the railroad station. Such celebrated names as Rockefeller and Vanderbilt had not often filled the notices of its newspaper, and the citizens were as delighted with the spectacle as the businessmen were with the new opportunities they perceived.

Considering the glittering guests, accustomed to the luxuries of such posh resorts as Newport, Superintendent Ogden must have thought his problems monumental. The board of directors had arranged for servants and supplies to be provided by the newly constructed Oglethorpe Hotel in Brunswick. The Oglethorpe and the Jekyl Island Club were having simultaneous maiden seasons. Since the late arrival and overflow of Jekyl guests were expected to provide a major clientele for the new hotel, it had seemed quite reasonable that the two establishments should cooperate in such a way. According to the post-season report that Ogden submitted on May 1 to the board of directors, Mr. Crittenden, manager of the Oglethorpe, was "to assume charge" of providing servants and supplies, thus relieving Ogden of this time-consuming task. Because he had relied upon this arrangement exclusively, Ogden had taken no other steps. He soon recognized, however, that Crittenden had quite enough to do to take care of the Oglethorpe and would be unable to do justice to the Jekyl Island club house.

By then it was too late to make other suitable arrangements, and Ogden had to seek assistance from whatever sources he could find. The best servants had already been snapped up by hotels in Jacksonville and Saint Augustine, and Ogden bemoaned the fact that "no competent cooks, caterer or steward could be found at such short notice, and we were obliged to start with such an unskilled force as we were able to pick up for the occasion."

One can imagine his consternation, a makeshift crew at his side, expecting the arrival of Alva Vanderbilt. And everything that could possibly go wrong did. Ogden, who had no background as a hotel-keeper, suddenly felt obliged "to exhibit all the qualifications only acquired by years of experience." No allowances, he felt, were made for his unique problems and inexperience. Hot water was insufficient for kitchen, laundry, and baths; gas fixtures provided inadequate lighting; and the stables were too small for all the members' horses. "All these annoyances that could not be foreseen," Ogden wrote with self-deprecating humor, "were charged to the incompetency of your superintendent, greatly to the detriment of his reputation as manager, and not much to his encouragement." He could not resist adding, with a tinge of sarcasm, that if his performance was unsatisfactory in any way, it was probably the result of "his inability to appreciate and adopt the vast amount of advice so liberally tendered" by "so many persons of conflicting opinions, each one expecting his suggestions should be adopted, taking offence if they are not."

He noted, however, that "in due time many of the deficiencies were supplied, the difficulties overcome, and things ran more smoothly, with the exception of occasional upheavals of criticism on the quality of the oranges or butter, the guests seemed pretty well satisfied, especially after predatory excursions to, and an experience with the many hotels in the vicinity." He happily reported that the verdict was in the final analysis "almost unanimously satisfactory" and announced that, contrary to members' expectations, the club house, showed no loss, but, in fact, a slight profit. Expressing "a natural pride and satisfaction in knowing that it had been made a most unqualified success" and convinced that he had done all in his power to launch the club well, Ogden tendered his resignation, explaining that he had "given all the time to the enterprise" that he could afford. Thus the Jekyl Island Club closed its first season, which had lasted from January 21 to mid-April.[11]

With the resignation of Ogden, club leaders were forced to find a replacement. Thomas C. Clarke, a member of the board of directors, highly recommended a man named H. M. Schley who received additional endorsement from N. K. Fairbank of Chicago at a meeting of the executive committee on May 31, 1888. Schley was hired to take "full charge of the island" and given a two-year contract, "unless sooner discharged for incompetency or mismanagement."[12] At the same meeting the previous season's clerk, a young Swiss immigrant named Ernest Gilbert Grob, was retained to manage the club house proper and to serve as cashier and accountant for a monthly salary of $125 plus room and board.

Under new management, the second club season promised to be an even greater success than the first. Guests began to arrive as early as November 22, and Secretary Finney predicted that rooms would

Lucy Carnegie, owner of Dungeness estate on Cumberland Island, was a frequent visitor to Jekyl. She arrived on March 10, 1889, during the second club season, with a party of fourteen. In 1903 her brother-in-law, Andrew Carnegie, accompanied her to Jekyl, and probably on this occasion was honored with a dinner. Andrew Carnegie is seated fourth from left. Beside him (third from left) is Joseph Pulitzer. (Jekyll Island Museum)

"be packed full" from February on. In answer to an inquiry from Henry Hyde about conditions at the club, he declared: "The house is in good order, the table excellent, and the weather perfection."[13] Unfortunately, Finney's prognostications for a packed house failed to come true. Attendance was low, especially in the months of January and February. A mild northern winter failed to motivate the members to depart for warmer climes, and a yellow fever scare in the Brunswick area was also a deterrent. As a consequence, the club house sustained a loss of almost $2,000.

Nevertheless, the club house manager's report of May 1, 1889, struck an optimistic note, indicating that, despite the deficit, receipts had increased. He projected that with an average of only forty guests, the club house could make a profit of $10,000 a season. But these roseate

claims concerning the future profitability of the club house turned out to be badly in error, for during the next nine years the house would realize a gain only twice.[14]

The general tone of optimism was warranted, however. Club property, which was constantly being expanded and improved, had increased in value. Indeed, promoters who recognized its intrinsic worth had by 1889 several times offered to purchase the island and its assets for a considerable profit to the club. But the membership, committed to the organization, declined to sell, preferring to pay hefty annual assessments to absorb the club's debts and expenses.

One thing was evident, however, by the close of the 1889 season. Schley would not continue as superintendent for another year. What prompted his discharge or resignation is unknown, but by June 1889 Ernest Grob had assumed the title and duties of superintendent, a post he would not relinquish for the next forty-two years.

3. A Life of Elegant Leisure

Luck had smiled upon the Jekyl Island leadership when they engaged Ernest Gilbert Grob as superintendent. His old-world charm, deference to the wealthy members, and constant attention to their every need became as much a part of the club's fabric as its island setting. His first season at the helm was, in fact, so successful that to dissuade him from accepting other offers, the executive committee increased his salary almost at once to $200 a month and by 1898 to $250.

As a rule, Grob, who worked at a northern resort during the summer, arrived at Jekyl in October or November, well in advance of the season, to make necessary preparations. The pampered life of the island's wealthy required enormous efforts on the part of the club staff. At Grob's side during the early years was an assistant superintendent, William Turner, who had been with the club since its inception. By 1892, however, he had been replaced by Julius A. Falk, who not only assisted Grob and managed the island during the summer but also doubled as bookkeeper and, from 1908, was secretary and assistant treasurer.

By the time of Grob's arrival, the assistant superintendent would already have set plans in motion to procure the multitude of waiters, chambermaids, and other employees the club season required. Ogden's earlier disastrous scheme of relying on helpers from the Oglethorpe Hotel had, of course, been totally abandoned. Now they hired the seasonal staff from various establishments in the North, where Grob had many contacts. One of these, Warren Leland, Jr., who had briefly managed the

Oglethorpe, as well as hotels in Chicago and New York, was urged by Falk in 1898 to "be on the lookout for a good Head Waiter . . . for our coming season." The headwaiter in question was to receive a salary of $70 a month and was expected to bring with him fourteen other waiters at $35 a month, a pantry man and woman each receiving $20, two nurse hall waitresses at $17, and a helps' hall waiter at $20.[1]

The most important and highest-paid seasonal employee, however, was the chef, who earned the handsome monthly salary of $125 to $150, depending upon satisfactory service. Failure to hire a topflight chef or head waiter inevitably brought a chorus of complaints about poor food or service from a membership not reticent about voicing its displeasure. Club member Henry Hyde tended to dismiss such grumbling as the product of sour stomachs or a bad night's sleep. "You cannot expect in a club with a hundred members [actually 86] that there will not be some disagreeable, snapping, snarling men."[2] After one such instance in 1897 club leadership briefly took over from Grob the responsibility for choosing both a head waiter and the chef. But Grob expressed his resentment at this intrusion into his domain, and by the following season he was once again fully in charge of hiring.

Like the head waiter, the chef was expected to bring with him a full complement of kitchen workers. "You are to get the best people for the money," wrote Falk to Charles Tamagin, who was hired for the 1898 position, "and be especially careful about your women, they must be first class and clean."[3]

Thus, in late December or early January of each year, Brunswick witnessed the arrival of a parade of specialty cooks, dish

Ernest Gilbert Grob, the club's superintendent for forty-two years, about 1890. (Everett Collection, Coastal Georgia Historical Society)

Servants arriving on the *Jekyl Island* steamer to work for the club season. The new steamer replaced the worn-out *Howland* in 1901. (Jekyll Island Museum)

and pot washers, laundry women, chambermaids, tray boys, porters, and sundry other workers. A mixed lot of immigrants and first generation Americans they were—from Ireland and Italy primarily, but also hailing from such diverse countries as England, France, Canada, Greece, and Germany. They arrived, dressed in their best, along with members' horses and heavy luggage aboard the Mallory Steamship Line.

Additional black labor was employed locally to serve as bellboys, stable hands, caddies, washerwomen, house cleaners, ditchdiggers, road workers, kitchen helpers, and day laborers on construction sites. They were paid minimal wages. An unskilled laborer received, for example, $1.00 per day, later raised to $1.50. Moreover, blacks were paid less than whites for the same work, as Grob clearly revealed in a letter in 1899. In replacing a "colored stable man," who had received the salary of $20 per month plus room and board, Grob proposed to the prospective employee that "if you would like the position, being a white man, I will pay you $25." Whites were preferred to blacks in jobs demanding special responsibilities or intimacy with the members. In requesting a man to teach bicycle lessons, Grob specifically stated: "I hope the man you send is white and not colored."[4]

Since the United States, North as well as South, was a segregated society, blacks on Jekyl lived in separate quarters. And the black servants' dormitory provided housing for males only, forcing married men to maintain their families in Brunswick and vicinity. In December 1915, in accord with the practices of major plantations in coastal Georgia, a plan was developed to provide

Above: Nine waiters arrived by Mallory steamer for the 1912 season. Among the group were Hector Delijanis (third from left) and George Harvey (believed to be fourth from left). (Jekyll Island Museum)

Right: Waiters on the beach on March 12, 1912. Before the day was over, Hector Delijanis (front row, third from left) and his friend, George Harvey, would drown in a freak accident. Funeral services were held in Faith Chapel, and both men were buried in the du Bignon cemetery on the island. The photograph was made by another waiter, Bert Stallman. (Jekyll Island Museum)

Opposite, top right: The chef and his family arrive to begin a new season. (Jekyll Island Museum)

Right: The white servants' annex was constructed sometime between 1888 and 1891. Heat was added in 1914 after Superintendent Grob complained that the "quarters are not fit for humans in cold weather." The black servants' dormitory is to the left. (Jekyll Island Museum)

Right: Servants enjoy a Saint Patrick's Day dance on March 17, 1909, in the stable of Frederic Baker. A social hall was eventually added to the white servants' annex. (Jekyll Island Museum)

Workers found time from their duties to relax on the beach. (Jekyll Island Museum)

black families with homes and garden plots on the island. Ten cottages were constructed the following year at a cost of $260 each. Although the club compensated itself by lowering wages again to $1.00 per day on a par with mainland plantations, black employees expressed satisfaction with the plan and felt they were better off in the long run under its terms.[5]

Blacks were also subjected to special rules, in some cases, perhaps, for their own safety, but usually to protect the club. In 1888, for example, the game committee adopted a regulation that "all negro employees shall follow the open roads and paths when coming to or going to work." And in 1900 when a smallpox epidemic broke out in Brunswick, the club quarantined the island. "We have not quarantined against Brunswick generally," Grob explained, "but have made such rules as will prevent the colored people from coming to or leaving the island."[6]

The club management and membership, by and large, harbored the stereotypical view of blacks shared in general by the nation's whites. Although official club correspondence always referred to blacks as "colored" or "negro," in private they were frequently called "darkies" or "coons." Viewed as inferiors with few skills, they were thus considered capable of only menial tasks and were often regarded as clownish people whose colorful dress was outlandish.

But there was also a paternalistic side to Jekyl Island racism, as was the case nationally among the upper class. Members contributed to a welfare fund for blacks, donated to their churches, and provided them with medical care and a chapel in which to worship on the island. Some seemed to develop a lasting affection for particular black employees, as did the Charles Maurices for their coachman and later caretaker, Charlie Hill. Other blacks worked for many years on the island and were viewed as trusted and loyal em-

Blacks were employed on Jekyl in a variety of capacities. Here caddies lounge while golfers practice putting. (Everett Collection, Coastal Georgia Historical Society)

John Cain (standing, right) in a wagon drawn by his mules, Pete and Julia. Cain's laugh was legendary among club members and was described by one visitor as "so loud and peculiar that when I first heard it I hurried to the window in amazement." (Jekyll Island Museum)

Club members, among them Edwin Gould (center, left of fiddler), celebrate a season's opening with a beach party that included entertainment by club employees. (Georgia Department of Archives and History)

ployees—among them Ophelia and Winslow Polite and Page and Aleathia Parland. One black employee who rose to a position of relative eminence among his fellows was Sam Denegal, foreman of road crews and forest workers and one of the few blacks entrusted with supervisory status. It was Denegal, for instance, who had been consulted by the club management before implementing the 1915 housing plan for blacks.

Segregation laws and customs, while observed generally, were not taken to the extreme, especially when to do so might interfere with the smooth functioning of club business. Thus when an employee of a Savannah supply and construction company who was working on the island caused trouble about his sleeping quarters because they were located in the proximity of blacks, Grob wrote indignantly to his employer:

> I beg to say that your Mr. Johnson is an ass, and he will be lucky if he will never have to put up with any worse accommodations than he had here. On the lower floor of our servants headquarters are two private coachmen (colored) belonging to Mr. Pulitzer, but there was no need of their meeting in any way. Our principal employees sleep in that part of the house in which he roomed. I cannot understand why he was able to sleep there one night, and could not do so one more, by which time he would have finished

his work. I was put to much inconvenience by his actions, in future unless you can promise to send a man who has some common sense, I will have to get our work done elsewhere.[7]

Not long after the arrival of the servants, members and guests began to pour into the club. A few arrived regally in their own yachts, but the majority reached Brunswick by train, although riding in private cars and compartments, to be sure. Travel arrangements to the island were normally made by the members themselves, but Grob and the club officers worked together with railroad officials to expedite runs to Brunswick and ensure that the trips were pleasant. To guarantee preferential treatment for members, Grob gained permission to spread a "light luncheon" for railroad officials meeting at the Oglethorpe Hotel in December 1898. He also used his influence with a new club member, Samuel Spencer, president of the Southern Railroad, to prevent the transfer of a popular conductor named C. A. Turner from the "Jekyl Island" train to another post. He "knows all our people," Grob explained, "and has been extremely nice to them, . . . stopping the train at the wharf where our boat lies, and having someone look after their baggage."[8]

Upon arrival in Brunswick, guests and baggage would be transported to Jekyl Island aboard the club steamer, *Howland*, with Captain Clark at the helm. Waiting to greet them at the Jekyl dock would be

Members and guests arrived at and departed from the Jekyl Island wharf, shown here as it looked before being remodeled later in the century. (Georgia Department of Archives and History)

Captain James Agnew Clark, left, is assisting guests aboard the club yacht. The third man from the left, in the white hat, is Henry Kirke Porter. (Jekyll Island Museum)

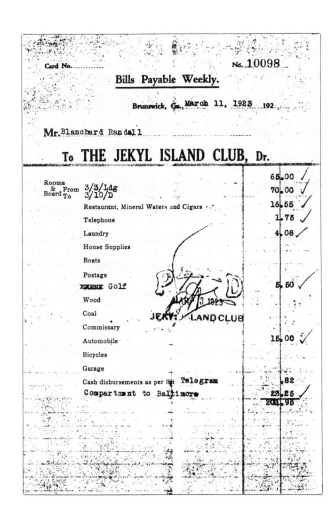

No. 4812
Folio 124
Bills Payable Weekly

Jekyl Island, ___ FEB 11 1909 ___ 190

M Hon Jos E. Willard
To the JEKYL ISLAND CLUB, Dr.
BILLS RENDERED EVERY SUNDAY.

Rooms	@ 15.00 per day	75 --	
Board	coachman price to Feb 7	85 -- / 5 50	
Mineral Water & cigars	✓	5 40	
Laundry	✓	4 97	
Boats	✓	5 --	
Postage		33	
Living	✓	3 75 / 50	
Bicycle	✓	3 --	
Express	✓	2 40	
Teleg to arrange RR reservation		50	
		$ 191 35	

Card No. _____   No. 10098

Bills Payable Weekly.

Brunswick, Ga., March 11, 1923 192

Mr. Blanchard Randall
To THE JEKYL ISLAND CLUB, Dr.

Rooms & Board	From 3/3/Ldg To 3/10/D			65.00 ✓
				70.00 ✓
Restaurant, Mineral Waters and Cigars				16.55 ✓
Telephone				1.75 ✓
Laundry				4.08 ✓
House Supplies				
Boats				
Postage				
Golf				5.50
Wood				
Coal				
Commissary				
Automobile				15.00 ✓
Bicycles				
Garage				
Cash disbursements as per list Telegram				.82
Compartment to Baltimore				22.25 ✓
				201.95

Bills presented to club members Joseph E. Willard (1907–13) and Blanchard Randall (1921–31) reflect the cost of room, board, and sundries at the Jekyl Island Club in 1909 and 1923. (Maryland Historical Society and the Library of Congress)

Grob or a club officer, often with a bouquet of flowers for ladies in the party. Debarking at the wharf, visitors would proceed to the club house to sign the register and then, at last, be shown to their lodgings.

Finding accommodations for the vast array of members, guests, and their private servants (valets, secretaries, maids, nurses, tutors, stablemen, housekeepers, and coachmen) was not always an easy matter. The club house originally contained sixty rooms for guests, with the top floor being set aside for servants. But upon the recommendation of Ogden in May 1888, a separate servants' annex had been constructed,

thereby freeing a number of servants' rooms in the club house for the use of members and guests. Quarters in the club house varied considerably in style and type, including singles and doubles with and without bath or parlor. Prices ranged from $1.50 to $6.00 per night, with guests being required to pay 20 percent more than members. A proposal to raise prices in 1896 met with considerable resistance.

Rooms with baths on the lower floors were inevitably in greatest demand, but space in the club house to suit one's exact needs was not always available. It could be obtained relatively easily in January but became more difficult in February and was often impossible in March. By 1900 conditions had become so crowded that a rule was adopted prohibiting guests after February 20, and reservation rules, even for members, became very strict. As Grob was obliged to explain to J. Herbert Ballantine, a manufacturer from Newark, New Jersey: "You of course are aware that we have a club rule which forbids our reserving rooms for any member to the exclusion of another member. A member always has the preference of a guest, and a guest can be turned out should a member want a room for himself or family, but a guest cannot be turned out for another guest, until the expiration of his two weeks limit."9

Thus, in any given year, Grob's letterbooks would be filled with telegrams warning of crowded conditions. When the club house overflowed, he could turn to the club cottage, the former du Bignon house, which now rented for $15 per day. In Grob's opinion, the lack of club house space had cost the organization several new members, and he urged old members to guarantee themselves good accommodations by investing in private dwellings. A number had begun to do so, and others eventually followed suit. Such members' houses, when not occupied by the owners, were sparingly and selectively let out. Private apartments in a complex constructed in 1896 were available on occasion at $25 per day, including linen and the service of a chambermaid and a bellboy.

But the club house was much more than a hotel. It was also the hub of Jekyl Island's social life, which centered around the daily ritual of dining. Swarms of kitchen workers prepared sumptuous luncheons and dinners, served in the beautifully appointed dining room by discreet waiters in swallowtail coats. The Jekyl cuisine was, according to one visitor, "on a scale to equal the best restaurants in the country." Although chefs were most often French and Italian, the food they prepared conformed, for the most part, to the native coastal setting, and the club menus regularly included the island's bounties of oysters, terrapin, venison, quail, turkey, pheasant, shrimp, and fish. In June 1897, Henry Hyde suggested the installation of a "general utility stove . . . to be used by a woman cook to make New England dishes," but his idea was promptly scuttled. Male chefs and native-grown dishes continued to predominate. Spinach and lettuce from the club garden formed the basis of two specialities of the house: cream of lettuce soup and spinach on toast. And "good light bread, rolls, [and] corn muffins" were baked in a wood-burning oven. Fresh cream and butter were imported from Franklin, Tennessee, and elsewhere until the early twentieth century when the club established a full-scale dairy of its own, which produced so much butter that the surplus had to be sold in Brunswick.10

A dinner at the club such as that served to the Maurices on February 17, 1902, consisting of caviar on toast, raw oysters, fish, roast beef, potatoes, peas, roast quail, sherbert, lettuce salad, chocolate pudding, sauterne, champagne, and coffee, was typical daily fare. Lunch was scarcely lighter. On March 22, 1903, club members enjoyed a delicious luncheon of oysters, soup, crab newberg, roast lamb, squash, eggplant, lettuce and tomato salad, wine jelly, whipped cream, champagne,

The Jekyl dining room about 1890. The faded photograph does little justice to the richly patterned carpet and the colors of the interior. (Jekyll Island Museum)

claret, coffee, cherry brandy, crème de menthe, almonds, olives, bonbons, and chocolate peppermints. Charlotte Maurice recorded almost every luncheon and dinner during her stays at Jekyl from 1899 until 1909, and her diary indicates daily feasts of the same order.[11]

Cuisine at Jekyl, as might be expected, was better in some years than in others. Whenever the food was less than superb, club leaders received a flood of "growling letters." Members and guests simply refused to drink poor wine. In January 1900,

Grob told club officials that the wines furnished by the Café Savarin Company, although expensive, were "simply abominable and a disgrace to such a club as this. Every bottle which is sent up to the Dining Room is returned." Even in good years the wine selection was small, as most members preferred "poland water" instead. Some enjoyed good beer, which was also kept on hand, and, at the behest of J. Herbert Ballantine, who joined the club in 1895, Grob put Ballantine's India Pale Ale on the list in 1898 and promised to add Ballantine's lager beer the next season.[12]

Dining at Jekyl, though leisurely, was hardly informal and not without social significance and a certain ritual. Members wore formal attire, reserved special tables, and frequently arranged private parties in the dining room. In the opinion of James W. Ellsworth, "the practice of giving formal dinners," to the exclusion of some members, threatened to have a detrimental effect on the social harmony of the club. His complaint, however, was largely ignored, and the practice appears to have continued throughout the club's existence.[13]

Children were not permitted in the dining room unaccompanied by parents or guardians. Special arrangements might be made, however, to serve them at an hour earlier than adults. The price of meals a day at Jekyl in 1896 was $4.00. Children seated at a guest's table were charged $2.50, but if seated at a servant's table, they paid only $2.00. Meals served in rooms or cottages cost an extra fifty cents.

Although the dining room was clearly an important feature, Jekyl Islanders used their club house as much more than a mere eating establishment. Members and guests gathered there frequently just to enjoy one another's company. Occasional grand balls were held, but such lavish entertainments were rare. The more usual after-dinner activities were simple but varied, allowing members and guests to select whatever best suited their tastes and individual life-styles.

The *New York Times* of October 4, 1896, described the typical Jekyl soirée: "Music and dancing and card parties are the evening amusements, and all hands usually appear in evening dress." Whist was the favorite card game at the time, and, for those who did not care for whist, billiards was always available in a room set aside for this purpose. Or one might prefer to retire to the solitude of the reading room.

Prior to 1896 a bar had attracted a mixed crowd for drinks both before and after dinner, "Jekyl Island Whiskey" (scotch) being one of the favorites. The open bar, "where men and women stand up and drink," however, offended the Victorian sensibilities of Frederic Baker, who denounced it as "against Club rules and disreputable." He preferred a "closed bar" or a "café."[14] Baker apparently had his way, at least for a time, for in the same article the *Times* reported: "There is not a barroom in the house, all the liquors sold being served by waiters from a bar in a house outside."

Perhaps the most popular room in the club house was the main parlor. Here around the cheerful fireplace one might encounter club president Henry Howland, a humorous after-dinner speaker, holding forth, or clusters of men chatting about business, exchanging investment tips, and discussing club and world affairs. It might have been at just such a gathering that Joseph Pulitzer mentioned to New York stockbroker John G. Moore that he had an idle $500,000 that he wanted "to place to advantage." Some members, accustomed to the seclusion of all-male clubs, mounted an abortive "scheme to forbid ladies sitting in that part of the building," but, as Henry Hyde predicted, it could "never be carried out." Although the club house had a separate "handsome ladies' parlor," obviously intended to keep women in their place, the *Times* reported that "The ladies play billiards in the common billiard hall and go anywhere they choose."[15]

The club house was also the business center of the island. Stockholder and committee meetings were conducted there, and just off the main entrance, which was adorned with game trophies, was the office of Superintendent Grob. Here he could be found on any given day talking with club officers, dictating dozens of letters and telegrams, and attending to the myriad details incident to the management of Jekyl Island. The "Club is run more on the plan of a large country house," he once explained to a newly elected member, "than like a hotel." He tried, therefore, to treat each person as a special guest, catering to his or her whims or solving his or her problems. One might find Grob variously distributing sample cigars among the membership, ordering orange buds for Vice President Fairbank, attempting to persuade Brunswick officials to lower taxes on Jekyl property, sending mockingbirds to William Rockefeller in Tarrytown, New York, or assuring Mrs. A. A. Preston (Laura Fitzhugh-Preston) that her piano score for the "Jekyl Island Club Waltz" was worthy of publication and advising her "to dedicate it to our President of the Club (as that would assure it a good sale) he being a very popular man in N. Y. society."[16] It was also Grob's duty to enforce club rules. This task required both firmness and tact, as was demonstrated in the case of Mrs. John G. Moore, who chose in 1898 to ignore the regulation that forbade dogs in the club house. Grob notified her politely that she would have to place her animals in the care of the gamekeeper, as the rules dictated, but since the thought of her pets mingling with the hunting curs was anathema to her, she ignored Grob's diplomatic request, thus forcing him to send a second, more peremptory notice. Reminding her that "this is a club, and all clubs have certain rules," he offered to place the dogs with the gardener and his wife instead.[17]

Serious problems, on the other hand, Grob dealt with forcefully. Learning that the mail to Jekyl Island was being rifled and money removed, he went first to the Brunswick postmaster and then, when nothing was done, addressed himself directly to the postmaster general in Washington. In another instance, when a dispute arose between club member David H. King, Jr., and the firm of Tutt and Ball of Jacksonville, Florida, which had billed him twice for work not done satisfactorily in the first place, Grob interceded with a compromise offer and the threat of legal action.

Settling such controversies was one aspect of Grob's job. Maintaining good public relations was another. Despite its reputation for exclusivity, the club tried to avoid any appearance of condescension toward the local community. During the summer months, organized groups of Brunswick citizens, such as the Humane Society or the Ladies Hospital Association, were allowed frequent but short excursions to the island.

Grob's value to the club was incalculable. On those few occasions when he became dissatisfied or his health failed, club officers were wise enough to meet his modest financial demands and to grant him extended vacations, recognizing that he was, as Frederic Baker described him in 1898, "a necessity," and a man of good taste with "capacity for his present position."[18]

Although he oversaw all facets of the operation in a general way, Grob was fortunate to have good help in many areas. Such members of the permanent staff as yacht captain James A. Clark and his engineer John F. Courier were invaluable assets. The carpenter, Torkel ("Chips") Torkelsen kept the facilities in good repair, while the gardener, Tom Scott, made an important contribution to the club table. The housekeeper, Minnie Schuppan, later

Clark Cottage, built in 1901 for Captain Clark and Minnie Schuppan after their marriage the previous year. (Jekyll Island Museum)

Key members of the club staff: (left to right) Minnie Schuppan, head housekeeper; Ernest Grob, superintendent; James A. Clark, yacht captain; and Julius A. Falk, assistant superintendent, enjoy a ride on the beach. (Georgia Department of Archives and History)

Jekyl Island's head game-keeper, probably Charles Brinkman. According to club rules, "under penalty of instant dismissal," the gamekeeper and superintendent were the only employees authorized to carry guns, use traps, or take birds and eggs. (Charles Lanier, *Jekyl Island Club,* n.p.: privately printed, 1911)

Mrs. James A. Clark, was the highest-ranking female member of the staff. Having replaced Kate Graf in 1891, she oversaw the daily maintenance of the club house as well as many of the cottages and later apartments. In her bailiwick her authority was supreme, to a degree extending even to privately hired maids. "My maid at Jekyl is going to leave," noted Henry Hyde in 1897. "She had some trouble with the housekeeper."[19]

Such oversight and minor contretemps, however, went on behind the scenes as far as most Jekyl members were concerned. They came down for rest and relaxation. And they enjoyed the island with a vengeance. In the club's early years, many members came to the island for its hunting, a favorite pastime for men and women

alike. "Many of the ladies," reported the *New York Times,* "wives of members and guests, are crack shots, and may well be proud of their achievements afield."[20]

The island had been well stocked with wildlife by John E. du Bignon even before it was purchased by the club, but because of the extraordinarily large amount of game killed each year, it was constantly necessary to restock. Several attempts were made to raise pheasants on the island but with only limited success, and these birds, along with hundreds of quail and turkeys, were purchased and imported annually. The pheasants were brought in from as far away as England. In 1897, several Virginia bucks were bought "for the purpose of infusing new blood into the stock of deer at present on the island."[21]

Thus few employees during these early years were more important than the head gamekeeper, Charles Brinkman, whose chief duties were "to take charge of the

The party of club member
William Struthers on a
hunt. (Jekyll Island
Museum)

Albert Maurice (right) and a friend display the deer they have shot during a hunt. (Georgia Department of Archives and History)

The taxidermist at Jekyl Island did a booming business but sometimes encountered problems. Grob informed Cyrus McCormick on June 19, 1909, that "Mr. Walbert the taxidermist reports that the 'coons' sent over by your son and Mr. Gould—were too far gone to do anything with them—they were in fact so far gone that even the hair was dropping off." (Georgia Department of Archives and History)

breeding, preservation, and care of game" and to maintain kennels. He received his instructions from the game committee through the superintendent to whom he was directly responsible.

The game rules posted in the club office conformed to the laws of Georgia, with shooting limits placed on certain types of game. "All game killed" was to "be turned over to the Club," with members and guests having "the first right, after the requirements of the Club are provided for, to buy a portion of their own shooting, at prices to be fixed by the Club." This rule probably accounted for the regular appearance of quail and other wild game on the club menu.[22]

While members and their families were free to shoot birds and animals up to the posted limits, there were regulations governing hunting privileges for guests, and boys under sixteen were not permitted to hunt at all. If a member was not on the island, he was entitled to transfer his hunting privilege to only one guest for one week. On the other hand, "If personally present," a member might invite up to three guests for each share he owned "to shoot at any one time. . . ." The rules were tightened in 1897 to preclude guests from shooting unless their hosts were present on the island, and even then only two visitors might be invited to participate instead of the previous three. Under the new rules, in accordance with members' Victorian values, shooting on Sunday was "strictly prohibited."

Members and guests were required to notify the superintendent whenever they intended to hunt and to record in the game books their kill for the day. During the first decade following the club's formal opening, an average of 1,302 quail were bagged per season with a record kill in 1898 of 2,815. In one fairly typical season, 1894–95,

members and their guests killed 1,551 quail, 1 pheasant, 31 deer, 73 ducks, 17 wild hogs, 3 alligators, 23 marsh hens, and 40 doves. Except for a bear allegedly sighted on the island and even mentioned once in the executive minutes (November 28, 1888), the only ferocious animals on Jekyl were alligators, wild hogs, and rattlesnakes. Several alligators were taken each year. The largest on record, over nine feet long, was killed on February 28, 1895, by William S. Ellis, a relative of club member Rudolph Ellis of Philadelphia.[23]

Grob supervised the game department using the same meticulous efficiency with which he handled his other duties, but not without some difficulties. When he insisted that the gamekeeper should release one of his two black helpers during the off-season, Brinkman protested, and Grob was obliged to appeal to the chairman of the game committee, then Eugene A. Hoffman, dean of the General Theological Seminary in New York, for support. But Brinkman was not the only person Grob forced to toe the line. Dean Hoffman himself was reported by one of Brinkman's helpers to have violated the rules by killing two deer with illegal shot. Grob reminded him that if the report were true, he owed a fine of $10 for each violation. Hoffman apparently ignored Grob's letter and had to be sent a subsequent reminder. There is no evidence that he ever paid the fine.

Hoffman's imperious attitude spilled over into his administration of the game committee, which paid little attention to its authorized budget and spent liberally and at will. Club treasurer Frederic Baker noted in 1897 that he had had "many a fight with

the Game Committee," which had "spent thousands of dollars without the by your leave of the Ex[ecutive] Committee." And in the summer of the following year, Julius Falk, in Grob's absence, pled for advice from William Struthers, for as he reported, "The Game Committee's appropriation of $2500 is now exhausted and the expense is still going on."[24]

But in 1897 plans to introduce golf to the island threatened Hoffman's little empire, as devotees of the game contemplated usurping certain hunting grounds for their course. Dean Hoffman objected. In his opinion, it would be "unwise to take . . . ground now used by the gunners for the purpose of making golf links." The area was too small and much too rough, he protested. Besides, it was the "best on the

The original golf course laid out in 1898 was apparently rough at best. When asked to join the club in 1911, Robert Todd Lincoln declined. In a letter to Cyrus McCormick on February 14, he wrote, "[Jekyl] is a very pleasant place, but in one particular it is not just what I want as a Winter Resort; that is, in the matter of golfing. There is, it is true (or was) a place where one could make a pretence of knocking balls about, but it was not at all interesting as a golf course." (Southern Historical Collection, University of North Carolina)

island now given up to game, it is especially the favorite with the ladies who shoot, and it is always a resort of large numbers of quail."[25]

In fact, the day would come when hunting would recede into oblivion on Jekyl. As late as 1913, the gamekeeper was still making glowing predictions that pheasant, quail, deer, ducks, and boar were abundant as never before. But shooting that season proved to be the worst on record, including the bagging of only 5 quail, 31 pheasants, 102 ducks, 13 marsh hens, 3 alligators, and not a single deer, boar, turkey, dove, or grouse. It did little to bolster the flagging interest in the sport. By 1919, the game committee, once of such supreme importance, had been reduced to a single member, Welland DeVeaux Woodruff, a paper manufacturer from Saint Catherine's in Ontario—a clear indication that hunting was no longer considered the major attraction at Jekyl. It had been superseded by the increasingly popular games of golf and tennis. By the 1930s, the game committee had ceased to exist.

Tennis, imported from England in the late 1870s, was played primarily at exclusive country clubs. Jekyl Island provided for a court in the 1887 club prospectus, although the exact installation date is unknown. But tennis would not really become popular at Jekyl until about 1903, when it clearly surpassed hunting and vied with golf in popularity. By 1905 Robert Pruyn, chairman of the committee on golf and sports, was able to assert that "For two years, tennis has been the most popular outdoor sport," and he urged the construction of additional courts. They were not put in until 1909, when two more courts

were installed. In 1913 Edwin Gould would erect a private covered court, and in 1930 the club built a similar covered court for members' use.[26]

Golf, however, was quite another matter. The decline of hunting and the rise of golf seem directly related in Jekyl's history. Like tennis, golf was a foreign import (from Scotland) and a recreation for the wealthy elite. Although Newport had a course by 1890, Jekyl officers did not begin putting in links until the year they ran afoul of the chairman of the game committee—1897.

The course, paid for by private subscription and laid out by Arthur B. Claflin, younger brother of John Claflin, was under way in the spring of 1898. It was anticipated that the links would be ready for play by the opening of the following season. But disaster struck. On October 2, 1898, a hurricane hit the island. Falk reported the entire golf course "covered with tide water." He predicted that there would be no grass and the course would not be in condition for the coming season. By December, however, Superintendent Grob seemed more optimistic about getting the links ready for at least a part of the season. "You can send a man down to lay out the putting greens and . . . bunkers at any time," he notified Claflin. By the first week of January 1899 a golf professional named Rawlings from Lakewood, New Jersey, was on the scene and hard at work on the course. Just when he finished his task is not recorded, but it is probable that the first game of golf played on Jekyl Island took place during the season of 1899.[27]

The popularity of the game so increased as time went on that the club decided to replace the old course with a new one. In

In 1910, a year after a new course was laid out on Jekyl to replace the old one, the club hired Karl Keffer (far right) as its golf professional. A Canadian champion, he came highly recommended by Walter Travis, one of the nation's foremost golf experts. Keffer would serve in this capacity for thirty-two years. (Lanier, *Jekyl Island Club,* 1911)

March 1909 the committee on golf and sports gave Grob the go-ahead to begin work. Operating "upon the principle of doing all that is necessary and doing it in the best manner possible, and not doing anything now which is not necessary," they planned for only nine holes (with provision for possible later expansion to eighteen), to be laid out on a marshy savanna north of the club compound in the vicinity of Captain Wylly Road.

Two experts, Donald J. Ross and T. Hutchinson, the golf professional at Dungeness, were requested to submit designs. Although the committee selected Ross's layout, they continued to seek Hutchinson's advice as the plans progressed. Because the course was to be located in an area subject to tidal flooding, drainage ditches and a wide culvert leading to Jekyl Creek had to be dug and dikes and a floodgate erected. An engineer who had worked on the Panama Canal, J. B. High, was brought in to oversee the pro-

ject. The course, completed at a cost of $11,300, was ready for play at the beginning of the 1910 season. Three years later a golf house on Shell Road would be added, as well as two new holes stretching all the way to the sand dunes overlooking the sea and prefiguring the celebrated "Dunes Course" subsequently laid out by Walter Travis, one of the foremost golfers in the United States. It was Edwin Gould who assumed the entire expense for the extension.[28]

Another outdoor activity that seemed to attract early Jekyl Islanders regardless of their other sporting proclivities was horseback and buggy riding. Some members were experts in horsemanship and coach driving. For example, Fairman Rogers of Philadelphia, an original member who published a manual on "coaching" in 1900, was recognized as one of the world's leading authorities on the art and etiquette of four-in-hand driving. And Cornelius K. G. Billings, multimillionaire sportsman, wintered a valuable stable of world cham-

Carriage rides along
the moss-hung roadways
were typical afternoon
pleasures for many Jekyl
families. This photograph
was made before 1911
on Oglethorpe Road, near
Half-Moon Pond. (Lanier,
Jekyl Island Club,
1911)

The Rockefeller children pose on the beach with their driver, attired in full livery, in March 1905. (Rockefeller Archive Center)

pion trotters on a farm outside Brunswick near the turn of the century. But the vast majority merely enjoyed leisurely rides around the island.

Carriage rides in particular provided fun for the entire family. C. S. Maurice, with his coachman Charlie Hill at the reins, took his family on such a drive every afternoon like clockwork. Every season Mallory steamers would arrive carrying a panoply of members' buggies, horses, hay and oats, stable boys, and coachmen complete with elegant livery and top hats. For members who did not bring their own mounts and carriage horses, the club contracted with H. S. McCrary of Brunswick to furnish high quality horses for the season and a man to handle them. Additional stables were built on the island in 1888 to house twenty horses, and extra carriages and buggies were ordered because the demand for them during the previous season had been much greater than the supply.

In the 1890s the horse met a rival in the new national fad—the bicycle. "The bicy-

cle craze is still extending, and no telling where it will end," proclaimed William Rockefeller in 1895. His daughter was taking lessons, and his son, Percy, had also learned to ride. "I was quite surprised that he was so willing to take the bicycle riding at the Michaux Club," Rockefeller continued, "but it is, I think, largely explained from the fact that a number of his young girl friends ride there." The craze was not confined to the young. The Reverend Dr. Charles Henry Parkhurst, the only man ever elected an honorary member of the Jekyl Island Club, rode regularly in the company of his wife in New York. The craze was just reaching its peak nationally when it hit Jekyl. "Bicycling has taken precedence among the amusements at Jekyl," announced the *Brunswick Times-Advertiser* of February 21, 1896. And so it had. Young and old, male and female, millionaires and workers alike joined in the fun. Being a competitive lot, Jekyl Islanders soon set about organizing bicycle clubs and races. On March 25, 1897, Jean Struthers took first place in the bicycle spoon and egg race for ladies, and on the same day, Nathalie Fairbank emerged vic-

Employees enjoyed biking on the island roads and the beach. In 1917 the tutor of the children of a club member wrote: "This afternoon I rode up the new bicycle path . . . , then along the beach. . . . It is like sailing to ride one's wheel along the water's edge, mile after mile before the wind." (Lanier, *Jekyl Island Club*, 1911)

Children on Jekyl joined the bicycle craze. (Jekyll Island Museum)

Visitors to the island enjoy the pleasures of a *chaise roulante*. (Everett Collection, Coastal Georgia Historical Society)

torious in the ladies' bicycle show race at a distance of 100 yards. If its name is any indication, the Ladies' Rough Riding Obstacle Bicycle Society staged even more grueling contests.[29]

To keep pace with the fad, a professional bicycle man named G. W. Evans was hired from New York in 1897 to rent, repair, and maintain bicycles and to give lessons to novice riders. Evans might have made a considerable profit had he been a more scrupulous entrepreneur. In 1899, unable to come up with ready cash and lacking the credit he needed to furnish equipment, he appealed to the club for a loan. Grob advised against it. "I don't think it wise to advance Evans any money, I should think if he were upright in his business dealings he would not have any trouble in getting the necessary amount of 'wheels' on credit. . . ." When the man

persisted in his request, Grob sent him a curt and final sally: "If you cannot scrape together enough money to take the position, the better way is to leave it. Mr. Lanier [then club president] does not want to be bothered with any more letters from you."[30]

There was the inevitable conflict between the old and the new. Henry Hyde was no doubt one of many who worried that bicycles might spook his horses. Through his private secretary he requested that Grob ask his coachman "when he is driving or exercising his horses" to take "the greatest care" on the shell road, which ran between the club house and the beach, "as a number of bicyclists will no doubt be on that road and the horses coming on them suddenly might get excited and trouble might ensue. . . ." To make both cycling and horseback riding safer and more pleasant, members began donating special bicycle paths. Gordon McKay had one constructed at his own expense for about $1,000, and in 1898 William Rockefeller donated another one on the express condition that it "be used for bicycles exclusively." In later years still others would be added.[31]

Clearly, there was no reason ever to be idle on Jekyl. If the major forms of recreation were not appealing, one might picnic on the beach, swim or wade in the surf, fish in Jekyl Creek, boat, take excursions on the club yacht to neighboring islands, target shoot at the butt, or participate in the innumerable tournaments held each year. If Henry Hyde's schedule was typical in the least, life on Jekyl was never dull. Describing it to his son, he wrote:

> You speak of my leading a life of elegant leisure. Between my correspondence, riding two hours and a half in the morning and

A picnic on the beach opens the 1901 season. (Jekyll Island Museum)

driving in the afternoon and talking, I was never so busy in my life. Hardly have a moment to read the newspaper or a book. Am dining out nearly all the time, one night with the Royal Boar Hunters, another night on the presentation of a cup to Mrs. Stickney as the Captain of the Rough Riding Obstacle Bicycle Society, and last night I dined with Mr. and Mrs. Stickney. They had a very big turkey from their farm. Tonight I dine at Mrs. Struthers' so that the bewildering excitement and fast pace I am leading is beginning to tell on me.[32]

The Jekyl Island Club manifestly was not the dull place that Cleveland Amory de-

scribed in his *Last Resorts*. To be bored to death at Jekyl as Amory asserted, one would have had to be unimaginative to the extreme. Jekyl, declared Grob to one would-be interloper from Murfreesboro, Tennessee, was "a resort of pleasure and rest" where "only members . . . and their guests are permitted to land. . . ." It was a place where one might pursue "a life of elegant leisure" in which recreational activities were as varied as the desires of the members. Thus it would remain throughout the club's fascinating history.[33]

4. The Early Cottage Colony

Thomas C. Clarke, who had heartily approved Alexander's design and execution of the club house in 1887, was equally pleased in 1888 when he visited once more during the opening season. After enjoying island hospitality for three days, he pronounced its atmosphere "home like," the food also "like that of a private home," the riding and driving paths "very beautiful," and the weather "perfectly delightful." In a letter to his business partner, Charles Maurice, he noted: "One man [McEvers Bayard Brown] has begun to build a cottage. What for I dont know. The club house is good enough for me."[1]

Most members agreed, but a few, like Brown, would choose over the years to construct individual dwellings, which would not only provide greater privacy but also guarantee fine accommodations during the peak season when the club house overflowed with guests. The club prospectus had anticipated such needs, and landscape architect Cleveland had laid out fifty lots, one lot for each of the two shares allocated to the original members. During the life of the club the lots changed hands many times, but only a small number of members actually built homes. In all, fifteen members' cottages would be constructed on Jekyl.

Their owners occupied a distinctive place in Jekyl's history, and Frederic Baker, himself one of the early owners, once referred to the group as the "cottage colony." His phrase, however, implied a greater homogeneity than existed in reality. Although the owners mingled with one another socially and had certain interests in common, they also included among their intimates many members who had no interest in obtaining cottages and, not surprisingly, preferred the company of some of their neighbors more than that of others.

Although the cottage colony was never an enclave at odds with the rest of the membership, nevertheless a degree of friction occasionally surfaced between the non-cottage people and the homeowners. As Baker observed, certain "backbiters" complained that the cottage colony did "not pay into the club its share of expenses, and wants to conduct matters quite in its own interest." Even though homeowners may not have used club house amenities to the extent of other members, it simply was not true that they pursued their own selfish goals without regard to the greater good of the organization. On the contrary, they were among the club's most loyal and consistent supporters. Because of their stake in the island community, they took a proprietary interest in the enterprise. They tended to come down annually and usually spent longer periods at Jekyl than most members, thus providing stability and continuity to club seasons otherwise characterized by constant turnover. Some, among them Charles Maurice and N. K. Fairbank, served as informal hosts in the president's absence, welcoming newcomers as well as oldtimers as they arrived at the Jekyl dock. Baker himself was club treasurer for years and spent many hours on club affairs. They gave freely not only of time but also of money to improve Jekyl's facilities. As Almira Rockefeller, wife of William Rockefeller, a later cottage owner, commented in a letter to her daughter, "The golf course is a great expense and kept up by voluntary subscriptions. We never use it but pay more for its upkeep than many that use it." Such a situation was not atypical among cottage owners.[2]

The house constructed in 1888 but never occupied by eccentric millionaire McEvers Bayard Brown was the first cottage built by any Jekyl member. (Georgia Department of Archives and History)

Ironically, the man who built the first member's house on the island, McEvers Bayard Brown, did not fit the congenial mold of most of the other cottage dwellers. The Brown house, already under construction during the first club season, was never occupied by its owner. It stood isolated and empty in a remote area just north of Wylly Road at an inhospitable distance from the club compound. Legend has it that Brown planned the cottage in anticipation of his marriage, but when his bride-to-be jilted him, he lost interest in the house and seemingly all else and fled the country aboard his yacht, the *Valfreyia*. Dropping anchor along the Essex coast of England, he kept his vessel fully provisioned and manned, ready to sail at a moment's whim. There he remained, growing increasingly eccentric, until his death in 1926. However, sniffing the stuff of myth, the *New York Times* declared: "There is the inevitable gossip about a love affair that drove Mr. Brown into exile, but somehow he did not act like a man thus disappointed."

Strange to say, though he never lived in the cottage and probably never saw the finished structure, Brown retained his membership in the club, authorized the use of his house by club employees, and even contributed a substantial sum in later years to the liquidation of the club debt. In short, it would seem that even so reclusive a character as Brown shared at least one attribute of the cottage colonists, namely loyalty to the organization.[3]

The second private dwelling to be built on the island was that of Nathaniel Kellogg Fairbank, a well-known and influential Chicagoan. Constructed in 1890, the house was located on what would be called "the most convenient and desirable site on the Island," just south of the club house. Fairbank had purchased the lot from his New York stockbroker and friend, E. K. Willard, who had resigned from the club in 1888 and who, ten years later, would be expelled from the New York Stock Exchange for fraud.

Sixty-one-year-old Fairbank, a distinguished-looking gentleman with a taste for small black cigars, had served for many years as president of the prestigious Chicago Club. Considered one of the city's leading cultural philanthropists, he had been instrumental in the construction of Chicago's great Central Music Hall and trustee of both the Chicago Art Institute and the city's symphony orchestra. He also made generous contributions to such causes as Saint Luke's Hospital and the Newsboys' Home. His concern for the downtrodden extended, at times, to controversial issues, and both he and fellow club member Wirt Dexter had been among the staunch supporters of the Reverend David Swing, a free-thinking minister who had been forced to resign from the pulpit of the fashionable Fourth Presbyterian Church in

Left: The club house (left) is shown here with the club cottage (extreme right), formerly the du Bignon house, and the second member's residence (center), constructed by Nathaniel Kellogg Fairbank in 1890. (Everett Collection, Coastal Georgia Historical Society)

Lower left: A rare photograph of the Fairbank cottage, purchased in late 1903 or early 1904 by Walton Ferguson, Jr., of Stamford, Connecticut. Ferguson was an executive in the Union Carbide Company and, until his death in 1922, president of the Stamford Trust Company. During the rest of the 1920s and 1930s the house was owned first by Ralph Beaver Strassburger and then by Marjorie Bourne and her husband, Alexander Dallas Thayer. (Jekyll Island Museum)

Lower right: Club vice president Nathaniel K. Fairbank, of Chicago, with one of his grandchildren. (Chicago Historical Society)

1875, when his views on such issues as evolution had become notorious.

Just before the construction of his house, Fairbank had allowed himself to become involved in another such unpopular cause, to his later regret. A recent divorce scandal, called by the *New York Times* "the most indecent and revolting divorce trial ever heard in the Chicago courts," had deprived a once-popular matron, Mrs. Leslie Carter, of her child and the support of her husband.

Suited for little else than the role of the wife of a wealthy man, Mrs. Carter decided to become an actress and appealed to Fairbank for financial assistance to provide temporary support and training. Although he agreed to help her, he wanted in no way to be associated publicly with the woman, dealing with her only through lawyers and bankers. Between July 1889 and March 1891, he paid more than $50,000 to one David Belasco who had agreed to undertake her training. No written contract had been signed, and as the months went by, Belasco demanded more and more money from Fairbank, apparently threatening him with unsavory publicity if he did not oblige. Finally Fairbank had had enough and refused categorically to contribute any more support to Mrs. Carter, whose career had been launched, albeit not to the greatest of reviews. But Belasco refused to drop the matter and sued Fairbank for an additional $65,000. The case went to trial before the Supreme Court of New York in June 1896. In what the *New York Times* described as a "remarkable verdict," the jury awarded Belasco $16,000 on the grounds that to do otherwise would have branded him unfairly as "a perjurer and blackmailer." The *Times* openly sided with Fairbank, describing him as "a generous and

public-spirited man" who had genuinely sought to help a woman with no other recourse.

His entanglement with Mrs. Leslie Carter must have been much on Fairbank's mind as he constructed his Jekyl cottage, and the respite of the island must have been most welcome. He would enjoy many seasons there with his wife and their seven children. He served from the 1888–89 season until his death in 1903 as vice president of the club and had significant influence over its development during those years. His granddaughter would later write of his association with the island that "he thrived on the sociability of the place." His wife, Helen, like some of the other Jekyl wives, did not share his fondness for the club. Much of her concern appears to have stemmed from the fact that the island still had no acceptable church. Although there was a small chapel, it was apparently too rustic for her tastes and held by no means the high church services she preferred. She would eventually erect a portable altar in her own cottage and invite visiting clergymen for services. "I think she likes the place," Fairbank wrote to his daughter, "though she may not like to admit it."[4]

Charles Stewart Maurice, a partner in the Union Bridge Company who hailed from Athens, Pennsylvania, also had a house under construction in the northern part of the club compound at the same time Fairbank's cottage was being built. Maurice, an original member of the club, had sold one of his two shares to his friend Albert E. Touzalin, president of the Chicago, Burlington and Northern Railroad, thereby allowing him also to become one of the founding members. The frequent business connections and consequent friendships that grew up between railroad executives and bridge builders are typified by their

relationship, which remained close until Touzalin's untimely death in 1889.

In July 1888, shortly after the close of the first season, Touzalin had suggested to Maurice that the time might be right to unload their shares of Jekyl stock "if we are so disposed." At the time neither man had yet visited the island, but "I have met two friends who have been there," Touzalin explained, "and I reach the belief that it will be a good Club for rich and young New Yorkers but hardly for staid old fellows like you and I."[5] But Maurice had no intention of selling. From the outset he took a deep interest in the affairs of the club and quickly became one of the organization's most respected members. Although he would never hold an office, he did serve as a director and worked enthusiastically on many important committees.

The construction of "Hollybourne," as he would call his cottage, was for him a personal matter, and he worked in close conjunction with his New York architect, William Day, significantly influencing the house's structure by insisting upon the use of bridge-building techniques. The finished house was a curious but pleasing blend of island materials and Flemish design. It suggested the great variety of architectural styles that characterized Jekyl Island homes and the Victorian period generally. Its tabby construction reflected the Maurices' interest in the island's history and natural resources. Tabby, a local mixture of lime, sand, and shells, was the substance that had been used for the Horton House, or "old tabby" as it was known by club members, the eighteenth-century ruin which stood on Jekyl. Charles Maurice and his wife, Charlotte, took a profound interest not only in the club but in the island itself. Maurice was well-known as the club authority on Jekyl wildlife, and the two of them together would become the island's first historians. It was appropriate that their house should harmonize so well with the island's natural resources. Built at a cost of $19,100, it was ready for occupancy by December 18, 1890, when the Maurice family arrived with a party of eighteen people, twelve of whom stayed comfortably in the cottage, while the rest took rooms in the club.[6]

By the time the Maurice cottage was completed, Frederic Baker, the wealthy head of Baker & Williams, an extensive New York warehouse firm, had already begun a new residence between the Maurice dwelling and the club house. Unlike Maurice and Fairbank, Baker had not been an original member. Proposed by Henry E. Howland and seconded by Newton Finney, he had been elected to membership on May 22, 1888. Throughout the 1890s and into the early 1900s, as club treasurer he was directly responsible for developing and implementing club policies. He had been a member but a short time when on March 3, 1889, he wrote to the executive committee requesting a plot of ground near the club house. The commit-

Maurice cottage, called
Hollybourne, shortly after
completion in 1890.
(Southern Historical
Collection, University of
North Carolina)

Solterra, the cottage of the
Frederic Bakers, would
house the President of the
United States, William
McKinley, during his visit
to Jekyl in March 1899.
(Lanier, *Jekyl Island Club,*
1911)

Frederic Baker, longtime
treasurer of the Jekyl
Island Club, and Elizabeth
Claflin. (Southern
Historical Collection,
University of North
Carolina)

Frances Emma Steers Baker pauses during a drive with her nurse companion in front of the home of J. H. Thompson, the south-end fisherman from 1907 to 1914. (Everett Collection, Coastal Georgia Historical Society)

tee, feeling that it was "in the interest of the club" to have Baker build, accommodated him.[7]

But Baker found the lot, located just north of the club house, a bit small to set his house off graciously and looked covetously at the contiguous lot owned by Henry Hyde. Hyde agreed to sell it to him, and Baker was able to complete his house in early 1891. The frame structure, named "Solterra," stood a stately distance from both the club house and the Maurice cottage. It was graced with ample porches, turrets, and a gazebo. In this pleasant setting the Bakers would host a multitude of parties and entertain a variety of guests— among them the president of the United States.[8]

Still another cottage under construction at the time at the southernmost point of the

club compound was that of Walter Rogers Furness, scion of a socially prominent Philadelphia family. At age twenty-six, Furness was the youngest of the original members. Following the lead of his uncle, Frank Furness, he had become an architect in the latter's firm, Furness, Evans and Company, and in all probability the design for the cottage was his own. It was a simple structure, compact but charming, built in shingle style with a rounded corner that contained both a downstairs and an upstairs porch.

In 1896, for reasons unknown, Furness sold his cottage to Joseph Pulitzer, but he remained a member of the club for several more years. Hunting was one of his favorite pastimes, and he served as an active member of the game committee and even as a club director. However, after sustaining an eye injury he was no longer able to hunt, and the Jekyl Island Club lost its appeal.

The cottage of Walter Rogers Furness, built in 1890 and later sold to Joseph Pulitzer. In time it would become the island infirmary. (Jekyll Island Museum)

He commissioned Superintendent Grob to sell his share, but when no immediate buyer could be found, he allowed his dues to lapse and informed Grob of his determination to leave the club. Grob responded in January 1901: "I am sorry to know that you do not think you will ever shoot again." Within three months Furness's share, in accordance with club rules, was sold at public auction for non-payment of dues, assessments, and debt. It was bought by the club itself and later taken over by a syndicate of members headed by Frederic Baker.[9]

In the meantime, in 1892, still another new residence was erected on Jekyl Island. The owner of this latest addition was Gordon McKay, one of the island's oldest members who was over seventy when he built his house. He had made his fortune during the Civil War by improving and patenting a process for sewing boots and shoes and by manufacturing the stitching machine that would do the job. The demand for army shoes had been very great, and it had not taken long for McKay's fortune to expand to an estimated $40 million before he retired in 1895.

McKay, divorced from his first wife, Agnes Jenkins, in the late 1840s, shocked society some thirty years later in 1878 by marrying his housekeeper's daughter, a young woman named Minnie Treat. Just two years before he began construction on his Jekyl house, the marriage had ended in divorce. McKay's affection and extraordinary generosity toward her remained undimmed. He brought her mother and sister, along with Victor, his nine-year-old son by Minnie, to visit his new home on Jekyl in 1895. And when his ex-wife, now calling herself Marian, married German diplomat Baron Adolph A. von Breuning in 1899, he gave the couple a wedding gift of $100,000. He would provide in his will an annuity for Minnie, her mother, and her sister. McKay was known at Jekyl as a kind and sociable gentleman who entertained frequently despite his advanced years.[10]

By the end of 1892, six private cottages—those of Brown, Fairbank,

The cottage of Gordon McKay was constructed in 1892 and purchased in 1904 by William Rockefeller, who named it Indian Mound. (Georgia Department of Archives and History)

Inventor Gordon McKay, club member 1891–1903. (Harvard University Archives)

Maurice, Baker, Furness, and McKay—were listed on the Glynn County tax rolls. Of the six, the Baker and Maurice cottages were valued the highest, twice as high as any of the others. But this would soon change. In the years 1896 and 1897 three more private homes and an apartment house would go up on the island. All but one of these structures would be valued at a higher rate than anything yet constructed on Jekyl.

The least expensive of the lot and the simplest in style was "Moss Cottage," built in 1896 by William Struthers, retired owner of a Philadelphia marble works. Struthers, his wife, and daughter, Jean, who subsequently married club member Henry Francis Sears, came to Jekyl almost every season to hunt, ride, and relax. They were hospitable neighbors and entertained as often and as lavishly as any family on the island. Jean Struthers was particularly active in the island's social and sporting life. She hunted, bicycled, rode, and held her own in the island's many competitions. Among her occasional riding

William Struthers constructed his Moss Cottage in 1896 on the lot adjacent to and north of Pulitzer's property. The "conservatory," visible here at the south end, was added a few years later. The Struthers family sold the cottage to George H. Macy in 1910 or 1911. (Southern Historical Collection, University of North Carolina)

Joseph Pulitzer, editor and publisher of the *New York World* and an original club member, 1886–1911. Jekyl Island was one of Pulitzer's favorite haunts, but it was never his wife Kate's idea of paradise, and she rarely joined him there. (Brown Brothers)

companions was newspaper magnate Joseph Pulitzer, whose wife detested the island and who enjoyed Jean's companionship, on one occasion sending her a little bouquet of violets.

Pulitzer, having watched the Struthers house go up, decided that the old Furness cottage was no longer adequate for his needs and that he, too, required a new residence. His wife, Kate, like Mrs. Fairbank, was not fond of Jekyl, its heat, or its sandflies. He may have hoped that the new house, a large and imposing structure designed by Charles Alling Gifford and built by W. H. Mann, would lure her more frequently to join him on the island. One feature that was absolutely necessary for his comfort in the house was soundproofing. The aging editor suffered from a variety of ailments—rheumatism, failing eyesight, asthma—but none more so than hypersensitivity to sound. One local anecdote relates that he once bribed a boat captain $100 a day to stop tooting his horn as he passed

Pulitzer built this substantial brick house in 1897. Extremely sensitive to sound, he had it thoroughly soundproofed. (Lanier, *Jekyl Island Club,* 1911)

In 1899 Pulitzer added a six-room wing, connected to his cottage by a forty-two-foot glass corridor or "solarium" (shown here). In 1904 he contracted with the local firm of Bowen and Thomas to build still another wing containing a music room, a billiard parlor, and a special bedroom for his wife, Kate, in hope of luring her more often to Jekyl. (Everett Collection, Coastal Georgia Historical Society)

through Jekyl Creek. The story contains a ring of truth, for in 1895 Pulitzer did offer to increase an already substantial donation to the club by $500 if the telephone were removed from the club house. "He does not want us to have the cable taken up," Frederic Baker reported to Henry Hyde, "but he does want the connection severed. What do you think about it?" There is no record of Hyde's reply, but telephone service continued, and no one used it more than Pulitzer.[11]

In good health or ill, he worked vigorously while on the island and kept his large retinue hopping. His staff endured, with a certain sense of humor, Pulitzer's illnesses (not untouched by hypochondria), his temper tantrums (he once was so enraged about a later addition to his house that "he danced a polka on the lawn"), and his incessant work habits. Even during a season in which he was described as "wonderfully tranquil," his companions suffered from his impatient demands. One of his aides described the plight of "poor old" Dr. G. W. Hosmer,

> who pad & pencil in hand stands patiently . . . repeating for the sixtieth time the last words of a telegram in response to the irritable query "have you got it?" After half an hour's labor a telegram of three hundred words is evolved, & the doctor retires to his room to *painfully* set it down in black & white understandable to the club clerk for telephoning. But just as he is slinking off by the back door to place it beyond the hope of recall a messenger reaches him with instructions not to send it until Mr. P. has read it again & the circus begins afresh.[12]

Pulitzer remained a paradox among the members of the Jekyl Island Club. As editor of the *New York World* and despite his own wealth and extravagance, he never hesitated to attack the moneyed interests and even to lampoon club member J. P. Morgan when he felt the situation called for it. On the other hand, he was always sociable toward his fellow islanders. Although he was never elected to an office or appointed to a committee, his opinions were sought and heeded on various matters, and he never experienced overt ostracism. Henry Hyde, for example, joined him for dinner on Jekyl in January 1898, not long after the death of the editor's daughter Lucille. Hyde reported to his son that Pulitzer "is very much cut up on account of losing his daughter; she was the only one of his children who possessed his mind. Very confidentially, I think he feels his boy [Ralph] will never make a business man. I said all that I could to comfort him and came home early."[13]

Despite the surface civility, there was a hidden antagonism that revealed itself from time to time in private correspondence. When Pulitzer tried to hire Grob away, contingent upon the club's consent, Frederic Baker was infuriated and grumbled to Henry Hyde that Grob would do "a wretched thing for himself, if he should go with the dirty Jew." Hyde, without resorting to anti-Semitic comments, agreed that it was "a wicked world" and suggested counter-offers to persuade the superintendent to stay.[14] Grob decided to remain with the club but also continued to enjoy a friendly relationship with Pulitzer. If the newspaper magnate was occasionally the recipient of hard feelings, he seemed oblivious to it and in under two years began looking toward a major expansion of his property on Jekyl, hardly the actions of a social pariah.

The house of David H.
King, Jr., a noted New
York contractor, was the
only one-story cottage
built by a club member
and the only one with a
swimming pool. He sold it
to Edwin Gould in 1900.
(Georgia Department of
Archives and History)

Pulitzer's house was finished in December 1897, at almost the same moment
that another club member, David H.
King, Jr., was preparing to move into his
new cottage. King was a well-known and
highly successful New York contractor who
had many important landmarks to his
credit, among them Madison Square Garden, which he had built for the famous
architectural firm of McKim, Mead, and
White, and the masonry base of the Statue
of Liberty. He had also entered into contract on May 5, 1886, to erect the statue
itself on the pedestal at Bedloe's Island.
King had purchased two lots adjacent to
Baker's Solterra. The house he constructed
there was unusual in that it was the only
one-story cottage a member ever built on
the island. It also had a swimming pool,
one of the earliest in the state of Georgia,
which had been built within a center atrium
to take advantage of the southern sun and
block the chilly winter winds. The architect

of this unique cottage is, unfortunately, unknown, although it is intriguing to note that
Stanford White had been King's guest on
the island during the 1892 season.[15]

The nine cottages constructed prior to
the end of the century were quite distinctive, manifesting both inside and out the
individual tastes and needs of the owners.
However, they all shared characteristics in
common. Without exception they blended
with the island life style and adhered to the
concept of simplicity which had been the
club's keynote from the outset. Though
large and comfortable, these structures
were, for their millionaire owners, truly
cottages, not mansions on the order of their
home residences or of those constructed at
the fashionable resort of Newport. They
all enjoyed magnificent views of Jekyl

Creek and the marshes. Finally, barring
the Brown cottage, they were all located in
convenient proximity to the club house,
where the owners regularly joined their fellow members and guests for meals and
play. The cottages served their owners as
important social assets, for there they entertained frequently at dinners, luncheons,
or teas, most often catered by the club
house dining room, although, contrary to
popular belief, at least some of the cottages
had kitchens where meals could be prepared or reheated. But, even more important, the individual homes provided a
private family domain, where members
could enjoy their children, their wives, and

their special friends without the scrutiny of
half of elite society.

During the twentieth century most of the
cottages would change owners one or more
times, and seven more houses would be
constructed. The new residences, though
they tended to be grander than some of the
older ones, still harmonized, with the glar-
ing exception of the Crane cottage, with
the natural setting of the island and its phi-
losophy of simplicity. But most important,
the new owners, like the old, would adhere
to the tradition of loyalty and generosity
established by the early cottage colony.

5. The Czar of Jekyl Island

Henry B. Hyde, whose prominence in the Jekyl Island Club would become so dominant that his own son dubbed him the "Czar of Jekyl," had been pleased in the spring of 1892 to learn of a number of proposals approved at a recent stockholders' meeting. The club house dining room was to be enlarged, new roads extended to the beach, and an electric plant installed, as soon as the directors thought it feasible. "From the accounts I receive of the Club and its ground," he wrote to Frederic Baker in May, "it must have taken a new departure for the better. The electric lights and other improvements . . . will make it a very charming place and I hope I shall have the pleasure of enjoying your society there next winter. . . ."[1]

Unfortunately, these fine new plans were cut short by a series of circumstances that created a vacuum of leadership into which Hyde would move with vigor. An outbreak of yellow fever in Brunswick in 1893 brought a sense of uncertainty and sparked a debate among members as to whether or not the club should even be opened for the season. "This is nonsense," scoffed Charlotte Maurice, "after they have had frost, . . . it kills all germs at once."[2] But conditions in Brunswick were considerably worse than she realized, and the epidemic did spread to Jekyl. In August Grob had reported the direness of the situation to her husband:

> We had another death from fever yesterday, and one new case. . . . I have discharged the most of my force, as all the stores in Brunswick have closed up, the steamers have stopped running here, also both of the railroads. So our only connection with the outer world is by wagon to Waynesville. . . . As there is likely to be a famine here, I thought I would get rid of as many people as we could.
>
> I took the liberty to have a deer killed today, as we have been a week without any substantial food.[3]

By September the Brunswick area was under quarantine, and the famine that Grob had predicted had indeed occurred. The Brunswick health officer wired Henry Hyde of the "great destitution" and asked his help in securing "subscriptions of food" for Brunswick "sufferers."[4]

Conditions on the island and in the Brunswick area clearly warranted the decision not to open the club officially for the 1893–94 season. Although seven members and thirty-one guests braved the yellow fever scare and enjoyed winter on the island anyhow, ironically, neither the Maurices nor Henry Hyde were among them.

To make a bad situation worse, a financial panic in May precipitated a stock market crash that plunged the nation into a major depression from which it would not fully recover until 1898. Hundreds of industries, banks, and railroads went bankrupt, and workers by the thousands faced unemployment and real hardship. Even before the panic struck, confidence in the economy had been sufficiently shaky to cause a run on the gold reserves of the United States Treasury. Frightened investors hurried to redeem silver certificates for gold, allowed under the terms of the Sherman Silver Purchase Act of 1890. The precipitous decline of gold in the treasury prompted such bankers as J. P. Morgan and James Stillman, both club members, to urge President Grover Cleveland to call a special session of Congress to cope with the crisis.

Left: Henry Baldwin
Hyde, the czar of Jekyl
Island. (Baker Library,
Harvard Business School)

Right: Ernest Grob during
the Hyde years. Grob, al-
though sensitive to criticism, learned to work with
the hard-driving Hyde,
who in turn came to re-
spect the superintendent's
managerial abilities.
(Jekyll Island Museum)

Lower left: Captain Clark on the steps of the Brown house where he lived briefly before the club built him a dwelling of his own. During the yellow fever epidemic of 1893–94, Clark remained on the island "caring for the sick, and protecting the interests of the club and its property," for which he received a note of thanks and a bonus of $100. (Georgia Department of Archives and History)

For the most part, members of the Jekyl Island Club were not badly hurt by the financial malaise that spread over the country, but they were definitely worried. Charles Maurice, whose bridge-building interests depended upon the solvency of railroads, was unable to conceal his anxiety from his family. "Papa is . . . disturbed about the money outlook for the entire country," his daughter observed in late June, but by December his concern had abated considerably.[5]

Despite the fact that the vast majority of Jekyl Islanders (fully 70 percent) were Republicans, they had been prepared to cooperate with the Democratic president in combatting the panic. They supported his efforts to repeal the Sherman Silver Purchase Act in the belief that such action would put a stop to the run on the gold reserves. The "silverites" fought bitterly to prevent it, but in October the act was repealed. Still gold continued to be drained from the treasury in alarming amounts. J. P. Morgan approached the president with a scheme to relieve the pressure by selling gold bonds both at home and abroad. Cleveland consented, and in a matter of hours a syndicate composed of Morgan and August Belmont had disposed of a bond issue worth $62.3 million.

The depression had focused public attention on two matters that would not disappear for years and which would come to have enormous impact on Jekyl members. One was the weakness of the national banking structure, which would manifest itself again during the Panic of 1907 and lead finally to the creation of the Federal Reserve System. The other was the free

silver question. In 1896 William Jennings Bryan and the Democratic Party made unlimited coinage of silver a central campaign issue, while William McKinley, the Republican candidate, championed the gold standard. Members of the Jekyl Island Club, Democrats and Republicans alike, viewed free silver as "a craze, a species of hysteria," or worse. So strong were their emotions on this question that Frederic Baker, a staunch Republican, sought to have club business thrown in the direction of gold rather than silver adherents. "I am anxious exceedingly," he declared to Henry Hyde, "that none of the money, which we propose to spend at Jekyl, shall go . . . to *free silver* men. You have many mechanics in Georgia who are sound money and do you not think it will be our duty—other things being equal—to search for such? I do not like to furnish the enemy with ammunition."[6]

Despite the deepening depression, the editor of the *Brunswick Times-Advertiser* predicted on April 29 the "biggest and brightest" Jekyl season ever for 1894–95. With greater zeal than usual, the newspaper kept local citizens abreast of the comings and goings of the rich and famous, noting on March 21 the departure of James Scrymser and a party of fifteen, who had no less than twenty-five trunks. Their passage through Brunswick, reported the editor, "was profitable to the baggage transfer men." The following day a private railroad car arrived, bearing "an array of Chicago brains and millions bound for Jekyl." The occupants including Marshall Field, N. K. Fairbank, Charles Fargo (of Wells-Fargo), and Marvin Hughitt, president of the Chicago and Northwestern Railroad. "It would be hard to get together a quartette representing more interests financial, mercantile, and social, than this one."

The Reverend Charles Henry Parkhurst, the only honorary member of the Jekyl Island Club. Proposed by club president Henry Howland on November 5, 1894, and seconded by Frederic Baker, he was elected on December 12, after an appeal to the membership from N. S. Finney for a "vote as nearly unanimous as possible." Parkhurst, a Presbyterian minister and president of the Society for the Prevention of Crime in New York, was a celebrated adversary of Tammany Hall politicians. Club member James A. Scrymser threw his influence and money behind Parkhurst's crusade against municipal vice and corruption. It was at the height of his fame that Parkhurst was elected to the Jekyl Island Club. He resigned in 1909. (Library of Congress)

The Jekyl Island Club had survived a year officially closed, endured the ill effects of both the yellow fever scare and the financial panic, and emerged fundamentally hale and hearty. It had become obvious, however, that the club president, Henry E. Howland, who had served for nearly a decade, had ceased to exercise any real leadership but had slipped into a figurehead role. Responsibility for the club's activities had fallen largely to its treasurer and executive committee chairman, Frederic Baker, a burden he considered "onerous." But he would find help from an unexpected source that would lead the club into one of its most vigorous growth spurts.

On January 9, 1895, Henry Hyde made a seemingly spur-of-the-moment decision to quit Aiken, South Carolina, where he had been spending the winter, and go to Jekyl Island. That visit to Jekyl coincided with an inquiry from Baker regarding club affairs, which opened a floodgate and released a stream of letters between the two men, increasing to an almost daily exchange between 1895 and 1897. What had been a matter of passing interest now became a near obsession with Hyde, for he was a man whose painstaking attention to detail allowed him no rest; once committed, he felt compelled to oversee everything.

Upon returning to New York from Jekyl, Hyde, who had reviewed the club's financial situation during his stay, wrote Baker suggesting that the club could save $5,000 a year by abolishing its New York office and letting some officer who was already in the city handle "what little work there is to be done at this end of the line. . . ." The abolition of this "sinecure office," as Hyde called it, and with it Newton Finney's $300-a-month salary, was approved at an informal meeting of shareholders in March. By May the whole New York operation had been turned over to Frederic Baker, whose service came free of charge and who was already doing the lion's share of the work. The club's headquarters was moved from Finney's office at 52 Broadway to Baker's at 512 Washington Street, and Finney's long involvement in the management of the Jekyl Island Club came to an end.[7]

In the same letter in which he had complained about the expense of Finney's New York office, Hyde had also expressed concern about the "gasoline lamps and fixtures in use throughout the club house," describing them as "dangerous to health as well as disagreeable" and providing insufficient light. His wife had complained about the smell continually during her visits to Jekyl, and Hyde agreed that it was "positively sickening." He urged that the club carry out the proposal approved three years earlier to install electricity on the island. Finally, he suggested a larger-scale remodeling of the club house than the dining room extension originally proposed in 1892. "The Club could be made the most desirable on the continent if the above matters were attended to properly." And he had every intention of seeing to it that they were.

Baker was delighted with Hyde's frequent suggestions and responded to one of his many notes on April 10: "Your letter did me a great good, to see a waking up of members as to this island, its excellencies and its wants, is most encouraging." In the past, he added, the burden of planning "seems to have fallen to me. . . . To see help coming gives me a great let up."[8]

Hyde seemed eager to bring a third party into the coalition—David H. King, Jr., a new member of the club whose professional expertise could be valuable. King had worked with Hyde in 1887 as contractor for his Equitable Life Assurance Building in New York. Hyde liked the man and his work and began almost at once to consult him on plans to improve the club house. "I believe in our approaching old age," he stated, "that a rendezvous of this kind would be a first class thing if every thing was arranged in a comfortable and agreeable way." After conferring with Baker, he informed King that he intended to push him for election to the Jekyl Island Club's board of directors, because "We want to make that thing 'hum.' "[9]

At the annual stockholders' meeting in New York on May 30, Baker and Hyde engineered the election of what they considered the "*right* ticket." Besides King, they

supported Cornelius N. Bliss, William P. Anderson, and Morris K. Jesup for positions of authority. The balloting resulted in a complete victory for the Hyde-Baker cabal. King was chosen secretary and placed on the board. Baker and his friend Howland were reelected treasurer and president respectively. At least seven of the thirteen club directors were in their camp (Anderson, Baker, Bliss, Howland, Jesup, King, and Hyde). And their group had won every seat on the powerful executive committee, which now consisted of Hyde, Baker, King, Bliss, and Howland. Finally, they monopolized the committee on purchases and supplies and retained a voice, Anderson's, on the auditing committee as well. Fairbank, who was still vice president, tried to exert some influence, but the triumvirate of Hyde, Baker, and King was dominant and determined to do their all to make the Jekyl Island Club a viable, successful organization.[10]

Hyde's hand can be seen in every facet of the club's operations during this period. Nothing escaped his hypercritical eye, and no one, not even Grob, was safe from censure. After looking over the previous season's purchases, Hyde confided to King that he found "the present Superintendent and his assistants . . . entirely incompetent for the work they are called upon to perform." He decried what he perceived to be the "waste, the careless management, and the surplusage of employes." He would soon change his mind about Grob, however, and in July 1897 commented: "I think well of Mr. Grob; he is a very useful man and has the interest of the Club very deeply at heart."

At the moment, however, he trusted no one's judgment but his own (and occasion-

ally Baker's) as he probed into every aspect of the club's affairs. At his behest, a full accounting of the organization's financial history was summarized, record-keeping became more orderly, and the books were audited by an outside firm. Convinced of "the superiority of the position of Jekyl Island, with its pure and bracing air," Hyde desired to make it "as nearly perfect as possible."[11]

Given his interest in the club, it was not surprising that Hyde would eventually turn his attention to constructing a private residence at Jekyl. But his idea was more grandiose than a mere house. It would be an apartment building with six individual units. Quite possibly, the scheme originated with William Rockefeller, who contacted Hyde's secretary, William H. McIntyre, in mid-May while Hyde was abroad, with the proposal of a "new arrangement," but it was unquestionably Hyde who took re-

sponsibility for the enterprise. By June 21 a site for the projected building had been selected between the dwellings of Fairbank and McKay. The fact that the du Bignon cottage, now known as "club cottage," already stood on the site and would have to be moved to a new location suggests the influence that Hyde was able to exert on club policy.[12]

By July 27, he had lined up six prospective apartment owners, officially called the "Jekyl Island Associates." They included, besides himself and Rockefeller, Joseph Stickney, head of Stickney, Conyngham & Company, an anthracite coal firm; William P. Anderson, former president but now director of the American Cotton Oil Company; James A. Scrymser, president of three Latin American cable companies; and an unnamed club member from Cincinnati who must have been either banker Briggs Swift Cunningham or William A. Procter, president of Procter and Gamble, the only two Cincinnati club members at the time. When the Cincinnati man decided to back out, construction plans got under way without a sixth partner.[13]

"They wanted to elect me President of the Associates," Hyde confided to Baker, "but I told them that although I was willing to do the work, the honor had better be bestowed upon someone else. They then elected Mr. Stickney President, and made me Secretary and Treasurer, which I suppose means the management of the whole thing. Under all the circumstances, I suppose I will have to do it."[14] This long-suffering stance was typical of Hyde. Professing to prefer no official position, or at best a secondary one, he would assume his

Henry B. Hyde's influence brought about extensive remodeling of the club house during the 1890s, as well as construction of the Sans Souci and a new stable complex. Here in 1896 work is progressing on the new billiard room wing and passageway leading to it. (Georgia Department of Archives and History)

duties with a sigh, but unless he had near absolute control he was never happy.

The new apartment house was designed by New York architect Charles Gifford and built by the Stewart Contracting Company, a "highly recommended" Savannah firm also employed to undertake the club house renovation, which was to include the enlarged dining room with skylights, a billiard room wing, a barber shop and toilet room, several extra baths, two new stairways, and a new fireplace.

On August 10, the du Bignon house was moved to its new site, and work began. In an effort to meet the associates' deadline, some 175 workers were on the project by mid-September. Their large numbers worried Grob who feared they might "become boisterous and do damage not easily made good." A. R. Stewart, the construction firm's general manager, assured club officials that they anticipated

"no serious trouble from the conduct of our men," but would "get rid . . . of any unruly element."[15]

As usual, Hyde left nothing to chance but barraged both the architect and the contractor with letters regarding the work on Jekyl. "Do not wait until you are about ready to build any one portion of the house to prepare the material; that means unnecessary delay," he lectured the contractor. "Keep well in advance of your work and we will all be happy." Hyde's officiousness and perfectionist tendencies had few bounds. The location of chandeliers and gas fixtures (the proposed electrical system was still in the future), the color of the carpets, and the correct manner of hanging pictures (Southerners, he believed, would "make a fizzle of it") were all grist for his mill.[16]

The rounded room at the north end of the club house was the enlarged dining room. The Stewart Contracting Company of Savannah began construction in 1896. (Everett Collection, Coastal Georgia Historical Society)

He was horrified when Baker suggested that Grob should take charge of having the club house furniture recovered and wrote accusingly that he "did not think that you, on reflection, would approve of leaving the question of taste for coverings, etc. to the Club's Superintendent." He had, he explained, gone to an "immense amount of trouble . . . since the beginning of the work on Jekyl Island, and my only anxiety now is to do everything to meet the approval of the members. . . . If they find there has been any lack of taste, or careless work, both of us will be cruelly criticised." Hyde personally selected and approved the frieze "of raised plaster work rubbed ivory" for the dining room, the olive green of the walls, the somewhat lighter shade for the ceiling, and the "nice tone of Indian red" for the wainscotting. He rejected a red carpeting that would "fight" with the wainscotting in favor of "some dark, rich colored carpet—something in an olive tone."[17]

Although King had been given responsibility for the structural aspects of the club house remodeling, Hyde was unable to stand back even here to let the two contractors, King and Stewart, and the architect, Gifford, make the final judgments. He had his secretary write Gifford, insisting that "there ought to be some additional ventilation there [in the club house] beyond what Mr. King arranged."[18]

Work on the island's new projects was progressing well when suddenly on September 29, 1896, a furious storm struck the Brunswick area, doing an estimated $350,000 worth of damage and killing at least seven people. But despite devastation in Brunswick and on Saint Simons, Jekyl had been left almost untouched, with only the windmill damaged. No one there was hurt, although Captain Clark had been buffeted about and knocked down by the winds as he tried to secure the boats at the dock.

Fortunately, however, no real harm was done to the island's new construction. Within a few days, work had resumed, and vigorous efforts were being made to meet Hyde's renewed expectations that everything be completed before the first of January and the opening of the season. By October 23 the work crew had swollen to two hundred men, and the local newspaper happily reported that nearly all of them "come to Brunswick every other Saturday night to spend their money."[19]

Throughout the remodeling of the club and the construction of the apartment building, Hyde expressed an acute cost-consciousness, a characteristic frequently manifested among the wealthy Jekyl Islanders. Whatever conspicuous luxury they may have had a reputation for enjoying, a solid majority of members were determined to get a good return for their dollar. Aware of this trait of frugality and subscribing to it personally, Hyde vetoed music in the club house so as not to be "charged with extravagance," preferred to have carpet strips laid on the floor beside the billiard tables rather than cover the entire room, as Grob had suggested, and ordered a selection of rugs which he did not wish "to be of a very expensive character."[20]

By November 5, the apartment house of the Jekyl Island Associates was virtually complete, but the sixth apartment owner still had not been selected. Hyde had suggested Morris K. Jesup, who met all the

necessary criteria: "He is rich and he has no children." William B. Isham and Eugene B. Hoffman had been interviewed but had apparently decided against the venture. Baker had nominated several people, but something seemed wrong with each of them: "One has young children. You do not want that. Another is a widow. Very agreeable—but I am afraid she would feel that being a woman, courtesies, not business like, should be given to her." The widow in question was Kate Papin, the first female member of the Jekyl Island Club, who had been elected in 1893 upon the death of her father, Samuel W. Allerton, whose share she acquired. Baker suggested as an alternative, "Wouldn't George Gould go into the association?" Gould had just joined the club and had an unsettling reputation inconsistent with the general sobriety of the associates, who, although they enjoyed themselves and rejected Marshall Field "because he would not be much of a card," limited their pleasure to the strict confines of Victorian society, which did not allow the extravagances and mistresses of George Gould. They preferred to keep that apartment empty for the moment.[21]

The associates met on December 28 to determine a name for the building and to "auction" or draw lots for the apartments. They chose the name "Sans Souci," "without care" in French. In anticipation of the meeting Hyde's secretary had instructed Gifford to "paint in large letters in the servants' quarters, 'Women' on that side over his bed-room, and 'Men' on the other side." Women, he explained, "will make much less noise overhead . . . and he wants to make sure that the women servants get on his side."[22] At the meeting, however, Hyde drew the apartment on the second floor south, which was, in Grob's

The Sans Souci under construction. "The spacious plaisance at Jekyl Island was, perhaps, never before in its history such a scene of busy activity as now," exclaimed the *Brunswick Times-Advertiser* of September 20, 1896. (Jekyll Island Museum)

The Sans Souci after completion included six apartments and twelve servants' rooms in the attic. During its history William Rockefeller, J. P. Morgan, Henry B. Hyde, and James J. Hill all owned apartments here. (Everett Collection, Coastal Georgia Historical Society)

George Gould, club member 1895–1916, shown here in 1908 with his first wife, actress Edith Kingdon Gould. (Library of Congress)

George Gould's life style was more flamboyant than that of most Jekyl Islanders. Shortly after the birth of his illegitimate son, George, to Guinevere Sinclair, shown here with their three children (left to right, George, Jane, and baby Guinevere), Gould's name disappears from the club rosters. Following the death of his first wife, Edith, he married Guinevere. (Library of Congress)

opinion, "the most desirable," if only because it was buffered from the servants' quarters by the floor above. Rockefeller drew the apartment adjacent to Hyde, while Anderson and Stickney shared the first floor, north and south respectively, and Scrymser had the third floor south. Thus only the apartment on the third floor north remained unsold and vacant throughout the 1897 season, when the Sans Souci was first occupied.

But in July of that year an owner was at last found. It was none other than J. P. Morgan, whose wealth and prestige by this time had made his name a household word. Some accounts of the Sans Souci credit Morgan with its construction, but he was actually a Johnny-come-lately who had nothing whatever to do with originating or implementing the project. Nonetheless, the associates were pleased to have him as a member, and Hyde, at Morgan's request, took charge of furnishing the banker's apartment for him, duplicating the decorations of his own apartment, down to the chair coverings and the last print on the wall. Morgan would use the apartment for the first time during the 1898 season.

On January 22, 1897, Hyde had arrived at Jekyl Island to move into his new apartment and to view the club house renovations and a new stable which he had recently constructed in conjunction with Frederic Baker. Three days later he wrote happily to his wife, Annie: "You can't imagine how comfortable I am here at Jekyl Island. My rooms are nearly put to rights, and everything pleases me very much. The Club House is beautiful. Everybody that arrives is delighted with it and thanks me many times for the care I have taken of their affairs during the summer." The stable, made from a renovated barrack used for summer workmen, he

Left: William Rockefeller, one of the original Sans Souci Associates, purchased apartment four on the second floor. (Rockefeller Archive Center)

Right: J. Pierpont Morgan became the sixth and last of the original Sans Souci Associates. Contrary to myth, he was not responsible for the construction of the Sans Souci. (Library of Congress)

judged to be "comfortable" and "just as convenient as if it cost $100,000." In short, "Everything is quite satisfactory."[23]

By February 1 his enthusiasm had waned somewhat, and he wrote to the architect to complain about rattling blinds, narrow shades, and badly built doors. But even before the foreman arrived to set things right, Hyde was in a better mood and informed Gifford that "I have but little fault to find." He was as happy as he had ever been. "If I ever had any doubts about Jekyl Island, they have been removed. This is the place for me. . . . I am booming everything down here as much as possible, under the circumstances."[24]

One of the things he was currently "booming" was a grandiose new private stable, much larger and more elaborate than the old club stable built a decade earlier or the simple structure he and Baker had recently had put up. Gifford was once again called upon to draw the plans and by

March 10 had prepared a sketch, which envisioned a courtyard bounded by stables with a total of seventy-one stalls, space for forty-eight carriages, quarters for stablemen, and provisions for future expansion. The estimated cost was $7,500.

Hyde intended to pay for the structure by selling stalls to individual members, and by mid-March thirty-seven people had indicated a willingness to subscribe. Objections to the cost of Hyde's grandiose plans, however, brought from Baker the suggestion that the livery section of the stable complex might have to be abandoned. Hyde was indignant, attributing the complaints to mere selfishness on the part of some members. "I intend to fight it," he fumed to Baker, "and if whipped, my interest in Jekyl Island will become much less than it is now. Selfishness must not have any place in the Jekyl Island Club. . . . Sharp New York tactics have got to be left out and the spirit of liberality prevail in everything we do."[25]

James J. Hill and his wife, Mary, 1906. Hill belonged to the Jekyl Island Club from 1888 to 1916. When Joseph Stickney died in December 1903, his wife offered to sell her Sans Souci apartment for $13,000, fully furnished. Hill bought it in March 1904 and demanded a detailed inventory of the contents. Superintendent Grob obliged down to listing a toothbrush rack, toilet paper holders, and a teapot with a missing handle. (Minnesota Historical Society)

In the end the plan was scaled down to more modest dimensions. Unlike the Sans Souci, which had been confidently constructed by five partners on the assumption that a sixth investor could easily be found to help absorb the cost, the stable size expanded and contracted during the ensuing months in direct proportion to the number of subscribers. By the end of the year twelve people had purchased a total of forty-six stalls: J. P. Morgan (four), Gordon McKay (four), Joseph Stickney (four), A. S. Van Wickle (three), Cornelius Bliss (two), James J. Hill (four), William Rockefeller (four), Robert C. Pruyn (three), James A. Scrymser (four), John Magee (two), William Struthers (two), and Joseph Pulitzer (ten).

Construction on the stable was to have begun in the summer of 1897 with David H. King, Jr., supervising this phase of the work. But even before a site could be completely cleared for the foundations, a "disagreeable controversy" erupted between King and Scrymser over the proper location for the new structure. As chairman of the building committee, King ordered Grob to cease clearing operations until further notice, leaving a spot that Baker later facetiously labeled "King's Clearing," and began sulking in New York in his Hotel Renaissance suite.[26]

Concerned that King might resign and "throw all the work on me," Hyde tried desperately to placate him. In private, however, he was less tolerant of King's pique. To Baker he grumbled: "The truth of the matter is, King has a bad reputation for being quarrelsome and the moment our restraining hand is removed from him he will drop to a great depth, so far as the Jekyl Island Club is concerned." After several efforts to contact him proved useless, Hyde, his patience wearing thin, wrote: "I assure you, my dear Mr. King, I would just as soon go on alone and build the stable as to try and find you at your hotel."[27]

On July 14, King resigned formally from the committee, as he had threatened to do for more than a month, and later withdrew entirely from the Stable Association. The selection of the stable site was finally left to Grob, who, in the view of Hyde and various others, chose badly, for when the stable was completed in late December, it was considered to be too far from the club enclosure. But, concluded Hyde, "we must . . . make the best of it."[28]

Costs had run over a thousand dollars above the original estimate, and talk of building a separate sixteen-room coachmen's house subsided abruptly. Hyde, who had advanced the funds for construction, was eager to be reimbursed, but collection turned out to be more difficult than he had expected. Even though members had started using the stable at the beginning of the year, several had not yet settled their accounts with Hyde by early March. Joseph Pulitzer, who had contracted for the largest number of stalls, was the last to pay. After futilely attempting to collect for three months, Hyde's secretary finally succeeded only by appealing to Grob, who tactfully intervened to collect the debt.[29]

The stable affair had barely run its course before tension developed between Hyde and Baker over yet another project—the construction of an interdenominational chapel that the latter had championed since at least February 1897. The club had set aside a site, and ten members had pledged $100 each toward the construction. Howard Constable of the New York firm of Constable Brothers, architects and engineers, whose identification with the Republican party endeared him to Frederic Baker, had been employed to design the chapel. A sketch of the exterior, which Henry Hyde certified as "certainly handsome," was ready by mid-March.[30]

Baker was eager to begin and anticipated Hyde's support. He wrote him on June 14 that "nothing will suit me better than to enter upon another campaign of moderate extent with you and we will build the Church." In his zeal, Baker failed to note a certain reluctance on Hyde's part to become too committed to this particular venture. Still brimming with excitement, Baker shared with Hyde on August 20 his hopes for a more elaborate chapel than the original plans called for. Instead of the "inexpensive wooden Church" with cypress shingles, he wanted "an adobe building, iron roof, bright tiling, and all that," even though it would increase the cost from $5,000 to approximately $7,000. "I am willing to stand under one-half of this debt. Do you feel like taking the other half?"[31]

Hyde, still piqued by the stable experience, indicated his unwillingness to "assume any responsibility in the matter of finances in connection with the erection of the new Church" until he had been reimbursed the $14,500 he had advanced for the club house remodeling.[32] Shortly thereafter, Baker, still club treasurer, sent Hyde a check for $7,500 out of the $9,333 that had been collected in a recent membership assessment. But Hyde had his secretary write Baker to demand the entire assessment. Baker complied but was insulted by "the tenor" of the letter and said so. On September 18, Hyde wrote a long letter to his Jekyl colleague, both angry and self-pitying in tone, justifying his position:

> I would not do the work that I have been doing for the Jeky Island Club for ten thousand dollars; . . . but I have done it out of regard for you and to help you in the administration of the affairs of the island.
>
> You must bear in mind that I have unsettled accounts now with the Club, with the

Robert C. Pruyn, a banker from Albany, New York, was a club member from 1897 to 1931 and chairman of the committee on golf and sports from 1901 to 1914. In 1899 he purchased Sans Souci apartment three (Henry Hyde's old apartment) from Louise Moore for $10,000. (Everett Collection, Coastal Georgia Historical Society)

stable, and with the "Sans Souci." I am now out of pocket, for everything, some twelve or fifteen thousand dollars; I do not know when I shall get the money back again—soon, I hope. . . .[33]

Hyde was not well and had begun to grow weary of the constant drain Jekyl affairs were putting on both his time and money. Baker accepted the situation, and the matter was closed. The little church would have to wait another six years before Constable's original plan would finally be carried out.

Arriving on Jekyl in January 1898, Hyde eagerly inspected the premises and reviewed the previous year's work. Hoping for perfection, he could only be disappointed. From the moment he set foot on the island, he began to fret over any flaw he found, and during the next few days he saw much to trouble him. A leak in the skylight of the club dining room, for example, had left a dark spot on the green carpet. "It was such a beautiful carpet," he lamented, "and everyone admired the dining-room so much."[34]

His own apartment, however, had been scrupulously prepared by his Savannah housekeeper, Mrs. Ray Lincoln. And J. P. Morgan's quarters had also been readied for his anticipated arrival on January 22. Since this would be Morgan's first stay in his apartment, Hyde was especially meticulous in his instructions. From New York he had cautioned Grob to "be careful in unpacking Mr. Morgan's lamps" and to use "due diligence and get his rooms in perfect order."[35]

Yet on the whole he managed to relax and even to resist trying to run every activity on the island. The results of his earlier labors were, however, well in evidence. The club was resplendent. Moreover, the season was highly successful, both socially and financially. Hyde's frugality and concern for careful management had paid off, for the club enjoyed in 1897 and 1898 two of its best seasons thus far. He no doubt would have continued indefinitely his efforts to influence the club's development, had his health not begun to fail.

It was clear that Hyde lacked the vigor he had had even a year ago. And, while he denied that his health was bad, he was forced to confess that "after thirty-nine years of hard work in the service of the Equitable, I at times become fatigued. . . ." His weariness was evident, although no one could know that this would be his last season as the "czar of Jekyl Island."[36]

At the beginning of the next year, on January 3, 1899, Hyde's secretary contacted Joseph Stickney to tell him that

Hyde would, in view of his ill health, "be glad to have some other member of the [Sans Souci] Association elected Treasurer in his place." The following day he notified Grob that Hyde would not be coming to Jekyl for the season, nor did he wish to rent his apartment. "His main object is to sell," he told Grob.

Before the end of the month, however, Hyde rallied and wrote to the superintendent himself, "I am gradually improving in health, and cannot help taking an interest in affairs at Jekyl Island." He requested Grob to send him a statement of income and expenditures and asked his advice on what he should pay Miss Schuppan for keeping his apartment clean. "I often think of you," he wrote poignantly, "and regret that I am not at Jekyl Island to have the pleasure of dropping in at your office for my regular morning chat."[37]

But he would never again have that pleasure. By February 21, his apartment had been sold to John G. Moore, the New York broker whose wife had run afoul of the rules in keeping her little dogs with her in the club house. On April 8, Hyde sent Grob a check for $250 as his commission on the sale of the apartment.

Hyde's rally had proven to be only temporary, for his health continued to grow worse. On May 2, 1899, he died quietly, surrounded by his family at his New York home on East Fortieth Street. Formerly a man of boundless energy and enthusiasm, he had been confined there for more than a year. Writing of his death, a perceptive *New York Times* reporter commented: "To the superficial observer, Mr. Hyde's energy, enterprise, diligence, capacity and uninterrupted work, have been chiefly conspicuous, but those who have looked beneath the surface have seen that he was no less remarkable for care, thoughtful deliberation, vigilance, and an understanding adherence to sound business and exact scientific principles."[38]

The Jekyl Island Club had, in fact, profited enormously from the care and devotion he had showered upon it during his last years. Never since the period of preparation for the club's opening had there been so much vigor and activity, such growth and improvement in the club's facilities. Hyde had reason to feel proud of his accomplishments there, which were finally crowned, six weeks before his death, by a long-awaited visit from the president of the United States.

6. The President's Visit

Before Henry Hyde's death and the decline of his "machine," as Robert W. de Forest called it, a new leader had already been elected and others were in the wings to take the place of the Hyde-Baker-King coterie. In May 1897, Henry Howland had voluntarily stepped down as president of the Jekyl Island Club. His replacement, hand picked by Hyde and elected without opposition that same month, was Charles Lanier, a partner in the firm of Lanier, Winslow & Company, one of the most respected banking establishments in the United States. Lanier had at first declined the honor but was urged by Baker, Hyde, and Howland to reconsider. Hyde knew him well, for Lanier had an office in the Equitable Building in New York. "If Mr. Lanier declines the second time," Hyde remarked wryly, "I shall think he had treated me very badly. I have kept a record of the men who have treated me badly during my life and it amounts to forty-seven thousand, eight hundred and ninety-three, so you see I am used to it."[1]

But Lanier telegraphed his acceptance from Europe, and soon after returning to the United States, he endorsed the plans Hyde was then promoting for improvements at Jekyl. "It was very pleasant to me to find Mr. Lanier so cordial and so much interested in the Club in every respect," wrote Hyde. "I believe he will stick and do a great deal to help us." Lanier did "stick" and would emerge during his tenure (1897–1914) as a popular and effective president who, though never a "czar," would lead the club to new heights.[2]

Hyde may well have sought him as president in part because of his intimate friendship with J. P. Morgan, who in 1903

would accept the office of first vice president. Lanier, an attractive and debonair New Yorker, was one of the founders of the famed Corsair Club, members of which dined regularly aboard Morgan's yacht, with each seeking to plan a menu more lavish and interesting than the one before. He and Morgan were so close that they were said to be "almost like brothers." Whether his connections with Morgan were a factor in his election as president of the club, they certainly did nothing to hurt him.

During Lanier's first season as club leader, Secretary of the Interior Cornelius Bliss invited President William McKinley to be his guest at Jekyl Island. Frederick Baker offered his cottage to house the chief executive, who accepted the invitation and planned to visit near the end of February or in early March.

But the explosion and sinking of the battleship *Maine* in Havana harbor on February 15 ended McKinley's vacation plans and forced him to remain in Washington. Upon taking office in 1897, McKinley had hoped that Spanish reforms in Cuba would be far-reaching enough to satisfy the rebels and lead to an armistice, thereby removing the possibility of U.S. intervention in the struggle. But the destruction of the *Maine*, even though Washington officials did not blame the Spanish government, intensified the war fever among Americans, who already sided with the Cuban insurrectionists. Pulitzer's newspapers, as well as those of William Randolph Hearst, staunchly supported Cuban independence and even armed intervention if necessary. And John E. du Bignon, who had purchased an interest in a vessel known as the *Dauntless*, had in 1896 stood trial with the other owners and been forced to pay a fine for defying United States neutrality

The restoration of "old
tabby" (the Horton
House) was undertaken in
1898 by a Brunswick con-
tractor, W. H. Mann. This
pose for photographers
was a favorite for both
club members and em-
ployees. (Jekyll Island
Museum)

Ray Marshall Etter (right),
wife of the club's book-
keeper, stands with her
son Howard and friend at
the Horton ruins across
the road from the old du
Bignon cemetery. (Cour-
tesy of Howard Etter)

laws by smuggling "a number of men and a large quantity of arms and ammunition" to the Cuban insurgents battling a repressive Spanish regime. But the defiant *Dauntless*, once the fine was paid, set to sea again to aid the rebels. Under pressure from an inflamed public, Congress passed a resolution on April 20 recognizing Cuban independence, and five days later, the United States declared war against Spain.

Club members, who had always been conscious of the island's history, were reminded that it was not the first time that the Spanish had threatened its tranquillity. The retreat of Spanish troops across Jekyl after the Battle of Bloody Marsh on Saint Simons in 1742 had destroyed the plantation house of Major Horton. He had rebuilt his home, the ruins of which still stood like a symbol of the early colonists' victory over Spain. With the Spanish once again looming as a threat, Charles Stewart Maurice and his wife, along with Colonel John Mason Loomis of Chicago, headed a subscription list to preserve the Horton House, raising $600 to restore it. The work was completed in early May 1898. Although done in a manner to "last many years," the results did not please Grob: "To my mind the picturesqueness has now been taken from the ruin, and it looks like a modern house."[3]

Prior to the outbreak of war, the federal government had sought to fortify Jekyl Island against a possible Spanish attack, and on April 9, Baker and King, representing the executive committee, gave their permission to Captain Cassius E. Gillette of the Corps of Engineers "to erect a temporary battery on the north end of Jekyl . . . for the defense of Brunswick harbor." The few families left on the island—King, Maurice,

and Struthers—made plans to depart, and
on April 29, the engineers moved in to begin
construction. Ten days later, Grob allowed
the captain to build another battery on the
south end of the island. "I am certain the
Executive Committee would have granted
this favor," he wrote, "for the south end is
really . . . where the danger lies, as there is
nothing to protect Saint Andrews Sound."[4]

Although the war scare had come at the
very end of the season and thus affected the
club's operation very little, it had had a
dire effect on Brunswick, and, as Grob
described the situation to Struthers,
"Brunswick harbor looks very sick for the
want of vessels." Grob took it all in stride,
however, and even viewed the situation
with amusement. "I am expecting every
day my commission as general of the 'Jekyl
Island troops,'" he quipped. Although he
had watched the progress of the batteries
and noted the government's haste to construct them as they worked weekdays and
Sundays, he was not really worried. "I do
not . . . look for any trouble along this
coast, as [there] are many more important
towns to bombard excepting Brunswick."[5]

Despite the onset of war, construction
work continued on the club's first golf
course. When it was nearly done, Grob
remarked, "I don't think the 'Spaniards'
will want to play 'golf' in our yard, they
will have all they can do to play with
Dewey and a few others." He was, of
course, alluding to the destruction of the
Spanish fleet in Manila Bay by Commodore George E. Dewey on May 1, only
eleven days before. On May 17, the government, having decided that the danger to
Jekyl and Saint Simons was no longer im-

minent, ordered the guns removed.
Through it all Grob never for a moment
neglected his responsibility to the club or its
members, sending them regular reports on
the restoration of "old tabby" and on the
new golf course.[6]

In July, however, Grob fell seriously ill.
While the "Splendid Little War" with
Spain, as Secretary of State John Hay
called it, raged in Cuba and the Philippines, the superintendent turned the care of
Jekyl Island over to his assistant, Julius
Falk, and departed for the Adirondacks to
recuperate. After his doctor advised a pro-
longed vacation and an extended rest in
Europe, he set sail in late August for a
two-month trip. By then the United States
and Spain had signed an armistice ending
hostilities between the two countries.

During Grob's absence, the club would
suffer a major setback. On October 2,
1898, "the most severe storm ever known
here" struck the island. This time Jekyl was
severely affected. With the hurricane came
a great tidal wave, which swept over the
island and left most of Jekyl and Brunswick under four feet of water. The new
golf course was ruined, the wharf was left
a wreck, all the bridges and bathhouses
were washed away, the windmill was blown
down, terrapin pens were lost, and the fishermen's houses at the north and south ends
of the island were destroyed by the winds
and rising waters. "Nearly all the buildings
sustained slight damage, principally from
the blowing off of shutters, gutters and
leader pipe and the rain beating through
the windows and shingles," Falk reported.
The apartments at the north end of the
Sans Souci, particularly those of Morgan
and Rockefeller, were the most damaged.
But, fortunately, "The boats were all
saved. The naptha launch was sunk, but is
now out of the water and can be repaired."

The only cottages left undamaged were those of Fairbank and Maurice.

King's property, which stood between the two, had, however, suffered considerably from the hurricane. Falk reported to him the day after the storm. "Your orchard is all knocked down, the palms are pretty well twisted. . . . Part of the ceilings in two of the bedrooms of your house came down. . . . The cellar as usual was full of water. I also notice that some of the gutter around the outside of the house leaks; otherwise," he noted with unintended irony, "the house is in good shape." King, it seemed, was getting more and more fed up with Jekyl Island. He and his son, Van, a student at Harvard, came down to the island in December to view the damage and make arrangements for repairs.[7]

By then, and well before the new season, most of the damage to the club property had been repaired, albeit at great expense. Grob, who had recently returned from Europe fit as a fiddle, responded jokingly to an inquiry about the condition of the island from Colonel Loomis: "Yes, I guess we will be poor again after paying for the damage done. It is entirely safe here, and Mr. Maurice, who has been here with his family since the 14th inst., begs me to say to you, that he and his have been able to get along without life preservers, as they are all good 'waders', and the water has never been over 'waist deep'."[8]

By the 1899 season, waters had subsided and damages had been repaired to the extent that club officers were preparing once again to host President McKinley. Bliss had issued the invitation on March 9. It was an opportune time. With the war at an end, McKinley had planned a much-needed rest at the vacation home of his

friend Marcus A. Hanna in Thomasville, Georgia. A side trip to Jekyl appealed to the president, who accepted the invitation. By March 14 his impending visit was announced in the Brunswick newspaper. Just as before, Frederic Baker had offered the use of his cottage to the presidential party, and Bliss, who was to be the official host, accepted without hesitation.[9]

Jekyl and Brunswick alike began to make ready for the presidential visit. On March 15, the superintendent of the Brunswick city schools sent a letter to McKinley inviting him to address the school children. "We have charge," he wrote, "of more than one thousand white and colored children, to each and every one of whom a few words from the lips of the President of this great nation will be an event to be treasured in memory and handed down to their children and their children's children."[10] That the president declined the invitation did little to dim Brunswick's enthusiasm for his visit.

Senator Hanna, who was arranging the trip, had served as chairman of the Republican National Committee and McKinley's campaign manager in 1896. The official party was to include President and Mrs. McKinley, Vice President and Mrs. Garret A. Hobart, and Hanna himself. Two days before the president's arrival on March 20, the press discovered that Thomas B. Reed, speaker of the house, who was at odds with McKinley over the annexation of the Philippines, would also be present on the island. Concluding that this was to be no mere vacation but a prelude to the political campaign of 1900, reporters poised in readiness. On March 19,

Cornelius Newton Bliss, an original member of the club from 1886 to 1911, served as Secretary of the Interior during President McKinley's first adminis-tration and as treasurer of the Republican National Committee in 1900. (Li-brary of Congress)

Thomas B. Reed, Speaker of the House of Represen-tatives, whose March 1899 visit to Jekyl overlapped with that of President McKinley. The two were bitter political enemies, and their simultaneous vis-its to the club created a nationwide stir. (Library of Congress)

the *Brunswick Call* carried the following unattributed poem on the front page:

> When Tom meets Bill at Jekyl,
>   With Mark as referee,
> There'll be some mighty talking
>   About the G.O.P.
> . . . .
>
> When Tom meets Bill at Jekyl,
>   The clubhouse walls will hum
> While each sets up his claim for
>   That 1900 plum.
>
> When Tom meets Bill at Jekyl
>   They'll fix things for the best;
> "You'll run the house," says Willie
>   "And I will run the rest."
> "Well, that suits me," says Tommy,
>   And gives his hand to Will.
> "I'll run you both," says Marcus,
>   When Tom meets Bill.

The anonymous poet clearly believed that the Republicans were planning to thrash out their party's political future. In fact, "Czar Reed," as he was often called, was no longer a viable presidential contender, but he was still a powerful force within the party, and it behooved McKinley to make his peace with the speaker. This, presum-ably, was to be the goal of the meeting so carefully engineered by Hanna and Bliss.

Reed was waiting on the Jekyl wharf when the presidential cutter, *Colfax,* ar-rived on the afternoon of March 20. From all outward appearances the encounter was quite perfunctory. As reported in the *New York Times* of March 21, Speaker Reed "smilingly raised his hat" and said, "How do you do, Mr. President?" McKinley bowed and replied, "How do you do, Mr. Speaker?" The president and his wife then departed for Solterra in a carriage, while the speaker "strolled off in the direction of the Sans Souci," where he was the guest of John G. Moore, staying in Hyde's old apartment.

McKinley spent the following day riding about the island and holding an informal reception at the Baker cottage attended by club members and their guests, including Maurice, Scrymser, Fairbank, and Stickney. Reed, who had earlier been in conference with Mark Hanna at the Sans Souci, reached the reception late but was cordially received by the president. They shook hands, chatted briefly, and parted company, from all appearances in perfect harmony. The Brunswick reporter on the scene concluded that "if the two are not now agreed then they are both good actors." They were both good actors, for, in truth, while Reed did not oppose the president's renomination, he never became reconciled to McKinley's imperialistic policies and would soon retire from Congress.

The presence of reporters on the island, despite a ban against them, was apparently the result of Pulitzer's efforts to scoop his competitors. The *Brunswick Call* claimed that "Mr. Pulitzer had taken advantage of his membership in the club to admit representatives of his paper to the island, while others were barred. . . ." Discovering this, Cornelius Bliss immediately dismantled "the Chinese wall" against the press and allowed reporters from five newspapers to land and interview the dignitaries. From Hanna and McKinley they learned little and from Reed even less. The speaker refused to talk politics, saying only that "Myself and daughter came down here for a little rest and recreation. Our stay has been a charming one and our visit to Jekyl has been delightful." Nevertheless, the *Call* reporter surmised erroneously that "McKinley and Reed have buried the hatchet deep, deep in oblivion and Mark Hanna is happy again."

On their last night on the island, the president and Mrs. McKinley had a quiet, private dinner at Solterra with Bliss, the

Hobarts, and Mr. and Mrs. Thomas Nelson Page. Afterwards, they were entertained along with the other members and guests at the club house by "an old-fashioned cake walk, participated in by the colored help." The next day, March 22, McKinley left Jekyl. As news of his departure swept through Brunswick, a large crowd of spectators and well-wishers gathered at the Mallory wharf and the nearby train station to greet the president. Boats in the harbor blew their whistles and dipped their flags in salute. Among the vessels paying their respects to the chief executive was the bark *Tataila,* which became, according to the *Brunswick Call,* the first Spanish ship to dip its colors to the president since the war. Then its captain presented the flag to McKinley "as a souvenir of the visit."

As the president stood on the rear platform of the train bidding goodbye to the throng, Mrs. McKinley retired to the parlor car, where "the head gardener of Jekyl handed her a large basket of pink and white roses," compliments of Ernest Grob. The hullabaloo over the political implications of the president's stopover concealed from public view a sad domestic crisis involving Mrs. McKinley, who was verging on a nervous collapse. At the Jekyl reception, she had lost control. As one of McKinley's biographers described it: "The President's cordiality was irresistible as always, but his wife could scarcely bring herself to acknowledge the introductions. Her face sagged in peevish, fretful lines. Her eyes clung to her husband. If anyone detained him in conversation, she tried to attract his notice by pulling at his arm and twisting his sleeve. . . . This breakdown in polite company was a much more serious lapse than any private tantrums." If the members were shocked by her behavior, they were certainly too polite to mention it to the waiting reporters.[11]

Club members were delighted with the visit from the president and the First Lady and viewed it as the highlight of the last club season of the century. But their eyes were clearly on the future.

7. The New Century

The twentieth century promised to be something really special. The country was young, the economy good, and the club at its peak. The year 1900 was to be what a Brunswick journalist ballyhooed as "Beautiful Jekyl's Brilliant Season." Club officials, anticipating a banner year, had taken steps to handle the record number of people expected. Servants' quarters had been enlarged to provide more space for valets, and guests were excluded from the club house after February 20, "except on special invitation of the Executive Committee," to make more room for members and their families. The cottages and club house were almost full, and there was, according to the *Brunswick Call* of February 11, "gayety and pleasure unbounded. . . . By night it's the music with its swish and swirl of the dance, or an impromptu concert in the parlors or billiards in the hall."

The time had come, members thought, to revise their constitution and consider a review of club finances. By the end of the year they had drawn up a new constitution, to take effect in 1901, reiterating the club's purpose to "maintain a hunting, fishing, yachting and general sporting resort" and "to promote social intercourse among its members and," it added for the first time, "their families." It went on to specify, also for the first time, that women as well as men were eligible for membership, a clause that was thought necessary now that the club already had several female members. Dues were to be raised to $300 a year, and the number of vice presidents was increased to two and would later be raised to three.[1]

The emphasis on renewal, which seemed so appropriate at the dawn of the new century, did not, of course, prevent problems from recurring. Robert de Forest still viewed the Jekyl leadership, with the possible exception of Frederic Baker, as "rather negative" and hoped to see changes made. "Oyster pirates," as they were called, continued to plague Jekyl, even though Georgia legislators had in 1899 passed a law to protect the offshore islands from poachers. And smallpox in Brunswick threatened the safety of the club.[2]

But little could dim the enthusiasm of club members and their optimism for the future. The progressive spirit and the country's growing reliance on technology could not be repressed, and on the day after Christmas in 1900, the island's quiet glades were disturbed for the first time by the sound of a "gasolene [sic] automobile." The vehicle had been brought down by William Struthers of Philadelphia. In anticipation of just such an event, the executive committee had voted to prohibit automobiles on the island, a fact of which Grob informed Struthers. "He is much wrought up about it," reported Grob, "and says he does not think such a resolution would hold good in point of law." Nevertheless, Struthers made arrangements to have the car sent home by Mallory steamer, but the executive committee, apparently recognizing the inevitability of automobiles on the island, met on January 10 to establish a new set of rules. Automobiles were to be permitted "only on the beach and on the back road connecting the Club House and Stables with the beach via the Wylie [sic] Road" between the hours of 10:00 A.M. till noon and from 2:00 to

The automobile was introduced on Jekyl in 1901. Mr. and Mrs. Richard Teller Crane, Jr., take a drive by the island chapel. (Jekyll Island Museum)

The *New York American* claimed on February 26, 1940, that "the Automobile is tolerated, rather than favored, and it's the ancient vintage type of vehicle one is likely to encounter on the beautiful drives of the island, driven by millionaires who maintain fleets of high-powered cars and yachts." In fact, automobiles had long been on the island, and by the 1920s, even the workers were driving cars on the beach. Here employees' children (left to right) Howard Etter, H. Clark Flanders, David Nielson, and John Marshall Etter (standing) play in the sand as adults look on. (Courtesy of Howard Etter)

Right: The construction of an electric plant required the employment of a full-time engineer and assistants. The chief electrical engineer was for many years Gilbert A. Kay, shown here at the far right. Others in the picture are (right to left) Mrs. Kay, John Etter, Ray Etter, Howard Etter (baby), and an unidentified woman. John Etter was brought on board in 1910 to work as bookkeeper and later assistant superintendent. He resigned his position in 1931. (Courtesy of Howard Etter)

7:00 P.M. They were limited to a speed of
six miles an hour and were to be "brought
to a full stop when meeting horses driven or
ridden."[3] At the same meeting President
Charles Lanier reported the purchase of a
new yacht, the *Jekyl Island,* to replace the
worn-out *Howland,* which had had several
near accidents in recent years and was in
the end sold to a newly formed boat company and put into service between
Brunswick and May Bluff.

Seeing the rapid technological changes
around them, Jekyl Islanders were becoming impatient for the long-delayed electric
plant, particularly since Brunswick had
had electricity for more than a decade.
Several of the houses (Struthers, Pulitzer,
Baker, the club house, and the Sans Souci)
had already been wired in anticipation. By
October 1900 serious thought was being
given to "putting in a dynamo," but 1901
came and went, and the power plant had
still not been constructed. Although years
later a legend would grow that Thomas
Edison personally installed the electric
power plant, the truth was that he had
nothing whatever to do with it. In spite of
the fact that several Jekyl members backed
Edison's enterprises, no evidence exists to
show that he ever set foot on the island. On
the contrary, the George A. Williams
Company was contracted in 1902 to build
the plant for $36,100. In the end, it would
cost $39,500, which was paid, as were
most improvements, by private
subscription.[4]

The electric plant, constructed for the
most part during December 1902, would
transform Jekyl in the 1903 season into a
brightly lit wonderland, its splendid new
incandescence flickering in the island
darkness and reflecting on the waters of
Jekyl Creek. Grob wrote enthusiastically to

Joseph Pulitzer's secretary on January 11,
1903, to describe the newly illuminated
Pulitzer cottage. "The house and
grounds . . . were all lighted up, and it
certainly makes a fine appearance. Mr.
Pulitzer cannot help but being pleased with
it. . . . Your house and grounds are the
best lighted of any on the island."[5]

Along with the need for electricity,
property owners felt it imperative to install
indoor plumbing in all the houses. At the
time the Sans Souci was constructed, no
one had given any thought to the matter,
and only after its completion did Hyde
write to inquire whether there was, in fact,
indoor plumbing. With an abundance of
servants to carry water and chamber pots,
its lack had not seemed a major problem.
Nevertheless, prior to October 1901, steps
were taken to remedy the situation. On
October 9 the *Brunswick Times-Call* announced that the contract for plumbing in
the Sans Souci had been awarded to a local man, A. H. Baker. The newspaper
expressed the city's appreciation for the
"friendliness on the part of Jekyl Islanders
toward home enterprises," which was due
in large measure to the good will and
efforts of Superintendent Grob.

That "friendliness" had also been manifested when the executive committee had
decided in February 1901 to construct a
grandly proportioned annex to the club
house and awarded the contract to the
Brunswick firm of W. H. Bowen and J.
W. Thomas. Cornelius Bliss announced
the decision to Edmund Hayes: "The
scheme to build an apartment annex to the
Jekyl Island Club House has been revived
with prospect of coming to a successful issue." Henry Hyde had originally conceived

Top: The club house with completed annex. The Jekyl windmill (background) was frequently damaged by storms. (Georgia Department of Archives and History)

Bottom: Looking north, a rare shot shows the Fairbank cottage as it once stood between the club house annex and the Sans Souci. (Georgia Historical Society)

the idea for the multi-storied annex containing private apartments and extra rooms for guests in 1895. Overshadowed by the Sans Souci construction and club house renovations, the project was not promoted until 1897 when Hyde returned to the idea and asked architect Charles Gifford to draw up plans. Canvassing various possibilities, Hyde concluded that the best approach would be to build south from the club house across the northeast corner of N. K. Fairbank's lot. But when he approached Fairbank about the use of thirty-five feet of his land, Fairbank objected and suggested rather that the annex be built "obliquely from the billiard room" to intersect only a small corner of his property in order not to block his view of Jekyl Creek and the marshes. Hyde was miffed. "I do not think that Mr. Fairbanks [sic], any more than any other man, has a moral right to stand in the way of the progress and improvement of the club and I must say he has acted rather selfishly in the first place and un-business-like in the second place." Discussion dragged on in a desultory manner, but neither man would compromise, so the matter was finally dropped.[6]

In the end it would be Fairbank's suggestion which was followed. The executive committee designated Charles Lanier and Cornelius Bliss to negotiate with Fairbank, and this time all parties were amenable. The new wing would angle across the back of his lot and obstruct as little of his view as possible. With this critical issue settled, construction was well under way by August and would be completed in time for the 1902 season. At first, the annex was to include only six apartments, but interest was so great that plans were expanded to incorporate eight units on the first two floors and twenty new sleeping rooms on

the third, thus increasing the cost beyond the initial $60,000 estimate.

One of the new annex owners was the club's president, Charles Lanier, who purchased apartment four. Both cousin and friend of poet Sidney Lanier, Charles was well liked by club members and was never dictatorial in his administration of the club's affairs. He would serve as its president for seventeen years, longer than any other chief executive. During his first stay in his annex apartment, he brought with him his niece, Kitty Lawrence, the future wife of Ambassador to Russia W. Averell Harriman. For many years she would be her uncle's regular guest at Jekyl.

Other owners included former Secretary of the Interior Cornelius Bliss (apartment two), bridge builder Edmund Hayes (seven), banker John S. Kennedy (one), his business partner, Morris K. Jesup (six), lawyer Francis Bartlett (five), and John J. Albright (three), who had made his fortune in coal, hydroelectric power, and Westinghouse Electric.

Apartment eight went to Samuel Spencer, the president of the Southern Railroad Company and one of only a handful of southerners ever to belong to the Jekyl Island Club. He had served in the Confederate army during the Civil War and in 1867 graduated from the University of Georgia. He then obtained from the University of Virginia a civil engineering degree, which led to his lucrative career in railroads. Spencer was delighted with his apartment and wrote his wife on October 21, 1901, that he had "drawn the choice apartment of all at Jekyl—that is the end one on second floor with the two extra South windows. Of course," he went on,

One could not simply buy one's way into the Jekyl Island Club. It was necessary to have a sponsor, usually a relative, a business associate, or a friend, and to be elected by a board of directors, with two negative ballots sufficient for exclusion. Annex apartment owner Samuel Spencer, whose candidacy was announced in March 1898, was duly elected in April. (Baker Library, Harvard Business School)

"that apartment has the draw back of over looking and being some what behind Fairbank's house, but the sun will shine on it all day . . . and it will certainly be the airiest and brightest of all. Everybody said 'what luck.'"[7] His was the only family that would continue to own an annex apartment until the end of the club era. Spencer himself would be killed in a freak accident on his own railroad in 1906.

The annex was not the only residential construction that characterized the early years of the twentieth century. The cottage colony saw the addition of three new dwellings between 1901 and 1904. The first of these was Mistletoe, the house of Henry

Kirke Porter, who decided to build in June 1900. Once again a club owner called upon Charles Gifford for a design.

No member's business career better typified the new attitudes and the growing reliance on the technological innovations of the young century than that of H. K. Porter. He had studied for the Baptist ministry after the Civil War, only to abandon the pulpit in favor of business and enter into partnership in the firm of Smith & Porter. The company evolved into the H. K. Porter Company, with Porter himself as president, a position he would hold until his death in 1921. At first the firm had manufactured light locomotives, but gradually it expanded to include all sizes and types of engines, which were used not only in the United States but also in such far-off places as Africa, Australia, Russia, and Japan. As a businessman, Porter was extremely progressive and was among the first to introduce into a firm profit sharing, group insurance, and the like. In 1903 he was elected to Congress, where he served for only one term before being defeated for reelection.

He had had the good fortune to marry a cultured and charming widow, Annie De-Camp Hegeman, who sparkled at the art of conversation and was considered a talented artist with a flair for entertaining. Her dinners and garden parties at Mistletoe, which was completed by February 1, 1901, were among the highlights of the Jekyl social season.[8]

The second cottage planned during the twentieth century was that of Frank Henry Goodyear, a wealthy lumber and railroad man from Buffalo, New York. After starting life as a schoolteacher, he gave up teaching to become a bookkeeper in a sawmill and ended up marrying the boss's daughter, Josephine Looney. His rise in life

Mistletoe Cottage, built by
Henry Kirke Porter in
1900. Porter was the only
person from Pittsburgh
ever elected to the club.
(Everett Collection,
Coastal Georgia Historical
Society)

Henry Porter prepares to
board the club yacht to
end his stay for the
season. (Lanier, *Jekyl
Island Club,* 1911)

Afternoon teas were
commonplace at Jekyl.
Here guests gather at
Mistletoe Cottage.
(Southern Historical
Collection, University of
North Carolina)

Frank Henry Goodyear, club member from 1902 until his death in 1907. (Courtesy of George F. Goodyear)

Josephine Looney Goodyear acquired her husband Frank's club share from his estate in 1909 and remained a club member until her own sudden death of a heart attack in 1915. Superintendent Grob and Edmund Hayes, who had originally proposed Frank Goodyear for membership, were pallbearers for her funeral in Buffalo, New York. (Courtesy of George F. Goodyear)

was phenomenal. With his older brother, Charles, he founded in 1887 a lumber firm that was reorganized in 1902 as the Goodyear Lumber Company. He was also president of the Buffalo & Susquehanna Railway, with other important interests in the coal industry. He had been proposed for membership by Edmund Hayes in March 1902. In April he purchased a lot on which he now proposed to build. He planned to follow a design by Thomas Hastings, of the well-known architectural firm of Carrère and Hastings, who had come to the island as Goodyear's guest on March 13, 1903. Although the plans were approved by the executive committee at the end of April, construction was delayed for some reason and the house would not be ready for occupancy until the 1906 season.[9]

The third new cottage—that of the George Frederick Shradys—would be completed in 1904. The Shrady cottage was actually proposed not by Shrady himself but by his son-in-law, Edwin Gould, who had joined the club in 1899 and in December 1900 had purchased the house built by David H. King, Jr. King had not been well, and his property, badly damaged by the 1898 hurricane, had become a perpetual headache. Its basement filled with water in every storm; the pool had sprung a leak; the doors jammed; the roof leaked. It was too much. He put the house on the market in 1899 at an asking price of $35,000 with Grob serving as agent. A year would pass before it was purchased by thirty-four-year-old Edwin Gould, the second son of powerful financier Jay Gould and a relative newcomer to the club.

Although Edwin's older brother, George, also a member of the Jekyl Island Club, had been trained by their father to manage the far-flung family enterprises, it

The Goodyear Cottage.
(Everett Collection,
Coastal Georgia Historical
Society)

was, ironically, Edwin who most resembled the old man in character and business acumen. While George enjoyed the social swirl of New York, Edwin, like his father, was an intensely private man, preferring the quiet of Jekyl to the Fifth Avenue glitter. According to Maury Klein, Jay Gould's most recent biographer, "While continuing to help George with the family investments, he [Edwin] also funneled his own money into a match company, banking, real estate, and other enterprises. By shrewd, careful management," he relates, Gould "quietly amassed a fortune of his own outside the family trust. His marriage was as happy as his tastes were simple. Where George delighted in champagne suppers, Edwin thrived on the outdoors and isolation of the woods. . . . He and Sally

doted on their children." Sarah Cantine Shrady, called Sally, was the stepdaughter of Dr. Frederick Shrady and had at the age of eighteen married Edwin Gould after an "unfashionably short" engagement. Her "reserved" personality blended nicely with her husband's quiet disposition.[10]

Jekyl Island, with its family orientation, suited them to perfection. It was a splendid discovery, where against the backdrop of the island's beauty and wildlife, they could rear their two young sons, six-year-old Edwin, Jr., and one-year-old Frank Miller, in relative safety and comfort. For Edwin Gould the setting of the King house more than compensated for its flaws. The abundant orchards, the palmettos, the lush hedges with which King had lined the drive in 1899, as well as its ideal location facing the river and near the club house, made it very desirable.

Edwin Gould and his wife,
Sarah Cantine Shrady.
(Lyndhurst Archives)

Chichota was the name
Edwin Gould gave to the
cottage he purchased from
David H. King, Jr., in
1900. (Lanier, *Jekyl
Island Club,* 1911)

George Gould (far right)
on one of his rare visits to
Jekyl, with friends and
some of his father's
associates in February
1891. (Lyndhurst
Archives)

Edwin Gould with his arm around his son, Frank Miller, hosts friends from Ardsley-on-Hudson, New York, around his pool. Edward S. Jaffrey took the photograph in March 1905. (Everett Collection, Coastal Georgia Historical Society)

Sarah Gould, framed in the doorway that led from the living room to the courtyard containing the swimming pool, plays a board game with her son. (Everett Collection, Coastal Georgia Historical Society)

This rare shot of the interior of the Gould house was taken not long after the Goulds purchased it. (Everett Collection, Coastal Georgia Historical Society)

The Edwin Goulds' love of
children is reflected here
as they help supervise
games on Jekyl beach.
Susan Albright, daughter
of club member John J.
Albright, is at far left.
(Jekyll Island Museum)

Gould's first stay in his cottage began on
March 6, 1901, when he arrived with his
wife and inscribed for the first time in the
guest register the name "Chichota," which
they had chosen for their cottage, most
likely in honor of an ancient Creek Indian
chief from the area. Despite their reputation for enjoying the quiet family life, the
Goulds loved to entertain their friends in
the informal atmosphere of Jekyl. One can
only imagine the reaction of the foppish
European nobleman with the impressive
title and name, the Marquis Marie Ernest
Paul Boniface de Castellane, who had with
great fanfare married Anna Gould, Edwin's younger sister, in 1895. He and his
wife arrived on Jekyl with their maid and
valet on February 19, 1903. As a rule,
the marquis had only scorn for what he
considered to be the inelegance and even
boorishness of American manners. No

doubt the deliberate simplicity of Jekyl Island life and the Goulds' cavorting around
their pool with their children and guests
were quite a trial to him. He and Anna
came to the island only once.[11]

Life on Jekyl, however, had not been
without mishap for the Edwin Goulds.
One evening in late March 1900, a year
prior to moving into Chichota, as the family
made the crossing between Brunswick and
Jekyl on the old *Howland*, the yacht had
been grounded on a jetty at the mouth of
Jekyl Creek, leaving the Goulds stranded
for forty-five minutes on the dark water.
The incident caused Superintendent Grob
to remark that "had it been a rough night,
it might have been a very serious affair."
Although such a beginning did not diminish
the Goulds' enthusiasm for Jekyl to any no-

Edwin Gould's private dock, built in 1901. Few club members lavished so much expense on their island property as did Gould, whose family enjoyed Jekyl's pleasures immensely. (Jekyll Island Museum)

ticeable extent, it made them acutely aware of the dangers of the island life, particularly insofar as their children were concerned, and they took every possible precaution to ensure their safety.[12]

One of Frank Miller Gould's boyhood comrades from Browning School in New York, Ernest Stires, was invited to the island and recalled, more than fifty years afterwards, the protective restrictions placed upon him by his hosts, who had every activity monitored by "a very watchful governess." As he described the visit, "Wherever we went in a sort of Irish jaunty cart . . . some sort of adult supervision was in attendance. Irksome."

Stires remembered the Goulds as "wonderfully unassuming and quiet." His memories, albeit a bit faded with time, nonetheless capture the spirit of a child's life at Jekyl.

I was dimly aware of odds and ends of famous names, but when I returned home my own family were exasperated because I couldn't remember the names of anyone outside the Gould family, except a few first names of some boys and girls I played with. Tennis was daily, also pony rides, the above mentioned Irish cart trips, and my swims [in the ocean] when I could manage to outargue my protectors.

The life was quiet, but I suppose elegant. We had ideal weather. We were not allowed to shoot, but the older members of the Gould family did some hunting. I tried to fish, but was so outdone because I was constantly supervised for fear I would fall out of the boat, that the few small fish I did get were not too noteworthy in my memories of Jekyll.[13]

The Gould indoor tennis court (1913) was a grand affair, containing skylights with leaded glass, marble showers, a large corniced locker room, electricity, and a telephone hook-up to the main house. (Jekyll Island Museum)

George F. Shrady, father-in-law of Edwin Gould. (*Medical Record: A Weekly Journal of Medicine and Surgery,* March 4, 1916)

Hester Ellen Cantine Shrady took over the share of her deceased husband in 1908 and remained a member of the Jekyl Island Club until her resignation in 1916, after which she visited rarely until 1924. (Edwin Gould Foundation for Children)

The Shrady Cottage, completed not long after Edwin Gould proposed his father-in-law for membership in 1904. The house would remain in the family until 1925, when it was sold to Dr. Walter Belknap James, then president of the club, who would name it Cherokee. (Jekyll Island Museum)

Edwin Gould was so impassioned about the island that he had set out almost at once to improve his house, first making all the necessary repairs required for comfort and then undertaking the changes that would turn it into the perfect winter resort for his family. In January 1901 he planned to construct a private wharf and boat house. With still more improvements in mind, among them a stable and a new orchard, he began to buy up surrounding lots. In 1902 he built what has been called a casino. Although primarily a bowling alley, it also contained, according to later sources, a shooting gallery and a game room. He would in 1913 attach to it the island's first indoor tennis court, designed by New York architect Walter Blair. The huge structure, costing more than $25,000, was believed to be "one of the handsomest and costliest [covered courts] in the country." Until 1920 it was open to fellow club members.[14]

Considering the many improvements Gould had made in his property, his pro-

posal in 1904 to build a house for his in-laws immediately behind his own cottage came as a surprise to no one. It would merely extend the Gould family complex on Jekyl. Although it was Gould who was responsible for his father-in-law's nomination and subsequent election to club membership on July 8, 1904, Dr. Shrady was, nonetheless, a welcome addition to the club, which was always glad to have another physician on the island, particularly one so notable. One of only ten physicians ever to belong to the Jekyl Island Club, Shrady was a graduate of the College of Physicians and Surgeons in New York and a skilled surgeon who had served on the staff of no fewer than eight major hospitals. His fame was such that he was called upon to attend former president Ulysses S. Grant during his last illness, to act as a surgical pathologist when President James A. Garfield was shot in 1881, and to consult with the physician of Emperor Freder-

The Glynn County Board of Education authorized the establishment of a school for white children on Jekyl in February 1901 and in June appointed Bertha Baker to teach for a salary of $15 a month. This photograph was taken at the school in 1911. A school for black children opened at a later date, with Anna Hill, daughter of Charlie Hill, as the teacher during the 1930s. (Lanier, *Jekyl Island Club,* 1911)

ick III of Germany. A contemporary sketch of Shrady depicts him as "a most agreeable and accomplished man and a brilliant conversationalist." His house, completed in 1904, was occupied for the first time in February 1905.

The Shradys took particular pleasure in being near their grandsons, Frank Miller and Edwin, Jr., who often stayed with them in their cottage. Unfortunately, they would not enjoy it together for long, for Dr. Shrady died in 1907. The year following his death, his wife, Hester, was accorded membership in the club under a constitutional clause which stipulated that the "widow or child of a deceased member may become a member of the club, without payment of entrance fee." She kept the house and continued to spend winters there near her daughter and grandchildren.[15]

The Goulds' life on Jekyl was idyllic until the season of 1917, when tragedy struck. Two days after Christmas, Edwin Gould arrived at Chichota with his sons, the younger on Christmas vacation from Yale, and several of their friends. This season was also to be the end of an idle existence for Edwin, Jr., who had not gone to college and found the structured academic life intolerable. As a boy on Jekyl Island he had fled from his tutor to join the workers' children in their schoolyard. He had run away as well from his preparatory school in New York after only three weeks there. He enjoyed the freedom of life at Jekyl and had become a full-fledged member of the club in 1914, when he was only twenty-one. Although it was unusual for anyone that young to be accepted for membership while his parents were still alive, the Gould family had been for eighteen years loyal, dedicated, and generous to the

School house interior. Bertha Baker is second from the left. She would remain a teacher on Jekyl until 1918. (Georgia Department of Archives and History)

club, and their son was given special consideration. Now he was twenty-three, and his father felt that it was high time his first-born learned to make a useful living. Thus this extended vacation at Jekyl Island was to be his last before his father introduced him into the banking world of New York. He intended to make the most of it and was delighted by the arrival on January 9 of the George Macys, for he was, according to one source, "quite mad about Kathleen Macy and . . . proposed to her every other day."[16]

The Tracy Dows family arrived on January 17, bringing with them their children's tutor, Noyes Reynolds, who became the hunting companion of Edwin, Jr., after his brother's return to college. One of their favorite hunting grounds was Latham Hammock, a marshy island of approximately 3,000 acres located on Jekyl Creek within sight of the club house. Edwin Gould, Sr., had purchased it in January 1914 and in-

corporated under the name "Latham Hammock Club." The purchase had sparked rumors that a rift had developed among club members and that Gould was planning to withdraw to form a rival organization. But Gould had, in fact, acquired the property both to prevent the construction of a factory or some other building that would spoil the Jekyl view and to expand his hunting options.[17]

Eddie Gould and Noyes Reynolds departed from Jekyl shortly after 7:00 P.M. on February 24 to check the traps they had set earlier in the day on Latham Hammock. Finding a raccoon caught in one of the traps, Gould, not wanting to damage the skin by shooting the animal, struck the coon with the butt of his gun. When he struck a second time, the gun, which he had carried with the hammer cocked, dis-

Frances Baker (not related
to Bertha Baker) was the
"guardian angel" of the
Jekyl Island School. She is
said to have subsidized the
teacher's meager salary
and to have donated funds
and materials for many
years to keep the school
operating. Here the class
of 1907 is shown on the
steps of Solterra, where
Mrs. Baker entertained
them on Washington's
birthday. Bertha Baker
stands at the top,
overlooking her pupils.
(Georgia Department of
Archives and History)

Bertha Baker's pupils,
the children of club em-
ployees, ranged in age
from five to nineteen. The
graduating class of May 5,
1911, poses with its
teacher in front of the
Jekyl Island School. The
taller of the two girls is
Ada Thompson, daughter
of the south end fisher-
man, and the boy at the
right is the son of the carpenter, Chris Nielsen.
Bertha Baker stands at the
top. (Jekyll Island
Museum)

charged, the barrel only inches from his body. According to the newspaper account, "the lower portion of the young man's body was literally blown to pieces."

Reynolds frantically tried to carry the young man to the boat but, realizing he was bearing a corpse, abandoned the body and set out in the canoe, turning it over several times in his desperate efforts to go for help. When those on the Jekyl dock heard his screams, Captain Clark set out in the club launch to find him. It was almost midnight when they returned with the body.

The boy's father was reached in Saint Augustine where he had gone on business. He gave instructions for the body to be prepared for shipment back to New York. He himself did not return to the island but went directly to Savannah. There he met the train pulling the Dixie, his private car and now the funeral car bearing his son's coffin. "It is an awful thing for him," wrote the tutor to the Valentine Everit Macy children, "for he was devoted to this boy." The hardest part was comforting Sally Gould, who had remained in New York with her sick mother. She was, according to the *New York Times*, "so prostrated by the news that she was placed under the care of a physician."[18]

Despite their love for the island and the great expense to which Edwin Gould had gone to make it a real pleasure resort for his family, he could not bring himself to come back for almost four years. His wife never set foot on the island again. Hester Shrady, the boys' grandmother, returned but found the island "rather sad." She made her last recorded visit in 1924, when her niece reported that Sally Gould "never will come to Jekyl . . . and does not even like us to be here."[19] After that final visit, Mrs. Shrady apparently acceded to her daughter's wishes and never returned, selling her house the following year to Walter James.

The century that had begun with such high hopes for the Goulds and so many others had dimmed somewhat. They were beginning to learn that even the Jekyl retreat could never completely shut out the more painful realities of life and occasional intrusions from the outside world.

8. A Paradise Imperfect

Although Jekyl in the early decades would fall shy of the Brunswick press's vision of it as "a regular garden of Eden," it seemed in January 1904 almost to have reached that perfection. The capstone project of the new century's building flurry—the chapel of which Frederic Baker had dreamed since 1897—was at last complete. It had been the final element that many thought necessary to transform Jekyl into a long-awaited earthly paradise.

Baker had not been the only person delighted to see Constable's little church become a reality. Charlotte Maurice, for many years the organizer of spiritual affairs on the island, welcomed it as well. Through her efforts, services had been held on a fairly regular basis in a building known as Union Chapel, and between 1898 and 1904 she had arranged for the bishop of the Episcopal Diocese of Georgia to furnish visiting clergymen, with the bishop himself agreeing to come on occasion. [1]

Although an Episcopalian herself, Charlotte Maurice held out her hand to people of other beliefs, among them Catholic missionaries and teachers traveling in the area. Six sisters of Saint Joseph and a priest named Father Dunn were her guests on March 21, 1908, at a luncheon that included Mrs. James J. Hill, who had been educated at a school founded by the nuns of this order. Three years earlier, she had befriended a Father P. J. Luckie, whose mission in Brunswick had been one of "hardship." Charlotte Maurice's willingness to embrace people of other faiths, social levels, and even races was a reflection not merely of her personal warmth and sociability but of her devout religious convictions and paternalistic class principles. [2]

She seemed as much at ease mingling with blacks at worship services in the old Union Chapel, which members donated for their use, as she was hosting the wealthy and famous. Her daughter, Cornelia (Nina), wrote to her grandmother of a Sunday when the family attended services conducted by a Reverend Perry, the black minister from Brunswick. She expressed the family's admiration for his church and school which were "more prosperous than anything else in Brunswick as far as we can see." The service was "pleasant indeed and with a good number of colored men we had quite a congregation." On March 23, 1901, on the other hand, Charlotte Maurice and her husband entertained with a dinner party that included John D. Rockefeller, his brother William, and their wives. No special to-do was made for the Rockefellers. She merely commented in her diary that "They do not drink wine except William," preferring "Poland water" instead. [3]

Charlotte Maurice also maintained good relations with members of white Brunswick society. Club attorney A. J. Crovatt and his wife and the James Dent family from Hofwyl Plantation were frequent guests at Hollybourne. On one occasion Mrs. Maurice was hostess to the entire Brunswick chapter of the Daughters of the American Revolution.

But no times in the Maurice household were more joyous than those spent with her own family. The Christmas season, when her eight children were most likely to be there, was one of the best. The Maurices usually arrived at Jekyl well before the opening of the club season to enjoy a classic Victorian holiday at Hollybourne. "The children have a little tree every year," wrote Nina in 1898, "which is put in my room by the fireplace." They hung their

Faith Chapel was constructed and dedicated in 1904. The architect, Howard Constable, paid two recorded visits to the island—once on February 19, 1895, prior to preparing the design for the church, and once on March 11, 1905, presumably to review his handiwork. Emily Maurice, daughter of Charles Maurice, was married here to Charles Whitney Dall on December 19, 1911, in the only recorded Faith Chapel wedding involving a member's family. (Everett Collection, Coastal Georgia Historical Society)

One of the finest features of Faith Chapel is its magnificent stained-glass window depicting the "Adoration of the Christ Child." It was designed by the father-daughter team of Maitland and Helen Armstrong, the former of whom had once worked with Tiffany, and was placed over the altar at the east end of the church where its clarity and jeweled colors could catch the sun's morning rays. The window was donated in memory of Joseph Stickney, who died in 1903. (Jekyll Island Museum)

Faith Chapel was the site of weddings, baptisms, funerals, and memorial services. Catherine Clark, daughter of Captain Clark, was baptized here by the Reverend Eugene A. Hoffman. Similarly, the first-born children of Emily Maurice Dall and Jean Struthers Sears were christened in the chapel. Rosetta Marshall and Hugh Flanders married here in 1918. The bride is at the center, holding a bouquet of flowers, with the groom to her right. The man holding the child is Chris Nielsen, the island carpenter; the child is his son, David. (Jekyll Island Museum)

stockings and, before daylight on Christmas morning, still in their dressing gowns and slippers, lit the fire and the candles on the tree. After opening presents, the family took the launch to Brunswick for church services, for there were too few people on Jekyl for regular services to be held on the island.[4]

Guests at the festive Christmas dinner always included Ernest Grob and frequently others on his staff. Nina described the event in 1898:

Our Christmas dinner on Monday was very pleasant with fourteen at table, ten of ourselves and the Club Superintendent, his assistant [Falk], the Housekeeper [Schuppan] (a very nice woman whom we like extremely), and the Captain of the Club boat [Clark]. We arrayed a small tree in the centre of the table and around it a present for each one with a ribbon attached to it & the pile in the centre about the tree covered with holly[.] When dinner was over each one pulled the ribbon nearest them & out came the presents from their hiding places. It caused a good deal of surprise & fun.[5]

The managerial staff attended a similar holiday dinner in 1899, but the following year, 1900, Captain Clark married Minnie Schuppan; the couple declined the Maurices' invitation, preferring to spend Christmas in their own home.

Along with Grob, the Maurices frequently invited the island's physician, William Hutchinson Merrill, of Pepperill, Massachusetts, and in later years other club doctors, to feast upon such delicacies as "Fish à la Maurice." Staff physicians had been present on the island since December 1897, following the first death there of a club member, the Reverend Charles F. Hoffman, brother of the game committee chairman, the preceding March.[6]

George Maurice (second son of Charles Stewart and Charlotte Maurice) and his family in front of the bath house on Jekyl beach. (Jekyll Island Museum)

Marian Maurice standing at the water's edge on Jekyl beach. (Southern Historical Collection, University of North Carolina)

After the physician's first season, which held some uncomfortable moments for Merrill, he made it clear to club officials that he expected to be treated more like a member and less like an employee. If the club desired "a physician married and of more experience than a recent hospital graduate," it must expect to make him an offer "on a more liberal basis." Evidently they came to terms, because Dr. Merrill returned to the island for many years, with one brief interruption in 1899, following his arrest in Rhode Island "due to a misunderstanding or lack of knowledge of . . . Rhode Island laws," as it was concluded, for practicing without a license. The matter was resolved, however, and Merrill was back at Jekyl for the 1900 season.[7]

The very presence of a staff doctor on the island was something of a concession on the part of members to the intrusion of life's realities. Club officers had since the founding of the organization boasted "the superiority of . . . Jekyl Island, with its pure and bracing air, freedom from malaria and

charming surroundings, and the comfort
and benefit to health that may be secured
there."[8] Charlotte Maurice herself had
been among the most outspoken in defend-
ing Jekyl's salubrious climate and its absence of disease. Nonetheless, illnesses like
smallpox, yellow fever, and typhoid continued to plague the island and the
Brunswick area.

At one of her many dinners in 1909,
conversation drifted around to the preva-
lence of typhoid fever at Jekyl and its
probable cause. Cases of it had been previously and repeatedly detected in the family of J. H. Thompson, the fisherman at
the south end of the island. Grob, who at
first thought dirty ice might be responsible
for the outbreak, had concluded that a carrier, perhaps even a club member, had
brought it to Jekyl. Dr. Merrill concurred
but was even more concerned about the
island's unsanitary conditions. He had advised the executive committee as early as

1905 to find a safer way to dispose of the
island sewage, but to no avail. In 1909, he
submitted another lengthy warning and also
presented his ideas to Edwin Gould who
agreed to contact an official on the board of
health to look into the situation and to have
his own family tested for the disease.[9]

Unfortunately, before the cause of the
problem could be diagnosed and remedies
applied, Charlotte Maurice contracted typhoid fever. Shortly after returning from
Jekyl to her home in Athens, Pennsylvania,
in April 1909, she fell ill. In May she
rallied and by July appeared to be almost
well again, but in August she suffered a
relapse. Just two days before her death,
Gratz Dent, son of the James Dents, wrote
to her from Hofwyl Plantation, "You have
had a dreadful siege of it all, and it seems
a cruel turn of fate that you should be selected for a case of typhoid fever, because
don't you remember the last precious day I
was at Jekyl, a Sunday evening before you
left for the North? Mr. Grob was dining

The interior of the
Maurice house with a
typical Victorian decor of
chintz and wicker.
Oriental rugs and animal
skins were used in
abundance. This
photograph, taken from
the dining room, shows
the entrance hall and
parlor. (Southern
Historical Collection,
University of North
Carolina)

Portrait of the Maurice
daughters (left to right),
Marian, Emily, Margaret,
and Cornelia. (Everett
Collection, Coastal
Georgia Historical
Society)

with you, and the discussion of typhoid came up, with you a champion for the island? I often think of that. And two weeks later you were ill with the disease."[10] Charlotte Maurice died on September 4, and Ernest Grob, as did many others, mourned deeply. "I too feel as though I have lost a Mother, as she was all that to me," he wrote to her daughter Marian. Club members poured out condolences to the family.[11]

They were distressed to hear of Mrs. Maurice's death, but more than that, they were alarmed. Before the next club season they had engaged a bacteriologist, one Dr. Charles Bolduan, to determine the cause of typhoid on the island. After consulting Dr. Merrill and conducting tests on the Thompson family and Page Parland, a black employee of the Goulds, he reported on December 2 that "the source of infection is probably associated with a chronic germ carrier" and hypothesized that a member of the Thompson family was the carrier. His proposals pointed to the need for better sewage disposal, window screens, correct and prompt destruction of garbage, better toilet facilities for black workers, and greater care in cooling and storing milk from the Jekyl dairy.[12]

Incredibly enough, no action appears to have been taken. When, during the 1912 season, typhoid fever broke out again, with six club members being stricken, the club once more engaged experts to examine the problem. On October 25, 1912, James A. Scrymser read to the board of governors a report from Dr. William W. Ford, which concluded that the disease was being spread through the oyster beds located too near the sewage disposal areas. The Thompson family had no doubt contracted it repeatedly because of a steady diet of infected oysters. He agreed with previous

Cyrus Hall McCormick, Jr., club member 1891–1936, was appointed to the committee on golf and sports in 1908 and for the next five years played a significant role in developing Jekyl's golf and tennis facilities. He was president of the International Harvester Company from 1902 until 1918, when he became chairman of the board. (Chicago Historical Society)

doctors that the Jekyl sewage disposal was "totally inadequate" and "highly unsanitary." This time the problem was not ignored, and the firm of Hering and Gregory was employed to install a modern new system. Work, though delayed by labor problems and quicksand, was finally completed toward the end of the 1913 season.[13]

Despite the blight that illness brought to the island, Jekyl had become, as its early prospectus had promised, a beautifully landscaped retreat where jessamine, wisteria, and Cherokee roses bloomed through the winter months, where palms lined the stately, well-kept drives inside the club compound, and where wild orange trees perfumed the air. Just beyond the fences that kept the wild deer at bay, Spanish moss hung mysteriously and alluringly from the giant live oak trees. The best facilities, among them a fine new golf course and new tennis courts, were provided.

But the presence of disease and the death of members from other causes maintained a constant pressure on club officers to seek new members. Near the end of 1911, within a three-month span, William Struthers, Cornelius Bliss, and Joseph Pulitzer had all died, the latter aboard his yacht *Liberty* en route to Jekyl. For the first time in the club's existence, an organized membership drive, headed by Charles Lanier and Cyrus Hall McCormick, was initiated. To this end, a committee was appointed to put together a book of photographs reflecting the island's charms for distribution to prospective members. It was privately printed by Lanier in 1911 and reissued in 1916. McCormick drew up a list of prospects from Chicago and invited them down for inspection.

Among those invited were Mr. and Mrs. Arthur Meeker. Although Grace Meeker professed to "love everything about the place," to feel "at home" there, and even to sense in the air a "tonic quality . . . one does not get in Florida," her husband did not join.[14] Whether or not cost was the reason, the club had in fact grown increasingly expensive over the years. Dues, originally $100, had been raised to $300 under the 1901 constitution and still again to $500 by a constitutional amendment adopted in 1910. Frequent assessments and other club expenses were far from negligible. Furthermore, club members were expected to support a variety of subscriptions, such as those which had financed the construction of the new golf course and tennis courts. Prospective members inevitably wrote McCormick to inquire about costs, and many may have been discouraged by the response.

In fact, the country had just recovered from another financial crisis, and even wealthy men were concerned about their

Joseph Pulitzer's yacht, *Liberty*, built in 1908. He died on this vessel en route to Jekyl Island in 1911. (Mariners' Museum, Newport News, Virginia)

economic well-being. In March 1907 the stock market had begun to decline, and by October, many were feeling the pinch. On October 21 of that year the Knickerbocker Trust Company, verging on collapse, had come for help to the club's first vice president, J. P. Morgan. Morgan decided, after careful deliberation, that the firm was too far gone to save and allowed it to collapse. Knickerbocker president Charles T. Barney, who had visited Jekyl Island as the guest of Henry Howland in 1892, committed suicide.

The failure of the Knickerbocker fueled the fires of the panic, and other banks began to feel its effects. On October 23, the Trust Company of America, headed by former Jekyl member Oakleigh Thorne, also appealed to Morgan for help when it was confronted with long lines of depositors demanding their money. This time Morgan was prepared to act, but not single-

handedly. He called upon fellow club members George Fisher Baker, head of the First National Bank of New York, and James Stillman, head of the National City Bank, also of New York, to assist him in dealing with this and other crises throughout the remainder of the panic. These three men would later be identified by a subcommittee of the House Committee on Banking and Currency (the so-called Pujo Committee) as the "inner group" among the major firms which controlled money and credit in the country. They were at the pinnacle of the banking profession, but it was Morgan, declared the *New York Times*, who "stood without a challenging American rival in the field of finance, and, in the public mind, was the supreme symbol of financial power." As the panic spread, despite the fact that the Trust Company of America had been saved, Baker, Morgan, and Stillman worked together with treasury secretary George B. Cortelyou to stem the tide.

The crisis, which had reached its peak in October, had begun to subside by

November, but its detrimental impact on business conditions continued into the ensuing year. "Never before in my experience was trade so paralyzed as during [the Panic of] 1907," dry goods dealer John Claflin wrote to Charles Maurice, "and in consequence orders were cancelled and stocks piled up on every side." Claflin, whose association with the island predated the organization of the club, resigned his membership because of his financial difficulties in 1912. And his New York firm, although aided liberally by his banking friends, never fully recovered from the depression which "laid the foundation of losses" that bankrupted him in 1914.[15]

The panic had focused attention on the need for banking reform in the United States. A central bank with ready reserves was clearly required so that the nation would no longer have to rely on a handful of private bankers to rescue the country as it had in 1893 and 1907. Thus in 1908 Senator Nelson W. Aldrich sponsored a bill to create the National Monetary Commission, which he would chair, to study the nation's financial system and determine what changes might be necessary.

Aldrich was himself a wealthy man whose daughter was married to the nephew of William Rockefeller. He had not at first been convinced of the need for sweeping reforms and a centralized banking structure, but, as the commission continued its work, he changed his mind. He also believed that the counsel of banking experts other than members of the commission was necessary in developing a plan. But the issue was so fraught with controversy, the motives of the representatives of financial institutions so suspect, and the senator himself so vulnerable to charges of conflict of interest that it seemed advisable to act quickly and quietly to avoid negative publicity that might undermine any proposal before it could be judged fairly on its merits.

Encouraged in this endeavor by James Stillman, who had a fetish for secrecy, Aldrich decided to organize a clandestine meeting of hand-picked advisors, to be held in a location where they would have "plenty of time" and be "free from interruptions." What better place than Jekyl Island off-season? Thus, sometime shortly after November 11, 1910, Aldrich, the five men he had chosen for the task, and his private secretary set out by train for Jekyl. Henry Pomeroy Davison, one of those selected by the senator, had been vice president of George F. Baker's bank until 1909, when he had joined the firm of J. P. Morgan. Either Morgan, Baker, or Stillman, in all probability, had given them permission to use the island, since none of Aldrich's group was at the time a member of the club. With Aldrich and Davison came Frank A. Vanderlip, who had replaced Stillman as president of the National City Bank when he had retired the year before to become chairman of the board; Paul Warburg, a senior partner in the banking firm of Kuhn, Loeb & Company and one of the country's foremost advocates of banking reform; A. Piatt Andrew, advisor to the monetary commission and assistant secretary of the treasury; and Benjamin Strong, vice president of the Banker's Trust Company, which had been organized by George F. Baker and his associates. All were highly respected in the financial world.

From the outset they maintained absolute secrecy "that would have delighted the

Right: Henry Pomeroy
Davison, club member
1912–17. (Everett
Collection, Coastal
Georgia Historical
Society)

Below: Senator Nelson W.
Aldrich of Rhode Island,
whose secret meeting on
Jekyl in 1910 led to his
becoming a club member
and to a proposal that was
the forerunner of the
Federal Reserve Banking
System. (Library of
Congress)

heart of James Stillman." Under cover of
darkness and posing as duck hunters, the
five financiers one by one boarded Senator
Aldrich's private railroad car, parked on a
siding in Hoboken, New Jersey. Vanderlip
described the situation: "We were told to
leave our last names behind us. We were
told, further, that we should avoid dining
together on the night of our departure. We
were instructed to come one at a time and
as unobtrusively as possible to the railroad
terminal. . . . Once aboard the private car
we began to observe the taboo that had
been fixed on last names." Vanderlip and
Davison even adopted false first names,
calling each other Orville and Wilbur for
the famous Wright brothers.

Work began immediately and continued
throughout the train ride to Brunswick,
where the men were met by the club yacht
and taken to the island. Vanderlip's account of the meeting contends that they
were cut off "without any contact by telephone or telegraph with the outside." His
memory on this score was flawed, for
Jekyl, of course, had both telephone and
cable service long before 1910. He further
gives the impression that they were alone on
the island except for "plenty of colored servants." But Captain Clark must certainly
have picked them up in the yacht, and on
November 18 Ernest Grob arrived to assume his duties. On the other hand, club
members had not yet begun to appear, and
by the time the Maurices registered on
November 29, the financiers may have already departed.

How long the surreptitious meeting
lasted is uncertain, although the group
spent Thanksgiving on the island, where

James J. Hill arm-in-arm with Jekyl Island Club member George Fisher Baker (right) and Charles Steele (left), May 5, 1910. Like many other Jekyl Islanders, Hill and Baker had close business connections and were summoned before the Pujo Committee. (James Jerome Hill Reference Library)

they dined on "wild turkey with oyster stuffing." They worked throughout the day and night, taking only sporadic time out to explore Jekyl and enjoy its delights. Aldrich and Davison were both so taken with it that they joined the club in 1912. Aldrich, in fact, was attracted back the following January in hope of improving his health and remained until March playing bridge, walking on the beach, and conversing with other guests.

Sometime after Thanksgiving, the Aldrich secret committee finished its work and left the island. The banking system that these six men developed became known as the Aldrich Plan. Acting apparently on the advice of Republican President William Howard Taft "to formulate your scheme into a definite bill backed by the Commission," Aldrich pushed forward his measure in 1912, but in the Democratically controlled Congress it died for lack of support, and on March 31 the National Monetary Commission was officially dissolved. Nevertheless, the Aldrich Plan became the forerunner of the Federal Reserve System, which was established in December 1913 under a Democratic administration.[16]

Suspicions about a "money trust" in the United States had by then been awakened, and in April 1912 a subcommittee of the House Committee on Banking and Currency was authorized to investigate the matter. Although it came to be known as the Pujo Committee for its chairman, Arsène Pujo, the chief counsel for the investigation, Samuel Untermeyer, would prove to be the more important of the two. Untermeyer was an outspoken critic of big business who was convinced even before the investigation began that, while an illegal

"money trust" might not exist, there was "a close and well-developed 'community of interest' and understanding among the men who dominate the financial destinies of our country."

A number of important Jekyl Islanders were called to testify before the committee. George F. Baker, J. P. Morgan, and James J. Hill led the list. Because Stillman was in Europe at the time, he was able to avoid the ordeal. Baker tried to explain the close relationship that prevailed among many banking firms with the simple statement: "We have always tried to deal with our friends rather than people we do not know." Morgan also testified for two days in a frank and vigorous manner, and his associate, Henry Davison, who had helped draft the Aldrich Plan, appeared as well.[17]

Also summoned before the Pujo Committee was William Rockefeller, who with the same grim determination as Stillman, Morgan, and Baker always sought to shun reporters and maintain his privacy. Pleading ill health, Rockefeller refused to submit voluntarily to questioning and went into hiding at Rockwood Hall, his estate in North Tarrytown, New York. In truth, he had been suffering for years from a chronic larynx problem that produced periodic coughing spells, spasms, laryngitis, and general debility. His physician, Walter Chappell, contended that it was potentially life threatening. An operation had only partially corrected the condition which flared up anew and rather conveniently as the House subcommittee undertook to investigate his banking connections.

Skeptical about the seriousness of his illness, the Pujo Committee subpoenaed him in October 1912 and sent process servers to Rockwood Hall. They were unable to find him, however; despite their surveillance, he managed to go motoring

J. P. Morgan testifying
before the Pujo
Committee in 1913.
(Brown Brothers)

William Rockefeller,
February 20, 1915, two
years after his abbreviated
testimony on Jekyl Island
before representatives of
the Pujo Committee.
(Library of Congress)

slumped in back of his car wearing earmuffs
and goggles, "so disguised that only those
who know him well can recognize him." By
the end of December the number of federal
deputies searching for Rockefeller had increased from four to forty and was reen-
forced by men from the Burns and
Pinkerton detective agencies. This army of
watchers, led by Charles F. Riddell, the
House sergeant-at-arms, not only besieged
Rockwood Hall and Rockefeller's house on
Fifth Avenue in New York City but also
staked out the neighboring homes of his
daughters Emma McAlpin and Geraldine
Dodge. After personally questioning the
maids and housekeeper at the Fifth Avenue
residence, Riddell told reporters: "We'll
keep him a prisoner in the house, whether
he is here or at Tarrytown until he sees fit
to come forth and surrender by accepting
service."

Unknown to Riddell, however, Rockefeller had long since slipped away. The first
inkling of his escape came from a reporter
in Brunswick, Georgia, whose story, filed
on January 2, 1913, appeared in the *New
York Times* the next day. It read: "While
process servers . . . have been watching
the New York home of William Rockefeller for weeks, he and his son, William G.
Rockefeller with their wives, were on Jekyl
Island." Riddell sent members of his staff
to Jekyl to investigate the rumor and concluded it was "absolutely unfounded." This
assertion amused Emily Maurice who had
just received a letter from her sister declar-
ing that "Dad had had the gentleman in
question out driving [on Jekyl] all a. m."[18]
The Rockefellers had arrived secretly and,
without registering in the guest book,
stayed three weeks in the Sans Souci before
sailing away on the yacht *Vanadis* belong-

ing to club member Cornelius K. G. Billings, who was wintering his world champion racehorses on a farm in Brunswick.

Riddell's siege was lifted on January 4, when Rockefeller's lawyer finally accepted the subpoena ordering him to testify in Washington on January 13. Still unresolved, however, was the question of whether his health would permit him to appear. Dr. Chappell declared that tension of any sort might trigger a throat spasm and result in Rockefeller's choking to death. The Pujo Committee relented to the extent that it agreed to allow the Standard Oil magnate to testify at Jekyl Island rather than in Washington. The private hearing was set for February 7.

On the scheduled day Pujo, Untermeyer, and a stenographer arrived on the island to represent the committee. Greeted by Rockefeller's lawyer, John A. Garver, and the club attorney, A. J. Crovatt, they were ushered into the parlor of his Sans Souci apartment, which was described as "a spacious, unostentatious chamber, at one end of which stood a plain square table covered with green baize. Chairs had been arranged for the party and a large rocker, for use by Mr. Rockefeller, was immediately behind the table. To its right was a small stand on which were Dr. Chappell's instruments and a small box of pills used by Mr. Rockefeller to soothe his throat when threatened with spasms." The room had been prepared like a stage set. Dr. Chappell came in for a brief conference and then went into the adjoining bedroom to bring back Rockefeller, and the hearing commenced.

Twelve minutes later, with only four questions having been asked, it ended. Rockefeller, whispering his replies, had a "fit of coughing and trembling which

brought sharp warning from his physician that the ordeal must cease or the consequence might be his sudden death." A report the following day elaborated on the scene:

It was a violent spasm of the throat. The witness's head had been swaying ominously and the palsey spread over his whole nervous system. He fell back into his chair, coughing. The trembling of his hands and the wagging of his head became more violent and the muscles of his face and neck contracted and expanded spasmodically. Dr. Chappell was at his side in an instant, administering a pill and treatment. Mr. Rockefeller became more quiet, but the physician was determined that the ordeal should go no further.

The *Times* reporter remarked ironically that "Not a word of information had been gleaned after the six months' chase and final running down of the financier. The only result was a demonstration that the National House of Representatives could reach out its long arm and compel the obedience of any citizen." The intruders into the island sanctuary, Pujo and Untermeyer, came away absolutely convinced that the illness was real, describing Rockefeller's condition to the press as "pitiable" and indicating that it would have been "dangerous and inhuman to go further."[19]

Even without Rockefeller's testimony, the Pujo Committee was able to submit a report on February 28. The seven Democrats on the committee found, as expected, "an established and well-defined identity and community of interest between the leaders of finance," which had resulted in "great and rapidly growing concentration of the control of money and credit in the

George H. Macy, club member 1902–18, with his wife in front of Moss Cottage. Macy succeeded Frederic Baker as treasurer in 1908. By the end of 1912, he had become third vice president (later moving up to second and first vice presidents) and chairman of both the executive and game committees. (Lanier, *Jekyl Island Club*, 1911)

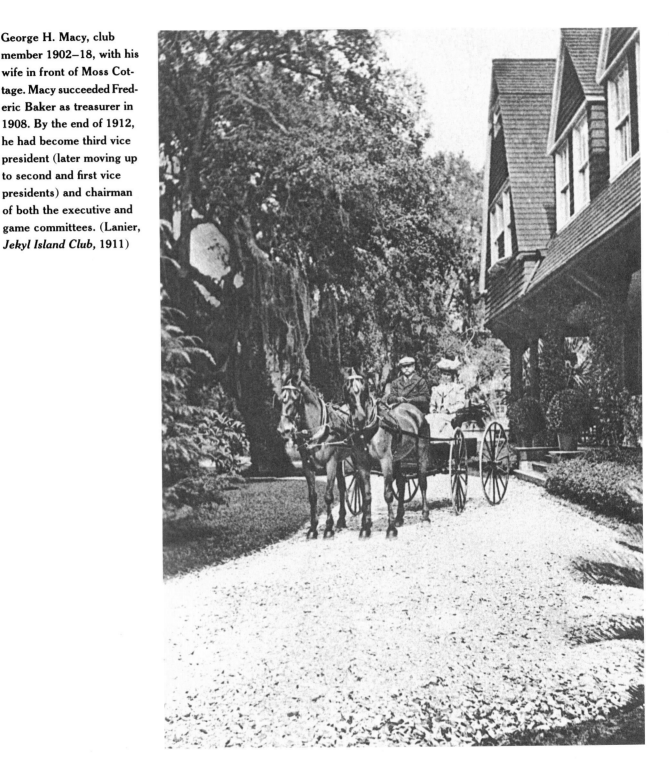

John J. Albright of Buffalo, New York, joined the Jekyl Island Club in 1890, two years after he sold his coal distributorship. He dabbled in real estate and the asphalt paving business for a few years with his brother-in-law Amzi Barber (also a club member) and in 1896 entered hydroelectric development in conjunction with Edmund Hayes. (Knox-Albright Art Gallery)

John J. Albright and his daughter Nancy in the solarium of the cottage purchased from the Pulitzer estate. (Georgia Department of Archives and History)

The Jekyl managerial staff included Miss Gross (left), who followed Minnie Schuppan as head housekeeper and who is shown here at her home in Tarrytown, New York, with her friend Bertha Baker. (Jekyll Island Museum)

hands of these few men"—in short, the money trust they had anticipated. The Republicans on the committee signed two minority reports contending that the majority report "did not prove the existence of a money trust" in the United States. In spite of their concern over the increasing concentration of power and influence of investment bankers, the committee gave the devil his due and acknowledged "the important and valuable part that the gentlemen who dominate this inner group and their allies have played in the development of our prosperity."[20]

Rockefeller was not the only person who had suffered great physical stress in testifying before the committee. J. P. Morgan, who had gone to Rome for a vacation following his own appearance, died on March 31, 1913. Family members felt that the Pujo investigation had contributed to the decline of Morgan's health, but his son, J. P. (Jack) Morgan, Jr., did not wish the investigators to think that his father gave a fig about the matter. Reacting to a press release given out by his father's physician, Morgan was disturbed at the suggestion that Pujo was "one of the causes of Father's illness. We have," he went on, "all here maintained the note which he struck so well in Washington that he was much too big to be annoyed by miserable little things like that."[21]

Morgan's death climaxed a long series of club losses stretching back to the beginning of the 1911–1912 season. In 1913, only two and a half months after Morgan's funeral, Frederic Baker, a club mainstay for two decades, also died. By the end of

1913, club membership had dwindled to seventy-two (counting four estates).

Although places vacated by the old guard were filled by their sons, some of them, the heirs of Joseph Pulitzer and William Struthers, for example, took little interest in Jekyl and wasted no time in disposing of their fathers' property there. George H. Macy, who had already emerged as one of the club's most important officers, acquired the Struthers house in 1911, while John J. Albright purchased the Pulitzer house in 1913. One among them, J. P. Morgan, Jr., who dropped the "junior" from his name to symbolize the changing of the guard, would become prominent in club affairs as well as national monetary developments.

With the death of his close personal friend and the club's first vice president, J. P. Morgan, it was not surprising that Charles Lanier decided to step down as president. The Lanier years, despite disease, depression, and investigative intrusions, had seen many accomplishments and had brought Jekyl as close as it would ever come to being the Eden that many had foreseen. New leadership would inherit not only fine facilities but also a competent, experienced managerial staff headed by Ernest Grob and James Clark, both of whom had served the club for more than twenty-five years. But the next generation of leaders would also be forced to recognize, as Lanier had, that Jekyl, although a special place indeed, still remained a paradise imperfect.

9. The Great War

The new president of the Jekyl Island Club, elected to succeed Charles Lanier, was Frederick Gilbert Bourne, former head of the Singer Sewing Machine Company. Although a wealthy man, he had not always been so. Born in 1851, the son of a Boston minister, and educated in the public schools, he started his career as a clerk at the Mercantile Library. One of those frequenting the library was Alfred Corning Clark, president of the Singer Sewing Machine Company, who had also heard Bourne sing on Sunday mornings in his church choir. Clark was so impressed with the young man's "good sense, mental alertness, good nature, and general capability" that he offered him a job. Bourne rose rapidly in the firm from Clark's secretary to president after his mentor's death. Under Bourne's presidency, Singer expanded significantly, and Bourne himself, commonly known as Commodore Bourne for his leadership role in the exclusive New York Yacht Club, had in the process become extremely wealthy. Despite his business acumen, he had a streak of romanticism; in 1905 he had built as a surprise gift for his wife a magnificent castle on Dark Island, one of the famed Thousand Islands in the the Saint Lawrence River.[1]

Elected to the club on April 8, 1901, Bourne quickly became a regular vacationer on Jekyl, his family failing to appear for only two seasons between 1901 and 1919. They sealed their attachment to the island in 1903 with the purchase of the Sans Souci apartment of Julia Anderson, whose husband, William, died in 1897, only days after they had buried their daughter, Ida. A popular club member, Bourne was elevated to the board of directors after only a year of membership. By

1908 he had accepted election to the executive and game committees and in 1912 was added to the committee on boats and wharfs.

The transition of leadership from Lanier to Bourne went smoothly, with the club hosting a sumptuous dinner to honor its outgoing president on February 18, 1914. Bourne had arrived on February 3 in time to bid farewell to his predecessor and assume authority. Although in certain respects the Bourne years would prove to be among the most successful the Jekyl Island Club ever enjoyed, they were marred at the outset by tragedies that struck thousands of miles apart.

The first of these was the killing of a club employee. The victim, J. William Hart, formerly a field agent in dairying at the State College of Agriculture in Athens, Georgia, was hired as assistant superintendent to oversee club affairs during Bourne's first summer as president. Hart's name appeared in the club register first on February 6 and again on March 21. Brought to Jekyl to make recommendations for improving the dairy operations, Hart, a Canadian by birth, so impressed club officials that they offered him a full-time job, giving him both complete charge of the island during Grob's absence in the summer months and the opportunity to carry out his own recommendations for the dairy.[2]

He had been at Jekyl less than a month when he initiated a number of reforms, particularly one limiting the territories of the fishermen at the north and south ends of the island. In fact, such rules had been in effect for some time but had been largely ignored. Hart, however, had redrawn the boundaries and announced his intention to enforce them. On the evening of May 29, Hart, accompanied by two visitors from Athens, went out to the beach on a turtle

hunt, with Freddie Clark, the ten-year-old son of Captain Clark, tagging along. The famous sea turtles of Jekyl, huge pre-historic-looking creatures, crawled onto the beach at night to lay their eggs. Fishermen were allowed to take the eggs on certain parts of the island, but some sections had been set aside for undisturbed nesting.

As the three men and the boy approached the beach, they became aware that they were not alone. The fisherman from the south end of the island, J. H. Thompson, who had worked at Jekyl for the last seven years, was sitting in his wagon. He had been gathering turtle eggs on a restricted part of the beach. The *Athens Daily Herald* recounted what followed. Hart ordered Thompson out of the forbidden area, but Thompson retorted resentfully "that he had been on the island longer than Professor Hart had, and that he intended to do as he pleased. . . . Hart told him that if he did not get back on his side of the line he would have to put him off

the island. Thompson said he would be a dead man if he tried it." At this point, Hart moved toward the wagon. Without warning, Thompson pulled out a pistol, opened fire at close range, and shot Hart three times in the face and head. He died almost instantly.

Freddie Clark and the two Athens men all testified that Hart was unarmed, and the coroner's inquest substantiated their story. Nevertheless, Thompson turned himself in the following morning to the Brunswick sheriff, insisted the shooting was self-defense, and "exhibited a bullet wound on one of the fingers of the left hand, claiming that Prof. Hart fired upon him first."[3]

Evidence against Thompson seemed strong, and, as expected, the grand jury charged him with murder. Grob, learning of the incident, had come immediately to Brunswick, arriving on June 2. According to the *Athens Daily Herald*, "the Jekyl Island club, the millionaire organization, is going to take part in the prosecution of Thompson, and . . . Superintendent Grob is coming for the purpose of employing counsel to assist Solicitor J. H. Thomas in the prosecution of the case."

Thompson and his family were well known in the area. His daughter Stella, who had the preceding April married an English club waiter, Bert Stallman, was described by the Brunswick newspaper as "a charming young lady loved by a large circle of friends." Her sister, Ada, was also popular, and her visits to the city were faithfully recorded in the press. Because the Thompsons were a local family while Hart was an outsider and a foreigner to boot, some Brunswick citizens believed that an acquittal was probable. A jury was selected on June 29, and the trial began. It lasted two days with Thompson pleading

Fishermen seining on the beach. The man second from the right is J. H. Thompson, the south end fisherman. (Jekyll Island Museum)

self-defense and the state contending that he had shot himself. Witnesses stuck to their stories that Hart had been unarmed, while the defense attorney countered with the argument that Thompson had expected him to be armed since he had been seen earlier in the day with a revolver. On July 1, the jury reached a verdict of not guilty, which, according to an outraged *Athens Weekly Banner*, "came as a surprise to a majority of the people of Brunswick, who had at least expected a verdict of manslaughter."[4] Despite the verdict, club officials decided not to allow Thompson to return to his job at Jekyl Island, and the unfortunate affair brought to an end the pleasant life his family had enjoyed there for so many years.

The trial had attracted considerable local interest and was reported in other parts of the state. It was, however, soon overshadowed by another killing that took place thousands of miles away in the small Bosnian town of Sarajevo.

On June 28, 1914, the day before the Thompson trial had begun, Francis Ferdinand, heir apparent to the Austro-Hungarian throne, was assassinated by a young Serbian nationalist named Gavrilo Princip. The event would escalate into a full-scale war by August. Ironically, the conflict would work to the benefit of the club, for as the *Brunswick News* proclaimed on October 7, "these men of millions . . . who almost annually go abroad in the winter will this season come to Jekyl owing to the European war."

As the press predicted, members in record numbers began to cancel their European plans in favor of a vacation on the Georgia coast. Anticipating the demand, George Macy, second vice president, apprised the membership that those "desirous of going to Jekyl Island on December 1st" might do so even though the official opening would not begin until January 1. Club officers came down even earlier. The first to appear was President Bourne, arriving on November 1 aboard his new steam yacht *Alberta* with a party of four men including Macy. The next day, Edwin Gould, third

Coal was an essential source of fuel for the Jekyl Island Club. One thousand tons were shipped to the island aboard the *Ampere* on June 13, 1914. (Jekyll Island Museum)

vice president, also checked in at the club. He was followed three weeks later by Samuel R. Bertron, a New York banker who had superseded George Macy as treasurer about 1912.[5]

The only club officer yet to arrive was the first vice president, James A. Scrymser. He would show up in February but, apparently growing tired of executive responsibility, had on January 26 resigned from the board of governors and all committee assignments. He was immediately replaced on the board by Edmund Hayes. When his term as first vice president expired, it was filled by George Macy, with Gould moving up to second vice president. The position of third vice president remained vacant.[6]

When the season began officially on January 1, 1915, the island was already abustle with members and guests, with more pouring in almost daily. The season sparkled, not only with the usual panoply of Albrights, Rockefellers, and Hills but with such notable guests as Secretary of the Treasury William Gibbs McAdoo and his wife, the daughter of President Woodrow Wilson; the family of Senator Nelson W.

Aldrich, who had by now become a club member; Myron T. Herrick, former ambassador to France; and Mrs. Stanford White, widow of the famous New York architect who had been murdered in 1906 by Harry Thaw, a relative of the Carnegie family on Cumberland Island. By the season's peak, every cottage and most of the rooms in the club house, the annex, and the Sans Souci were filled to capacity.

It was fitting that such a grand season as 1915 should be capped by some momentous event, and the man who made it happen was Theodore N. Vail, president of the American Telephone & Telegraph Company. For many years Vail had dreamed of developing a truly national telephone system stretching from coast to coast. It was from Jekyl Island on January 25, 1915, that he saw that dream fulfilled. The transcontinental line had been completed on June 14, 1914, and successfully tested on July 29. The call on January 25 was to mark the ceremonial opening of the new line.

Theodore Vail speaks from Jekyl Island as he opens the first public transcontinental telephone line on January 25, 1915. William Rockefeller (seated) listens. Standing are (left to right) W. Welles Bosworth, S. B. P. Trowbridge, and J. P. Morgan, Jr. (AT&T Corporate Archives)

That Jekyl was involved at all was a matter of chance. The AT&T president had originally intended to participate in the event from his New York office, but an injury to his leg forced him to abandon this plan. He arrived on the island to convalesce on January 6, and shortly thereafter began preparations for the call.

Vail had no intention of risking such an important moment with faulty equipment. Jekyl had had telephone service since 1892, but the cable between the island and Brunswick had "never worked satisfactorily and often it was impossible to talk to a person in a distant city." Grob had also had problems with the transmitter, complaining to Southern Bell that "we are compelled to talk so loud, as to be heard throughout our Club House, and of-course our people sending telegrams etc dont want everyone in the house to know the contents."[7]

Since the celebration was to be a public affair, with the president of the United States, as well as Alexander Graham Bell and his assistant, Thomas Watson, all joining the coast-to-coast conversation, a new

cable and modern equipment were imperative. Sydney Hogerton, divisional supervisor for AT&T, was put in charge of coordinating technical arrangements to ensure a perfect connection. To make certain that the newly installed line would function properly, "a perpetual test" was maintained between Brunswick and Savannah and a technician patrolled the line to respond to any emergency. And well he did, for on the morning of the call, a tree caused interference with the service. "Everybody along the line was sweating blood, wondering what was going to happen," but the break was quickly repaired. It was unthinkable, as the chief engineer would later remark, that the line should fail and deprive Vail of his supreme moment.[8]

On the afternoon of January 25, Vail was ready at Jekyl, President Wilson in Washington, Bell in New York, and Watson in San Francisco. Other company officials awaited their turns as well. With Vail on the island were J. P. Morgan, Jr., William Rockefeller, W. Wells Bosworth, architect of the AT&T building in New York, and S. B. P. Trowbridge, architect of the J. P. Morgan building.

The call lasted several hours and was interspersed with speeches to the assembled dignitaries. It was 6:00 P.M. before Vail finally spoke with the president:

MR. VAIL: Hello, who is this?
PRESIDENT WILSON: This is the President. I am glad to hear your voice. I have just been speaking across the Continent this afternoon.
MR. VAIL: Oh, yes.
PRESIDENT WILSON: Before I gave up the telephone, I wanted to extend my congratulations to you.
MR. VAIL: Thank you.
PRESIDENT WILSON: I am very sorry to hear that you are sick.
MR. VAIL: I am getting along very nicely. I am sort of a cripple, that is all.
PRESIDENT WILSON: I hope you will be well soon.
MR. VAIL: Thank you.[9]

It had not been a very memorable exchange. But its real value, as company officials repeatedly mentioned throughout the day, was that the multiple voices on the line traveled farther than had any other voices in history. The whole country recognized the magnificent accomplishment, but President Wilson summed it up best when he congratulated Vail first and then Bell on "the ultimate triumph of your great ideal. It makes me realize how much I would rather be Bell than be President. But I am humbly proud even to be President when this splendid achievement is realized." It had indeed been one of the greatest technological achievements of the decade, and Jekyl members were proud to have had a part in it.[10]

The success of the 1914–1915 season prompted the unprecedented decision to open the club officially for the ensuing year on December 1, a month earlier than usual, perhaps sparking the rumor that President Wilson intended to spend his honeymoon at Jekyl with the bride he planned to wed on December 19. Although the rumor proved unfounded, such a vacation might well have provided him a brief rest prior to beginning a reelection campaign in which United States neutrality in the Great War would be a significant issue. From the outbreak of fighting, Wilson had urged all Americans to remain impartial, but administrative sympathies, as well as those of most of the American people, were clearly with the Allies.

Jekyl Islanders, who were no exception, had been outraged to learn of the attempted assassination of J. P. Morgan on July 13, 1915, by a deranged German sympathizer who despised Morgan's pro-Allied activities. Shot twice in the stomach, Morgan recovered to continue his work on behalf of the Allies, acting as purchasing agent for France and Britain and playing a principal role in extending loans and credit to the Allied governments. When he had recuperated from his ordeal, he wrote to James Stillman on February 4, 1916, "Of course everyone who counts at all in New York is doing his best to show sympathy with the allied cause, and to give it every assistance in his power." On March 17, 1917, three weeks before the United States finally declared war on Germany, he offered his *Corsair III* to the U.S. Navy, which would use it as a submarine chaser.[11]

Stillman, who had been living in France when the conflict began, also supported the Allies. He donated his house on the Rue Rembrandt in Paris to the French govern-

J. P. Morgan's *Corsair III*.
(Library of Congress)

James J. Hill during his
last visit to Jekyl Island in
February 1916.
(Minnesota Historical
Society)

ment for use as a hospital and gave large sums of money to war victims, especially French war orphans and widows. On January 27, 1915, the French government sent him a letter of thanks for a contribution of 500,000 francs.

Morgan and Stillman were by no means alone among Jekyl Islanders in helping the Allies behind the scenes. Both George F. Baker and James J. Hill had also been involved in arranging the Anglo-French loan of 1915. Hill's first concern when war broke out, however, had been to get his children back safely from Europe. His daughter Gertrude and her husband Michael Gavin, who would join the Jekyl Island Club in 1924, had been abroad at the time, as had another daughter, Clara. Once home in Saint Paul, Clara Hill worked with her father on Belgian war relief. But Hill's health was failing, and his effort with Morgan and others to finance the Allied cause was one of his last major acts. He made a final trip to Jekyl Island in the spring of 1916 and on May 29, only a few months after his return to Saint Paul, died.[12]

When Grob arrived in Brunswick on October 30, 1916, to prepare for the 1917 opening, he predicted not only a re-election victory for Woodrow Wilson, who still hoped to keep America out of the war, but also "the greatest season in the history of the club." With the conflict still raging in Europe, he expected guests to flock to Jekyl as they had in the two preceding seasons. "Everything on the island in the way of extra rooms . . . [has] already been engaged," Grob told the reporter for the *Brunswick News*, "and the island will be crowded from the time it opens until the closing." He would not be disappointed.[13]

Among those who savored Jekyl that season was the family of Valentine Everit Macy, a cousin of tea merchant George H. Macy, who had come to play such an important role in club leadership in recent years. Everit Macy, a Democrat who had joined the club in 1909, served in the Wilson administration during the war years on the Council of National Defense and as arbiter to the War Labor Board. During the trip from New York, the Macy family had enjoyed the hospitality of Edwin Gould and the company of Gould's frequent companion at Jekyl, Nelson B. Burr, aboard Gould's train car, Dixie.

With the Macys was their children's new tutor, Kate Brown, from Worcester, Massachusetts. Her letters to her family provide a fresh and extraordinary glimpse into Jekyl life during the war years. Her astute observations, keen eye for detail, and sense of humor shine through all her letters. No other documents more clearly reveal what a retreat Jekyl really was during those years and how far away from its shores the war and its horrors seemed.[14]

Ecstatic about her new job, Kate Brown described the "luxurious and delightful" trip down. Having slept on the train, she awakened to a rainy morning, but as they approached the Georgia coast the skies cleared, and Kate caught her first glimpse of the live oaks with "festoons of moss hanging from the trees." When the train stopped at Savannah, she got off to touch her first palm tree "to see if it was real." As the journey progressed, she related her initial impressions of the South, describing, in language typical of the times, the "funny little run down houses, . . . mule trains, and . . . pickaninnies" dressed

in colorful garb. When they arrived in Brunswick about 2:30 in the afternoon, the boat to the island was not yet ready, so they "motored" about the town. "The young man who drove the car was so sweet with his, 'Ma'm?' to everything he didn't hear at first and his beautiful drawl," she observed.

Finally, the Macy party embarked on the forty-five-minute boat ride to the island and Kate Brown got her first glimpse of Jekyl. Although she was right in exclaiming "It is a wonderfully lovely place," she was misinformed about a few things. She commented, for example, that "On the ocean side there is a wonderful beach, very hard, where people motor and ride and drive. For there are motors here this year for the first time." Automobiles, of course, had been coming to Jekyl since the turn of the century. Indeed, at the close of the 1916 season, the *Brunswick News* had described with wry amusement the "large number of automobiles, electric cars and even ponies" that were loaded onto trains in Brunswick as the millionaires and their chauffeurs prepared to return to New York. "William Rockefeller alone had three electric cars sent over the A. C. L. [Atlantic Coast Line], while a large number of cars of various sizes and shapes were seen being taken from the boat." The reporter had found it "almost humorous" to witness so many inexpensive Fords among the millionaires' vehicles.[15] But Kate Brown's mistake was only a minor slip. For the most part, her depictions of Jekyl were accurate and vivid moments of captured time.

Once on the island, Kate discovered that aside from the servants "the only other people one meets are bright lights in the social world or noted millionaires, etc." She liked her employers, describing them as "charming people and I enjoy them more

Valentine Everit Macy, club member 1909–27, registered to stay in the Sans Souci on February 19, 1917, with his family and his children's tutor, Kate Brown. (Everett Collection, Coastal Georgia Historical Society)

Kate Brown, tutor of the Macy children, Edytha and Noel. (Courtesy of Katherine G. Owens)

all the time." The George Macys were likewise "hospitable" and "absolutely kind in every way. . . . Even the butler seemed unusually pleasant."

But she also had wry observations about other club members and guests. Nelson Burr during the train ride down had been "most attentive, not to say flirtatious which seems a waste of time as he is married and middle aged." And, after only a few minutes of conversation with William Rockefeller's son, she decided that "he would be a good deal of a bore," but that "His mother . . . was charming." Kate's charge, thirteen-year-old Edytha, she saw as "selfish, or rather, very full of herself. . . . But," she concluded affectionately, "as she is also very young, in spite of seeming quite grown up, she will probably come out all right." Although she liked individual guests and members, she summed them up as a group rather unfavorably: "If you could only see it all!" she wrote her family. "It seems like a rare collection of very high bred and exclusive animals, perfectly useless to society in general but enjoying their gilded cage very much."

Although Kate Brown saw the millionaires as "very exclusive and . . . far removed from the 'common people'," it was clear that they were not so snobbish as to let class stand in the way of including her in their activities. She played tennis with Charlotte Delafield, had tea and played the piano with Kathleen Macy, and was invited to join games of golf and cards with club members.

She took dinner with the Macys at the club house, where she found the food "delicious and everything of the most luxurious. After dinner everyone stays around and chats, just like a reception, or there is dancing or cards or something of the kind." But she found terrapin "a great disappointment" and after eating three elaborate meals a day for three days in a row began to long for a simpler diet. "The food is delicious but I would gladly give up . . . my three daily chances for indigestion and have some meals of bread and milk."

The one aspect of the customary dinner at the club house that she found most trying was the necessity of dressing formally, which put a real strain on her wardrobe. Unaccustomed to vacationing where, despite the proclaimed simplicity of island life, one "had to spend several hours a day in dressing," Kate surmised that her employers were "so used to it that I suppose they don't mind." Mrs. Macy decked herself in splendid jewels and wore "a dressy evening gown every night for dinner (usually a new one each evening)." Kate, however, had brought only one white net formal dress, which proved "very useful indeed" and was getting quite a workout. Before the end of her stay she was compelled to inform her family that "I am darning it already!"

Once, when invited to tea by Mrs. Richard Teller Crane, she "giggle[d] inwardly to think of the way I had entered their house . . . —announced by a perfectly trained man in perfectly fitting plum-colored livery—and then to think of the way people came to see us at Choate Island—taking off their shoes and stockings and wading ashore if the tide were low. These little contrasts . . . do make life here amusing."

Her days, when she was not tutoring her charges, Edytha and Noel Macy, were spent in pleasant pastimes, reading or bicycling, which could prove very adventurous. On one ride, Kate "heard a rustling sound and suddenly a wild boar ran out from the palmetto and crossed the path ahead of me, then another, and then six or eight baby pigs, all black as night." Deer and rabbits would also dart frequently out of the underbrush, and she held out hope of seeing an alligator.

At other times there were bicycle races on the beach among the young people. According to Kate, "Nearly everyone won a prize, lovely silver vases. . . ." On Washington's birthday, a celebration was always held "with flags, paper hats and a very good speech." And she especially enjoyed the young people's outings on the beach, describing one moonlit evening when they "cooked eggs, . . . bacon, fried potatoes, tea, and had sandwiches and cake" beside the sea in "one of the loveliest settings for a picnic I ever saw."

It was with some regret that Kate Brown would depart from Jekyl Island on March 15. A threatened railroad strike spurred some of the members to leave early, among them George Macy, who was not well despite his long sojourn on Jekyl. His health was so bad, in fact, that the Everit Macys had decided that they should accompany him on the return trip. He would die the following January 18. For Kate Brown, the season on Jekyl had been an unforgettable and "very wonderful experience," but she left little doubt that she preferred her own Choate Island.

One evening several weeks before her departure from Jekyl, Kate Brown and most of the members and their guests had attended a lecture at the club house given by a young Frenchwoman telling of her

Jay Gould II, son of
George Gould, was a
championship court tennis
player. Unable to defend
his title in Europe during
the war years, he visited
Jekyl, where he spent
much of his time playing
on his uncle's indoor
court. (Library of
Congress)

work in Belgian war relief. "She was a
charming speaker," Brown exclaimed,
"very vivid, and the contrast between her
daily life in Belgium and the life of these
resting millionaires all around me was
rather striking—at least to my fresh eyes."

But although Kate Brown had no way
of knowing it, many of the millionaires, including some of those then "resting" on
Jekyl, were already deeply involved in aid-
ing the Allied cause and preparing the
United States for armed conflict. The conflict came finally on April 6, 1917, when
Congress declared war on Germany. To
the minds of some club members, the U.S.
intervention was long overdue. Reacting to
the declaration, J. P. Morgan wrote to a
friend in October 1917, "Of course, I
personally am still much ashamed that
America is so late in the fight, which is the
only cloud in my joy in really being in it at
last."[16]

Morgan and others at Jekyl increased
their efforts to support the cause. Morgan
himself helped the Red Cross and became
active in Liberty Bond drives and French
orphan relief. Henry P. Davison, a Morgan associate, acted as chairman of the
American Red Cross Council and
launched a successful campaign to raise
millions of dollars for food, clothing, and
medical supplies. Vincent Astor served as
an ensign and later as a lieutenant in the
navy. He donated his yacht, the *Noma*, as
Morgan had done, to serve as a submarine
chaser, and he himself commanded a gun
crew on the *Noma* which helped capture a
German U-boat.

Vincent Astor, whom the *Brunswick News* described as "probably the richest young man in America," arrived at Jekyl aboard his yacht, the *Noma,* with its crew of seventy-five, on February 12, 1916, the guest of Tracy Dows. Within three weeks, sponsored by Dows, he had been elected to membership. The following year Astor brought to Jekyl a "new patented beach boat" and was seen "making 35 miles an hour off the island beach." He would remain a member of the club until 1945. (Mariners' Museum, Newport News, Virginia)

Although George F. Baker was too old at almost eighty to participate that actively, he, too, offered his yacht, the *Harvard,* to the navy. Theodore Vail, for his part, sent personnel from his firm to build a telephone system in France. When the United States nationalized the AT&T system in 1918, Vail continued to serve as manager and advisor to the government and chaired the Communications Council, a subcommittee of the Council of National Defense. And Samuel Bertron departed in 1917 on a diplomatic mission to Russia on behalf of President Wilson.

Through it all, however, on Jekyl itself, the war remained but dimly in the background as the traditional cycle of winter vacations continued. Improvements went on as usual, and in the summer of 1917 a $45,000-club house renovation, to include a new dining room wing and twenty guest rooms, was undertaken.[17] But the construction most representative of the splendor of the war years on Jekyl was the new cottage of Richard Teller Crane.

Crane, a manufacturer of plumbing fixtures and supplies, had been enticed to Jekyl initially in 1912 during the membership drive spearheaded by fellow Chicagoan Cyrus McCormick. After nine days on the island he wrote that he was "delighted with the place" and thanked McCormick for nominating him for membership. "Mr. [Robert W.] Goelet was here and seconded it and I am now a full-fledged member. It is just the kind of place that suits me and I hope we can get here every spring."[18]

Two years later he contemplated the acquisition of two lots on which to build a cottage but deferred his decision while the executive committee debated whether or not to revise its unpopular policy of only leasing lots rather than deeding them to members. The delay coupled with a disastrous fire in the home of Mrs. Frederick Baker turned out, oddly enough, to be fortuitous for Crane.

On the morning of March 9, 1914, a fire broke out in the attic of Frances Baker's cottage Solterra, probably caused by a faulty flue. Despite the general alarm and firefighting efforts, the frame house went up like a tinderbox. By the afternoon nothing but smoking ashes was left of the grace and elegance that had once housed the president of the United States. Mrs. Baker, who had been spending her first season on Jekyl since the death of her husband the year before, bravely announced her intention to rebuild, but in time her resolve weakened; instead she sold the site to Crane, who considered it superior to the lots he had been considering.[19]

Once the land lease had been transferred, Crane asked Chicago architect Henry C. Dangler to draw up plans for a new "cottage," which were ready by February 14, 1917. The Chicago firm of Gage and Company was brought in to do the construction. In the meantime, Dangler died, and his friend David Adler completed the project in time for the 1918 season. The cost, if the *Brunswick News* was correct, was over $100,000. The most expensive cottage ever built at Jekyl, it was depicted by the press as a "winter palace . . . the handsomest to be found anywhere in the south."[20]

The splendor of the new cottage did not go unnoticed by Jekyl Island members. James W. Ellsworth, a former Chicagoan who had made a fortune in the coal mining industry and who had joined the club at the end of the 1915 season, objected to "the building of pretentious houses on the Is-

Construction on Jekyl
Island continued during
the war years. Here work
had begun on a new dining
room wing added to the
club house in 1917 to
replace the old rounded
dining room that had been
built under the supervision
of Henry B. Hyde.
(Georgia Department of
Archives and History)

Interior of the new dining
room wing added in 1917.
(Georgia Department of
Archives and History)

On March 9, 1914, at the height of the club season, Solterra, the island home of Frances Baker, burned to the ground. According to a newspaper account, "The blaze . . . started in the attic presumably from a defective flue. . . ." The fire was discovered about eight o'clock in the morning. (Jekyll Island Museum)

Servants and island employees rushed to remove "valuable furnishings, bric-a-brac and pictures" from the house and succeeded in saving most of its contents. (Jekyll Island Museum)

Because of the hazard
from fires, which had not
only destroyed Solterra
(1914) and the machine
and carpenter shops
(1906) but also damaged
various cottages at other
times, fire escapes were
added to a number of
buildings as shown here
on the servants' annex.
(Jekyll Island Museum)

Mr. and Mrs. Richard
Teller Crane, Jr. (seated
right) and guests relax
aboard their yacht
anchored in Jekyl Creek.
(Jekyll Island Museum)

land." In his judgment, such construction
would overshadow the club house, the island's chief architectural feature, and
would contribute to the destruction of
"what may be considered the greatest
charm [of the club], this atmosphere of
simplicity." Although the Cranes were not
mentioned by name, there is no doubt that
Ellsworth was referring to their proposed
"cottage." His complaint, addressed to
chairman George Macy, was read at a
meeting of the executive committee on May
9, 1917, discreetly tabled, and never alluded to again.[21]

The 1918 season would open with more
cottages and club house accommodations
than ever before in its history. Despite the

The splendid house that Richard Teller Crane, Jr., built on the site of Solterra was the most expensive "cottage" ever constructed on Jekyl. (*Architectural Record,* November 1924. Reproduced by permission of McGraw-Hill, Inc.)

James W. Ellsworth, club member 1915–24. (Everett Collection, Coastal Georgia Historical Society)

success of the war years, President Bourne reported at a meeting of the board of governors on March 9, 1918, that a floating debt of approximately $92,000 had been contracted over a five-year period. He was concerned about the indebtedness for two reasons. First, unless they liquidated the obligation, he warned, "our borrowing capacity from the Banks would be impaired." Second, failure to pay "might interfere with our renewing the First Mortgage Bonds which are due in principal the first of April 1918." The first mortgage bonds issued in 1886 were to have matured in 1905. However, the Central Trust Company of New York had purchased them from the original holder, the Mercantile Trust Company, and had advanced the maturity date to 1910. It had subsequently been extended to 1915 and again to 1918.[22]

Above: Crane Cottage, looking north. The rooftops of the Gould and Maurice residences can be seen. (Everett Collection, Coastal Georgia Historical Society)

Right: Crane Cottage courtyard. (Jekyll Island Museum)

Opposite, top left: The interior of the Crane living room. (Georgia Department of Archives and History)

Opposite, top right: Crane cottage loggia. (Jekyll Island Museum)

Opposite, bottom: A barbecue given by the Cranes. (Jekyll Island Museum)

George W. Cowman (left), a long-time resident of Brunswick and close friend of Ernest Grob, in front of the club commissary which he built in 1916. During the 1890s W. H. Mann and the Stewart Contracting Company were the primary builders on Jekyl. They were displaced at the turn of the century by W. H. Bowen and J. W. Thomas, but just before, during, and after the war years, construction on the island was monopolized by Cowman. Virtually every private home on Jekyl was repaired or altered in some way, at some time, by him. (Georgia Department of Archives and History)

Christian Nielsen, club carpenter, and his wife, Nikolme Lindstrom Nielsen, on the porch of their house, which was originally built in 1916 for boat engineer John Courier. The cottage was occupied from 1923 to 1926 by the Etter family. (Jekyll Island Museum)

The club wharf was remodeled in 1916 by Cowman and beautified by the addition of windows and a cupola. (Jekyll Island Museum)

This photograph was taken from the club house looking south. The Rockefeller boat house (far right) was moved to a spot south of the Albright cottage to make room for a sea wall in 1916. Shown also (foreground to background) are the Ferguson cottage (formerly Fairbank), the Sans Souci, Rockefeller's Indian Mound, and the roof and chimneys of the Porter cottage, Mistletoe. (Lanier, *Jekyl Island Club*, 1911)

Built in July 1916 by J. W. Fitzgerald of Savannah, this sea wall was designed to link with a bulkhead that the club planned to put in during the summer of 1917 on either side of the wharf. As the *Brunswick News* described it, "The seawall in front of the Rockefeller home will be one of the most elaborate pieces of architecture of the kind ever built in the south and will make it probably one of the most beautiful of all Rockefeller's homes, which he says is proper, as he enjoys it more than any other." (Jekyll Island Museum)

Jekyl workers and wives of workers seated on a sliding board outside a beach house in 1914: Rosetta Flanders (top), Ray Etter (third from top), and baby Howard. (Courtesy of Howard Etter)

To deal with the club's debt problem, Bourne launched a subscription drive, calling upon J. P. Morgan, who had previously loaned $5,000 to cover the cost of the new additions, and others to double their subscriptions. Morgan readily agreed to do so. In response to his generosity, Bourne wrote: "Thanks for your timely help. I never expected to be placed in the position of 'handling a drive' for Jekyl Island but I am happy to say we are doing very well to date and I believe we will succeed in raising the necessary funds to clear off the entire floating debt." His optimism was not misplaced. Pledges poured in, and by April 25, 1918, more than the required $92,000 had been raised. Moreover, at a meeting in New York on May 2, the shareholders voted to approve an agreement with the Central Trust Company to extend the maturity date of the first mortgage bonds once again, from April

1918 to April 1919, with an increase of interest from 4½ percent to 5½ percent. Thus Robert S. Brewster, the club treasurer who had succeeded Samuel Bertron in 1917, was able to inform the stockholders that "It will be gratifying to you to know that the present financial condition of the Club is more encouraging than it has been for a long time." The floating debt had been paid off in entirety and "we shall soon start afresh with a clean slate."[23]

The Jekyl Island Club came through the period of the Great War successful and solvent, with members rallying to President Bourne's call for help as they had to the needs of the nation as a whole. For six months longer the war continued to absorb much of their attention. The armistice, signed on November 11, 1918, brought an end to the conflict in which Jekyl Islanders had played personal, financial, and symbolic roles in helping to bring about Allied victory. For their country, just as for their club, they were prepared to make contributions in time of need.

10. The Golden Years of Dr. James

President Woodrow Wilson departed for the Paris Peace Conference on December 4, 1918. Four days later, club members began to arrive on Jekyl for the 1918–1919 season. This first post-war season, which started with a "clean slate," would turn out to be a great success financially, with the club house actually making one of its rare profits, this one over $8,000.

Club members were just beginning to grow accustomed once more to an atmosphere of peace and plenty when news came on March 9 of the death of their president, Frederick Bourne. The following day, at a special meeting at the club house called by Vice President Edward Harkness, who had been elected to replace George Macy, a committee was formed to draft condolences to the family and a resolution was passed to suspend for the day of his funeral the golf tournament then in progress. For Jekyl Islanders, for whom golf had become not just a primary pastime but a virtual obsession, it was a major concession and a sign of the genuine esteem in which Bourne was held.[1]

Bourne and Macy were only two of the valued members who died between January 1918 and December 1919. Death had also claimed James A. Scrymser, James Stillman, and Mrs. Frederick Baker. Memberships dropped precipitously following the war years, in part because of the demise of the aging members but also because of the growing resorts of Florida and the renewed appeal of the European spas. One of the major responsibilities of the new club president would be to arrest that decline.

The man chosen to take Bourne's place was Walter Belknap James, a sixty-one-year-old physician, former president of the New York Academy of Medicine, and later trustee of Columbia University. Much of his career had centered around the College of Physicians and Surgeons of New York, where he had taken his own degree and been a professor of clinical medicine. He had also served as head of the Medical Service at both Presbyterian and Roosevelt hospitals. Highly respected and admired professionally and personally, James was described as a man of "ability, insight, imagination and charm." Widely read in both English and German, he combined an interest in literature, music, and theater with a good business sense and excellent administrative abilities. His qualities as a clever speaker, a good listener, and a fine sportsman, combined with his "wonderful knack of getting along with people of all kinds," made him perhaps the most popular president in the history of the Jekyl Island Club.[2]

His wife, Helen Goodsell Jennings, herself came from a prominent family; she was the sister of Walter Jennings, director of the Standard Oil Company of New Jersey and former president of the National Fuel Gas Company. Their father, Oliver Burr Jennings, was a brother-in-law of William Rockefeller and, like the father of Vice President Harkness, one of the original Standard Oil stockholders. Whereas Dr. James was content with the rustic pleasures of the wilderness and the company of a few friends, Helen James enjoyed the sparkling social life of New York and Newport. Jekyl provided them a pleasant middle ground.

James had been elected to the club on February 19, 1917, only two years before his elevation to the presidency. He had every reason to feel confident about the future. He was solidly backed by a seasoned group of officers, a board of governors,

As a lasting memorial, a stained glass window by Louis Comfort Tiffany, portraying the theme "David Set Singers Before the Lord," was installed in Faith Chapel and dedicated to Frederick Gilbert Bourne on March 27, 1921. There was doubt ever after about whether this was an allusion to Singer sewing machines or simply a remembrance of Bourne's early choir days. (Jekyll Island Museum)

Dr. Walter Belknap James, Jekyl Island Club president, 1919–27. (Everett Collection, Coastal Georgia Historical Society)

Dr. Walter James lining up a fairway shot. Golfers who landed in the rough sometimes encountered snakes, "which seem to have struck terror to the hearts of certain golfers and to have made their drives wild and their putts tremulous," James observed with amusement in 1920. (Jekyll Island Museum)

and an executive committee that included men of the caliber of Rockefeller, Lanier, Harkness, Crane, George F. Baker, and Valentine Everit Macy. The financial condition of the club had been declared "satisfactory" by the treasurer, Robert Brewster. A recent spat with Grob, who complained of overwork and threatened to resign, was resolved by giving him permission to hire a stenographer-typist, and "a responsible and capable assistant who will relieve him of much of the detail work particularly at the office."[3]

Of course, there were pitfalls. Even without the aggravation of a floating debt, the struggle to keep the club in the black went on, as it had throughout the organization's history. With the increased cost of goods, services, and labor that had resulted from wartime inflation, making ends meet had become especially difficult. But James was confident that with some effort Jekyl could maintain its attraction for the elite. Young people particularly, more than ever since the war, required lively activities if they were to be happy at Jekyl, and such guests were essential for the club house to operate profitably. Clearly, Walter James had his work cut out as he approached the first full season of his presidency.

James reached Jekyl on January 10, 1920, accompanied by two friends, to stay in his annex apartment purchased from John J. Albright in 1917. "All the men like the early part of the season when they can bring their cronies," claimed Almira Rockefeller. "Eddie Harkness had a party here when we arrived. Walter James brought some men down and they seem to be having a good time." James agreed with her assessment, noting "enthusiastic accounts on all sides." He was especially pleased at the number of "young people" among the guests.[4]

John and Elizabeth Claflin had dropped out of the club in 1912, presumably because of his business difficulties. They were enticed to return by Walter James in 1921, and Claflin remained a member until his death in 1938. He purchased Mistletoe cottage from the Porter estate in 1923 or 1924. (Everett Collection, Coastal Georgia Historical Society)

Under his leadership, which stretched from 1919 to 1927, not only did Jekyl not lose ground to the increasingly popular Florida resorts, but it gained in financial strength and membership. After dipping to sixty-eight by the end of 1920, membership climbed steadily during the James years, hovered in the nineties, and finally, albeit briefly, touched one hundred. "For the first time in its history the club now has a waiting list," board member Alvin Krech proudly informed Winthrop W. Aldrich, who sought to join the club in the spring of 1927, but he added, "our custom has been to give priority to the families of deceased members" provided they were "satisfactory to the Board of Governors." As the son of the late senator who had died in 1915, Aldrich was perfectly acceptable and was inducted on June 2, 1927, after being proposed by Krech.[5]

In his efforts to attract newcomers and rekindle the flagging interest of some of the old-timers, James employed a warm, personal touch. With the help of Charles Maurice, he was able to entice the John Claflins back into the club after an absence of nine years. They were "both charming people," James averred, who had managed to overcome their financial setback following the collapse of the H. B. Claflin Company in 1914. Upon learning that Cyrus McCormick, who had not been on the island since 1915, might be considering the purchase of the cottage that Walton Ferguson had previously obtained from the N. K. Fairbank estate, he wrote encouragingly to tell him "how glad I am if you are thinking of taking to Jekyl and making more use of it." He and Mrs. James, he indicated, had "bought an apartment there

Dr. James bought the
Shrady house in 1925 and
named it Cherokee.
(Georgia Department of
Archives and History)

a few years ago . . . [,] have been spending a good deal of the time there in the
winters and are . . . delighted with it." So
great was their enthusiasm for Jekyl that
they would purchase the Shrady house,
which they named "Cherokee," in 1925.
James urged McCormick likewise to "catch
the spirit of the place and settle down for a
little while every winter." Perhaps remembering McCormick's fetish for golf, he
threw in for good measure: "Our golf
course has been steadily improving and is
now good enough for anyone, and all together we think the island an exceptionally
pleasant place for a winter vacation. And
with pleasant companions."[6] Unfortunately, McCormick's wife died in 1921,
thus undermining his incentive for buying
Jekyl Island property. However, by 1923,
despite "a great grief" which he still felt,
his zeal for club affairs had revived, thanks
to James, and he was soon inviting guests
down and urging friends to join.[7]

Although a family-like camaraderie
would be the hallmark of James's administration, he also understood that up-to-
date facilities were an ingredient vital to the
club's success. His attempt to modernize
Jekyl Island was manifested in many ways,
but his two most significant accomplishments were the construction of another golf
course and the installation of an outdoor
swimming pool.

The existing golf course, built in 1909
largely through the efforts of Cyrus Mc-
Cormick and George Macy, had been
gradually expanded, as planned, from nine
to eighteen holes. In describing the attrac-
tions of Jekyl, club members invariably referred to the excellence of this course which
was now staffed by a golf professional,
Karl Keffer, and his assistant. Yet golfing
zealots wanted more and craved a new,
modern, first-class course set in picturesque
surroundings. In 1926, the well-known golf
expert Walter Travis, the same man who
had some years before recommended Keffer
as Jekyl's golf pro, was employed to ex-
ecute their wishes. Work on the links,
which stretched along the beach among the
sand dunes, was under way by November
and continued throughout 1927 and into
1928. A major tournament held on Jekyl
in January of 1928 suggests that the course
may have been ready for play by that time,
but finishing touches were still required, for
in March, Cornelius ("Connie") Lee, a
New York stockbroker who served as
chairman of the greens committee, reported
that "work was progressing very satisfactorily and we hope next year to have one of
the best courses in the country." It would
come to be known by the name Travis gave
it—the "Great Dunes Course."[8]

Golfer putting on the new Dunes Course designed by Walter J. Travis. (Georgia Historical Society)

Golfers and caddies in front of the tea house at the beach. (Georgia Department of Archives and History)

As was always the case with major improvements of this kind, a subscription was necessary, and the contributors to this project included prestigious members both old and new. George F. Baker, Edwin Gould, Richard T. Crane, Cyrus McCormick, and J. P. Morgan were among the former, and Connie Lee represented the latter. Walter James gave one of the largest donations ($2,500), and his wife, who had been elected in her own name in November 1926, contributed another $1,000.

The new swimming pool, described as "superior" in a club circular, was also constructed in 1927, replacing a small round reflecting pool that had graced the front of the club house for years. It would become a focal point where members and guests frolicked, lounged, or simply gathered for chats during the late twenties and throughout the thirties.[9]

The round pool in front of the club house, 1925. (Everett Collection, Coastal Georgia Historical Society)

A new swimming pool, in approximately the same location as the earlier round pool, was completed in 1927 under the administration of Walter James. (Georgia Historical Society)

Club members of all ages loved to cavort in or sit around the pool. Rachel Hammond and Betty Holter ride rubber sea serpents near steps. (Everett Collection, Coastal Georgia Historical Society)

Norman James, brother of the president, and his wife, Isabella, cool themselves beside the pool. (Everett Collection, Coastal Georgia Historical Society)

James was by no means alone in his efforts to create an environment of relaxed congeniality and post-war modernization. He had help from a legion of friends and a number of natural allies in the form of relatives—the Brewsters, Jenningses, Coes, Auchinclosses, Rockefellers, and the Norman Jameses—many of whom, like his brother Norman and his friend Robert Brewster, a relation by marriage to Mrs. James, served as officers or held committee posts in the club. The tangle of family connections exemplified by the James clan was by no means unusual on Jekyl, but Dr. James's extended family was probably the largest and most complex of any on the island, for it was also linked to the Rockefeller-Stillman-Aldrich-Jenkins combination through William Rockefeller's wife, Almira Geraldine Goodsell, who was Mrs. James's aunt.

William and Almira
Rockefeller during their
last years on Jekyl.
(Rockefeller Archive
Center)

One of those particularly supportive
during James's administration was William
Rockefeller, who with his wife had been a
regular participant in the club since its
founding but particularly so since the Pujo
Committee hearing. He still owned an
apartment in the Sans Souci as well as a
house, Indian Mound, which he had purchased from the Gordon McKay estate in
1905 and remodeled extensively over the
years.

Probably as wealthy as his more famous
older brother, John D., who sometimes visited him on Jekyl, William Rockefeller was
less pious and austere, less philanthropic,
and less cautious in business. Although
overshadowed by his brother, he had
played an important part in the early for-
mation of the Standard Oil Trust and had
been primarily responsible for developing
the firm's export markets. When the trust
was dissolved by court order in the 1890s
and reorganized into separate entities, albeit with interlocking directorates, he had
taken charge of the Standard Oil Company
of New York and been its president until
1911.

With James Stillman and Henry H.
Rogers, he had moved boldly into numer-
ous corporate fields, finally concentrating
on railroads and gas companies. It had
been the speculative tactics of this so-called
"Standard Oil Gang," luridly exposed by
Thomas W. Lawson in his *Frenzied Finance*, that had generated unfavorable
publicity and eventually attracted the attention of the Pujo Committee. But even crit-
ics of Rockefeller's more dubious ventures
were willing to concede that he was a man
of solid character, jovial, congenial, and
considerably more sociable than his
brother, who never cared for clubs or club
life. One relative remembered him as "a
lover of nature and little children" and lamented that the "great public" would never
see him in that light.[10]

After 1911, Rockefeller had begun to
distance himself from active control of his
various enterprises and to spend more time
on Jekyl Island. "Mr. Rockefeller never
feels so well," the *Brunswick News* stated
on January 30, 1917, "as when he is enjoying the secluded and exclusive life which
only this paradise on earth affords." Although he had served for many years on the
board of governors, he accepted for the
first time in 1914 a position on the club's
executive committee, which reflected his renewed interest in the island and his willingness to take a larger hand in the regular
operation of its affairs. By 1920 his wife
was writing to her daughter: "Father is
busy all the time and it is a good thing for
himself and the club. . . ."[11]

Almira Rockefeller shared her husband's
fondness for Jekyl and expressed it in her
letters, which were filled with such matters
as the island's weather, milk cows dying
from fever, the efficiency of the club's Ford
trucks, and the difficulties of the current
housekeeper, Miss Gross, who had "so

many apartments to get in order and only the southern help to depend upon. . . ." A young cousin once described her, not incorrectly, as "always so queenly and with it most kind and thoughtful." Even when chiding her Jekyl neighbors for being quarrelsome or selfish, she did it without malice. "The Eddie Goulds have given orders that no one is to use their squash or tennis courts," she wrote; "they have always been free to the members of the club. I know it is a great expense to keep them up, but it would have been a friendly thing to have permitted the club to use them, provided they kept them in condition." Of course, she commented further, the courts had been used primarily by "the young people who do not trouble themselves about what things cost as that never *concerns* them."[12]

It was disturbing to Almira Rockefeller to witness any sort of disharmony in what Maurice had called "our little Jekyl fold," even if it was confined to a single family. "I do hope when father and I are gone our children will not quarrel among themselves," she wrote to her daughter on January 14, 1920. "Be sure to prevent it. Bear and forebear. There are three or four members of the Bourne family coming to the Club and all are at logger heads."[13]

Three days later Almira Rockefeller was dead. She had been suffering from a heart condition for years but, while on the island, had seemed reasonably well, complaining of only "a few twinges" of neuritis at night. On the morning of January 17 she rose at her accustomed hour but, feeling ill, went back to bed "and in a few moments she quietly passed away."[14]

Although her sudden death, only twelve days after their arrival on Jekyl, was a shock to her husband, it did not prevent Rockefeller from returning for the next two seasons. Joined on Jekyl by a host of relatives and friends, he spent his time quietly walking on the beach with his daughter Emma, riding in the "electric," which once got stuck in the sand with Emma and her father aboard, and playing bridge. He enjoyed tea at the Cranes', dinner with the Jameses, and chapel on Sunday followed by hymn singing at the club house. On

Rockefeller crowd on the beach, 1921, identified as "Laura Harding, Sally Sage, Margie James, Gerrie [Geraldine Rockefeller McAlpin], Dr. [Walter] Dandy, Emily Hammond, and Phillip von Hemert." Dandy was a club physician and on good terms with Grob whom he treated for jaundice in 1923. (Rockefeller Archive Center)

Routh Ogden (left), a friend of Rockefeller's granddaughter, Geraldine McAlpin (right), injured her left arm during her stay on the island in 1921. The 1921 season was hazardous for the Rockefellers and their guests. Geraldine broke her leg during a bicycle ride that same year and spent the rest of the season on crutches. (Rockefeller Archive Center)

Walter James (left) spends part of a day at the beach in 1921 with the Rockefeller grandchildren and their friends and relatives (left to right), Hamilton Armstrong, Mrs. Rufus Patterson, Helen James, Routh Ogden, Connie Jennings, Laura Harding, and Catherine Harding. (Rockefeller Archive Center)

During his visit in 1921, Ben McAlpin ventures along one of the moss-hung bicycle paths that the club provided. (Rockefeller Archive Center)

February 15, 1921, everyone went to the movies ("Father's first movie," noted Emma in her diary).[15]

With these simple pastimes, William Rockefeller's long association with Jekyl Island would end. He died of pneumonia on June 24, 1922, at his home in North Tarrytown, New York. His Jekyl house, Indian Mound, remained vacant throughout 1923 but was finally purchased near the end of 1924 by Helen Hartley Jenkins, the aunt of his son-in-law, Marcellus Hartley Dodge. Rockefeller had belonged to the club for thirty-six years and spent many happy hours there. At the time of his death, the organization was on the upswing, having entered the golden years it enjoyed under the presidency of Walter James.

Even so, as the niece of Hester Shrady noted in 1924, the "Old Guard" was "growing pitifully small."[16] Only a few of the names on the membership list would have been familiar to the average American—Astor, Gould, Morgan, and perhaps Baker. But the majority, though wealthy and successful, simply were not very well known nationally and did not capture the imagination of the public as had the men that Frederick Lewis Allen called "the lords of creation." Such a person was Blanchard Randall, one of the new faces that came into the club during the early James years. A grain exporter with the Baltimore firm of Gill and Fisher, he had been proposed for membership by his cousin, Dr. Frederick C. Shattuck, at whose invitation he had visited the island with his wife, Susan, and daughter Elizabeth (Bessie), in February 1921.

Two days after their arrival Susan Randall conveyed her impression of the surroundings and pace of life on Jekyl. "This is not Europe where every moment should have its conscientious requirement," she related to her daughter Emily. "But even here one is looked at askance who idles all the time. However, having idled, it becomes a pleasure as well as a duty to work later. . . ." She especially enjoyed the quiet moments: "I am sitting in our own round tower in the 4th story overlooking the harbor," she wrote. "I am sure we could not have pleasanter quarters. . . . Nothing but green between this window and the water, and no sound but the dripping rain." As Susan Randall whiled away the day writing letters, her daughter Bessie and cousin Fred Shattuck were out on the golf links in a "pouring rain" and, jested Mrs. Randall, "will probably have to be rendered first aid at least from drowning."[17]

Her husband was also favorably impressed with the island and wrote his delighted reactions to Emily: "We are drifting along day after day with a beautiful sky, Japonicas, purple magnolias, & violets. Mocking birds fill the air. The grounds are lovely and the Club House most comfortable." Bessie, he continued, had been to swim in the ocean, played golf every day, as he did, "sometimes twice," and at the moment was engaged in a game of bridge in an adjoining room "with some new friends." Unquestionably, the Randalls had been embraced by the "Jekyl fold." Blanchard became a golfing crony of Robert Pruyn, Susan found a kindred spirit in Mrs. James Ellsworth, and Bessie lunched with the Rockefellers and played in a golf tournament against Erasmus C. Lindley, whose wife was a daughter of James J. Hill. She rode with Dr. James's niece, Connie Jennings, in one of the is-

Blanchard Randall, club member 1921–1931, on porch of the club house. (Everett Collection, Coastal Georgia Historical Society)

The James era saw the introduction of the Jekyl Island red bug, a miniature motorized vehicle powered at different times by gasoline or electricity. They were popular during the 1920s and 1930s among members and guests of all ages. Here two employees' children, Howard Etter (left) and David Nielsen (right), play on a red bug in one of the earliest known photographs of the little vehicle. (Courtesy of Howard Etter)

land's newly introduced "red bugs," miniature motorized vehicles named for the insidious island insect that had tormented the club house architect so many years ago. "This place grows on one," admitted Mrs. Randall. "It is all so refreshing that we have decided to remain here till the last moment."[18]

Consequently, when Randall was formally proposed for membership by Fred Shattuck and seconded by Norman James, he accepted with alacrity. "I am asked to join the Club," he informed his daughter, "and while it seems a great piece of self-indulgence, yet it has advantages in the way of invitations to others, both to come with me and to invite others here when and as you please, without the necessity of coming too. The cost is less than Florida hotels."[19]

Considering the delight they took in their first Jekyl vacation, it would have been surprising indeed had some of the Randalls not come down again the following season. Although his wife would remain in Baltimore in 1922, Randall and his daughter Bessie caught the train for Georgia on February 10, arriving at the rail junction south of Savannah five hours late. "The bobtailed train waited for us," wrote Randall, "but there was in attendance also a very sumptuous automobile which we took and which bore us into Brunswick over a beautiful road, to the waiting steamer, to arrive here at 10:30. Miss Bourne and Mrs. Lindsay were on the dock also Mr. Grob. Our rooms are more beautiful than ever and huge glasses of milk and crackers awaited."[20]

Greeted like old friends by the John Claflins, Connie Lees, Charles Maurice,

In 1925 Jekyl Islanders congregated on the beach for an afternoon of red bug racing, swimming, picnicking, and fellowship. The entrance to Shell Road can be seen in front of the beach house. (Everett Collection, Coastal Georgia Historical Society)

Bicycling and tennis remained popular on Jekyl. Here (left to right) Josephine Prentice, whose husband, Bernon, would become the last club president, Susan Clark, Mrs. Frederick P. Keppel, and Alice Fisher prepare to ride to the tennis courts, March 1925. (Everett Collection, Coastal Georgia Historical Society)

The *Corsair III* under way. In 1921 the steam yacht, with a crew of fifty-five, docked at Brunswick, having cruised for a month in the West Indies. Its owner, J. P. Morgan, Jr., and a small party of guests stopped briefly at the Sans Souci before going on to New York by train. Morgan brought the yacht down again in 1926. (Peabody Museum of Salem)

and many others, the Randalls, father and daughter, threw themselves vigorously into the activities of the club. Randall renewed his golf rivalry from the previous season with Robert Pruyn who at seventy-five could still beat him "savagely" at golf. "Think of it—Pruyn! whom I used to chew up," he exclaimed, "yet Keffer, the coach, says I have improved and that my form is allright!" Their camaraderie carried over into the club house where Randall was made an integral part of Pruyn's circle of friends, among them Jack Morgan, who gathered for cocktails every evening before dinner.[21]

Bessie, for her part, was once more in demand as a golf, tennis, or bridge partner and was popular with the staff as well as the members and their guests. "Grob had lovely roses for her on her arrival," noted the father proudly, "and all the people in the house, even the Bar Keeper, addressed her by name and a smile."[22]

Amidst her busy schedule, Bessie still found time for her father, and together the two took a walk one evening "to the colored church in the woods, where there was going on a mild revival. We spent an hour . . . hearing some really wonderful singing and not bad preaching. . . . The scene," Randall recounted, "might have been in darkest Africa, the night, the moon, the strange chanting in the little church, . . . came out to us in the forest."[23]

The next day Jekyl Island's white congregation was graced by the presence of the famous bishop of the Episcopal Diocese of Massachusetts, William Lawrence of Boston, who came as the guest of Dr. James. The bishop and his wife, Julia, had vacationed on Jekyl as far back as 1898, but beginning in 1920 they came annually to the island and were invariably welcomed with delight and deference by the members. Randall was thrilled with the news of the bishop's impending arrival and proclaimed it in a letter to his wife: "We went to bed

The presence of Walter James (left) and William Lawrence, bishop of the Episcopal Diocese of Massachusetts, typified the 1920s on Jekyl Island. James's efforts to create a congenial atmosphere and Lawrence's sermons based on his "gospel of wealth" created a general sense of well-being. (Jekyll Island Museum)

last night with the news that Bishop Lawrence would be here this week and will conduct the service on Sunday next! That is the best that Jekyl has offered this year so far. Nothing could be better than that except word *from you* to the effect that you were on your way here." Randall was waiting with Grob on the dock when the club steamer, *Jekyl Island*, docked with the Lawrences on board. The bishop was most "appreciative" of the reception and as his wife rode ahead with the superintendent strolled to the club house with Randall, chatting intimately and "picking up all old threads."[24]

The presence of Bishop Lawrence on the island, like the presidency of Dr. James, would in a sense characterize the 1920s. Preaching a gospel of wealth which insisted that "it is only to the man of morality that wealth comes" and that "Godliness is in league with riches," the Right Reverend Lawrence not surprisingly felt at home on Jekyl. In his 1926 reminiscence, *Memories of a Happy Life*, he remarked favorably upon the island's "fine forest" and "beautiful beach" and upon the many

"warm friends" he had in the club. "Dr. Walter B. James presides, and makes of the group of from eighty to a hundred one congenial family, while Mr. George F. Baker is the beloved and recognized patriarch."[25]

The bishop's sermons in Faith Chapel inevitably drew a full congregation. "He has made some of these knobs sit up and listen," said Blanchard Randall. Lawrence was also willing to direct the church choir, the composition of which might change from week to week as guests came and went. "I train the choir," he wrote during one visit on the island, consisting of "Mrs. Joe Colton at the organ, Mrs. James, Mr. & Mrs. Hugh Auchincloss, Bayard Hoppin & wife, the headwaiter, the telegrapher etc."[26]

For all his prestige, Lawrence was no puritanical stuffed shirt. He had a good sense of humor and participated, if unskillfully, in the sporting life on Jekyl. "Today I think that I shall try a bicycle for the first time in 20 or 30 years," he told a clerical friend, "& get in my hand a little at golf. But one can do just what he pleases and as no one does anything very well, one is not abashed." His wife, on the other hand, seemed to Randall a little stiff at first, as she staked her claim on the deference normally accorded the bishop's wife. Under usual circumstances, it was Mrs. J. P. Morgan who held first rank in island social situations. With the arrival of Mrs. Lawrence, however, protocol was put to the test. Randall and his daughter discreetly observed the initial encounter between these two grandes dames of New York and Boston society in 1922: "It was interesting to watch which of the two, Mrs.

Bishop Lawrence, despite the dignity of his office, threw himself into club activities. He is shown here (left) enjoying a red bug ride with club member William Warren Vaughan of Boston in 1927. (Everett Collection, Coastal Georgia Historical Society)

Helen Hartley Jenkins, the daughter of arms manufacturer Marcellus Hartley. (Jekyll Island Museum)

J. P. or Mrs. Bishop, would make the first advance. J. P. himself rushed over to the Bishop's table and spoke to both, but his wife passed on up the dining room; after dinner, on the way out Mrs. J. P. crossed over and saluted Mrs. Bishop, the Rt. Rev. having paid a visit to the lady. It was fine play!"[27] Social tensions aside, Mrs. Lawrence had quickly relaxed and proved to be as gracious and popular as the bishop himself.

Inspiring an altogether different feeling was Helen Hartley Jenkins, one of the eight women stockholders who frequented the island in the 1920s. She had arrived the day after the Lawrences to a less enthusiastic reception, as Randall hinted in a comment to his wife on February 14, 1922. "Last night arrived that old Mrs. Jenkins and her nephew, Mr. Rockefeller's son-in-law that nice Mr. Dodge. . . ." Susan had met them both the previous season and agreed with her husband that Dodge was "a very nice fellow" but that Mrs. Jenkins was a "character." "Personally, I should not like to have many dealings with the poor lady. It is pitiful to see one so gifted as she may have been develop into such a misanthrope and so extremely volcanic." Nonetheless, neither the Randalls nor the other club members ostracized Mrs. Jenkins, and she appeared to be as much a part of the swirl of bridge and teas as anyone else.[28]

It would be hard to dispute Randall's assertion that "we are getting out of Jekyl all there is here, and some besides." His physical condition improved (he looked younger and leaner after his trips to Jekyl), and his personal appeal grew steadily among the members, as was expressed by an ovation when he entered the dining room for the first time after his arrival for the 1926 season. Mrs. Jenkins declared that it was "the biggest fuss I have seen over any arrivals." Their cousin Fred Shattuck of Boston, who had been in the club since 1912, also seemed to thrive on the Jekyl atmosphere. In his mid-seventies, he still bounced "merrily from one party to another—dispensing his wit and enjoying the good things offered," dined on terrapin washed down with champagne, played golf daily, and joined in the fireside chats.[29]

After-dinner conversation among the male members had been a club tradition since the days of Henry Howland. Over the years Jekyl had had its fair share of raconteurs, the latest and not the least Dr. James himself, who on any given night during any season might be heard telling "Scotch stories" or reminiscing about the island's past. James's recollections of the club's bygone days prior to his 1917 membership were based on hearsay, but accord-

ing to a statement attributed to him, he firmly believed that "The real core of life in Jekyl Island's great days was to be found in the men's after-dinner talks. It was always of great things, of visions and developing. If they didn't have a map of the United States or the world before them, they had a map of industrial or financial empires in their minds." Bishop Lawrence, himself no mean conversationalist, was impressed by the serious content of the after-dinner talks. "One of the pleasures here is the conversation with men: last evening I sat for three hours in interesting talk upon race amalgamation, . . . birth control, Germany, England, &c &c—with men who are really conversationalists."[30]

Besides conversing in the parlor, club members enjoyed "letting their hair down," not only for such traditional celebrations as Washington's birthday but also on many festive occasions of their own concocting. One Saturday night during the 1926 season they organized a costume ball. "This is the middle of a fancy dress evening so if I sound incoherent, you'll know what the trouble is," Bessie Randall Slack explained to her husband Harry, whom she had married in 1922. "Emily & I constructed some terrible red trousers & wore our Chinese coats, but the majority of the costumes were just as clever as they could be. Connie Lee as Bacchus, Mrs. James in a highland costume and many others. They are all dancing now, but I slipped away to have a little talk with you."[31]

It was perhaps the same event to which Ray Etter, wife of the club bookkeeper, alluded in her diary on February 27 when she noted that she had gone to the club "to see fancy dress costumes." Only two weeks later the island employees had their own

Costume balls were popular among the elite in America and at the Jekyl Island Club. Carolyn Stickney is dressed as Lady Liberty, January 16, 1911. (Library of Congress)

Opposite, top left: Two prominent club members, Connie Lee and Michael Gavin (son-in-law of James J. Hill), don costumes to amuse the guests in 1927, belying the reputation for staidness attributed to the club by later writers. (Everett Collection, Coastal Georgia Historical Society)

Opposite, top right: Robert Fulton Cutting, on the front porch of the club house in 1928. Cutting was the sole heir of his cousin, the eccentric and reclusive McEvers Bayard Brown, who had died on his yacht off the coast of England in 1926. (Everett Collection, Coastal Georgia Historical Society)

Opposite, bottom: An excursion to Saint Simons, 1925. Walter James is standing to the left. (Everett Collection, Coastal Georgia Historical Society)

Upper right: Helen James (right), wife of the club president, and a friend, Mrs. Gary, enjoy a brief interlude under the eaves of the "Snow House" at the beach. (Everett Collection, Coastal Georgia Historical Society)

costume party, an echo of that held by members, to which Mrs. Etter wore a "Red clown suit." Such parties were not uncommon among the Jekyl staff and were frequently sponsored, as was this one, by club members.[32]

At the beginning of the twenties, only four original members had remained: Hayes, Rockefeller, Claflin, and Maurice. Hayes resigned in 1921, and Rockefeller died the following year, leaving two lone stalwarts by mid-decade. But Charles Stewart Maurice was extremely ill, and on February 20, 1924, he died at his home in Athens, Pennsylvania. Maurice, like his

wife, had evoked genuine affection from fellow club members, and letters of condolence poured in to his children—from Walter James, from the Cranes far off in Italy, from Ernest Grob, Minnie Clark, and dozens of others. But none captured more clearly the spirit of Charles Maurice's intimate relationship with Jekyl than the one penned by Howard Elliott, president of the Northern Pacific Railroad: "to me he was always an integral part of Jekyl. He loved it so. He knew it so well—its birds—its flowers—its trees—its shrubs—its paths and all its history and development. He was really Jekyl Island in many ways."[33] Maurice's death left John Claflin, who had helped du Bignon acquire the island and hence had facilitated the club's purchase of the property, the sole surviving original member.

On December 30, 1926, Dr. and Mrs. James registered at the club to spend the season, but on March 11, he suffered a severe heart attack. J. P. Morgan wrote to his cousin Ellen Vaughan who was then on Jekyl: "I have been terribly distressed . . . over Walter James' illness, which is a bad blow. I am very glad to hear the somewhat encouraging accounts which I have received in the last day or so." James remained on the island to convalesce, for he was considered too ill to make the trip home. On March 18, Ellen Vaughan replied to Morgan's letter, "The dear Dr. goes on & yesterday was his best day, but I fear he has a long time of quiet before him & one aches to think of that kind & ardent spirit fettered."[34]

Finally, James seemed well enough to travel to New York, but once there, his condition grew worse, and he died on April 6, 1927, at his home at 7 East Seventieth Street. Cyrus McCormick expressed the sentiment of many members when he wrote to the club's assistant treasurer, A. L. Berthet: "I feel that the Club has lost one of its most strong supporters, a man whose position can hardly be filled by anyone else."[35]

The James years had passed in peace and harmony, without economic upheaval and in general prosperity, both for the club and the nation. The board of directors quite understandably hoped that this "atmosphere of hospitality and kindliness" would continue, along with the healthy membership rosters and the general well-being of the club. But Dr. James would be the last club president who would serve his entire tenure in what might be called the golden years of the Jekyl Island Club.

11. "They Doubled The L . . ."

Finding an acceptable replacement for Dr. James seemed at first an impossible task. The sentimental choice proved to be his brother-in-law, Walter Jennings, unanimously recommended by the executive committee on November 21, 1927, and subsequently elected by the board of governors. Jennings had the good fortune of inheriting few problems and of coming to the presidency in a period of prosperity and optimism, when Jekyl Islanders were bullish about their club and shared the overweening national confidence that the good times would last forever. He accordingly had little difficulty in getting members to assess themselves at the rate of $100 per share and to amend the constitution to permit an increase in the annual dues from $600 to $700. The old method of relying on "gifts" from a handful of generous members to meet club obligations was deemed "no longer advisable." It was thought, rather, that in these affluent times the financial burdens should be spread equitably among all the stockholders.[1]

Jennings's personal faith in the future of the club was expressed by his construction of a new house on the island—the first in more than a decade. It was to be no mere cottage, but a "villa," designed by one of the nation's foremost architects, John Russell Pope, who had to his credit such landmarks as the National Gallery of Art in Washington.[2] It was completed in November 1927 at a cost of almost $50,000. As a tribute to the island's past, Jennings christened his house "Villa Ospo" after the first name given to Jekyl by the Guale Indians.

Jennings was not the only member to harbor an optimistic outlook. Less than a year later, Frank Miller Gould, who had joined the club in 1924, engaged a young New York architect named Mogens Tvede to plan a similar villa. Gould's happy boyhood memories had outweighed the tragedy of his brother's death at Jekyl, and he and his bride, Florence Amelia Bacon, had vacationed in 1925 and 1926 at Chichota. But now they wanted a place of their own. The cottage, built according to an architectural design similar to that of the Jennings residence and reminiscent of the Spanish style that Addison Mizner had popularized in Florida resorts, was virtually finished by mid-October 1928. Gould named it "Villa Marianna" for his little daughter and moved in during the 1929 season. It would be the last member's house ever constructed at Jekyl.[3]

The 1929 season was in full swing and the club flourishing with a membership in the high nineties when the newly elected president of the United States, Herbert Hoover, proclaimed in his inaugural address on March 4 that the future of the country looked bright. Jekyl Islanders, most of whom were Republicans, must have felt jubilant at the thought of four more years of government administered by men who were committed to fiscal policies favorable to business and who shared some of Bishop Lawrence's notions that "material prosperity" would help "make the national character sweeter, more joyous, more unselfish, more Christlike."

That summer there took place a seemingly insignificant incident which would, in historical perspective, take on a symbolic meaning for the club. At the instigation of club members, the Georgia legislature passed a resolution to "correct" the spelling of Jekyl by adding a second l. Signed by Governor Lamartine G. Hardman on July 31, 1929, the resolution noted that the is-

William W. Vaughan (left)
and new club president
Walter Jennings on the
front porch of the Jekyl
Island club house in 1928.
(Everett Collection,
Coastal Georgia Historical
Society)

Jean Pollock Brown
Jennings (right), wife of
the club president, sits on
the club house steps with
Susan Clark, wife of club
member Stephen Carlton
Clark, 1928. (Everett
Collection, Coastal
Georgia Historical
Society)

Villa Ospo, the Jennings
cottage, designed by John
Russell Pope and built by
George Cowman in 1927.
(Georgia Department of
Archives and History)

Interior of the Jennings
house. (Georgia Depart-
ment of Archives and
History)

The last of the millionaire "cottages" to be built—the Villa Marianna. Even after his parents no longer came to Jekyl, Frank Miller Gould continued to enjoy the island. His daughter stands in front of the house that bears her name. (Everett Collection, Coastal Georgia Historical Society)

Walter Jennings with his wife, Jean, and his daughter, Connie, relaxing on the beach at Jekyl. (Everett Collection, Coastal Georgia Historical Society)

land had been "named by General Oglethorpe, in honor of his friend, Sir Joseph Jekyll" and that the "correct spelling" had been corrupted through "long usage . . . by the omitting of the last letter." It was resolved, therefore, "that the correct and legal spelling of the name of said island is and shall be Jekyll Island."[4]

The change in the spelling of Jekyll was like a jinx that came upon the club. Less than three months later, on Black Thursday, October 24, 1929, the stock market plummeted. In a scene reminiscent of the Panic of 1907, a throng of alarmed people collected outside the New York Stock Exchange while banking leaders gathered at the offices of J. P. Morgan and Company to devise a means to stem the tide—to no avail. Tuesday, October 29, saw another disastrous decline. Panic swept the country and eventually undermined public confidence in the soundness of the American

The Goodyear Infirmary (formerly the Furness-Pulitzer Cottage), in its new location and completely refurbished, was donated to the club by Frank H. Goodyear, Jr., in memory of his mother. (Georgia Department of Archives and History)

Frank H. Goodyear, Jr., club member 1916–30, was killed in an automobile accident in 1930, the same year that the new infirmary was dedicated. (Courtesy of George F. Goodyear)

economy. In brief, the advent of the Great Depression marked the beginning of the end of both national prosperity and flush times for the Jekyll Island Club. In Brunswick, a proverb captured the event in terse terms: "They doubled the l, and they all went to hell."

At first, the depression had little or no impact on Jekyll Island affairs. The 1930 season went on much as before, with members opening their pocketbooks as they had in the past for the benefit of the organization. Cyrus McCormick, for example, gave a new truck that year and arranged with his company, International Harvester, for the club to buy all its farm and road machinery ("the best that can be found") at half price. Frank Goodyear donated a long-needed infirmary, dedicating it to the memory of his mother, Josephine Looney Goodyear, who had been a well-known

James Memorial Wall at the north end of the swimming pool, under construction by George Cowman in 1930. (Jekyll Island Museum)

New indoor tennis court under construction, 1930. This club court has been known traditionally as the Morgan Tennis Court, although no evidence has been found to indicate any particular association with J. P. Morgan. (Jekyll Island Museum)

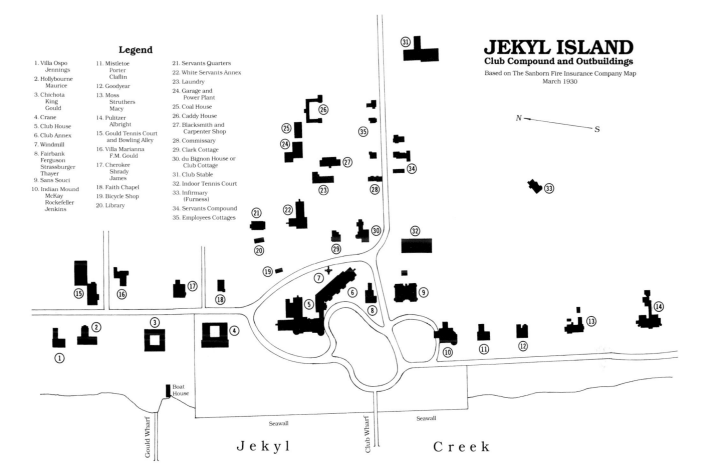

JEKYL ISLAND
Club Compound and Outbuildings
Based on The Sanborn Fire Insurance Company Map
March 1930

N → S

Boat House

Gould Wharf

Seawall   Club Wharf   Seawall

J e k y l   C r e e k

The Jekyl Island Club facilities evolved for more than four decades, as buildings were erected or moved to new locations. This plan shows the location of major buildings in 1930, at which time most island construction had been completed. (Based on the Sanborn Fire Insurance Company Map, March 1930)

benefactor of hospitals in Buffalo during her lifetime. "This most suitable memorial," as Walter Jennings called it, had been accomplished by acquiring the old Furness cottage from John J. Albright, whose financial affairs had been deeply affected by the stock market crash, and converting it into "a completely equipped" facility for the care of "both black and white," but "in separate wards, of course."[5]

Members also gave generously that year for appropriate memorials to Walter James. A committee headed by Richard T. Crane, Jr., quickly raised $16,000 to construct a new dormitory for the golf caddies (hired seasonally from Fort Valley School), who had been especially close to Dr. James's heart. In addition, an outdoor memorial designed by club member Eliot Cross was erected at the north end of the swimming pool.[6]

The expenditure of private funds for such projects in 1930 temporarily masked the fact that the club, like the nation, was facing serious problems as a result of the depression. In 1931, however, bank failures, farm foreclosures, industrial stagnation, and unemployment told a grim tale of worsening economic conditions and had inevitable repercussions on club membership. To be sure, the very rich—Morgan, Astor, Baker, and McCormick—could weather the storm with relatively little sign of financial strain, although even Morgan was not totally unaffected by the crisis and indicated in 1932 that he was "cutting down as far as possible on all expenditure in my houses" and "doing nothing except that which turns out to be absolutely essential."[7] How much more, then, did men of lesser wealth—the Barkers, Blakes, and Randalls—feel the pinch. Giving up expensive club memberships was one way to cut costs.

The *Viking.* On March 20, 1930, the *Brunswick News* announced: "Probably the handsomest yacht that ever entered the port of Brunswick was moored in mid-stream opposite the terminals of the Atlantic, Birmingham & Coast Railroad, this morning. It was the *Viking,* owned by George F. Baker, Jr., prominent New York financier." (Mariners' Museum, Newport News, Virginia)

George Fisher Baker, the "Sphinx of Wall Street," belonged to the club from 1901 until his death on May 2, 1931. Baker, described by the *Brunswick News* as "the lone survivor of a powerful group of financiers who commanded money and industry at the beginning of the twentieth century," celebrated his ninetieth birthday on Jekyll on March 27, 1930. "Mr. Baker is the best example of his own advice," the *News* quipped. "He often said: Business men of America should reduce their talk at least two thirds." (Everett Collection, Coastal Georgia Historical Society)

Membership in the Jekyll Island Club on January 1, 1931, had stood at ninety-seven, one of its highest points ever. By the end of the year it had dropped precipitously to seventy-one and would continue to dwindle throughout the thirties. Equally devastating was the fact that in those hard times few new people could be persuaded to join. During 1931, for instance, a year that saw twenty-nine resignations, only three new members were elected, and two of the three were affluent widows, like Ruth Hill Beard Lorillard, daughter of James J. Hill, who had been previously connected with the club through their husbands.

As one might expect, the finances of the Jekyll Island Club also suffered. Club treasurer Robert Brewster attributed insufficient revenues for 1931 to three factors: decreased attendance, increased expenditures for repairs, and a miscalculation in the budget estimates based on previous attendance records that were no longer valid. By the end of fiscal year 1932, he was forced to report a staggering deficit of $28,000.[8]

Jekyll Island, 1930, showing roads and bicycle paths. On March 28, 1930, Walter James wrote to Cyrus McCormick that "We had a memorable day here yesterday . . . not only because of Mr. Baker's 90th birthday, but because four roads were dedicated to four of our members." The roads in question were Palmetto Road, renamed for George Fisher Baker; Pine Road, for the Maurices; Oak Road, for John Claflin; and Willow Pond Road, for Walter Jennings. The Morgan Road on the map was completed in 1926 and the McCormick Road in 1927. A new entrance to the latter was added at Shell Road in 1930. Still another road was developed on the island during the 1930 season. It was paid for by Marjorie and Alexander Thayer and named in honor of Mrs. Thayer's father, Frederick Gilbert Bourne. It was laid out over the old bridle path and, as the executive committee explained, was to be "used as a motor road, as there are many more motors in use on the island today than saddle horses."

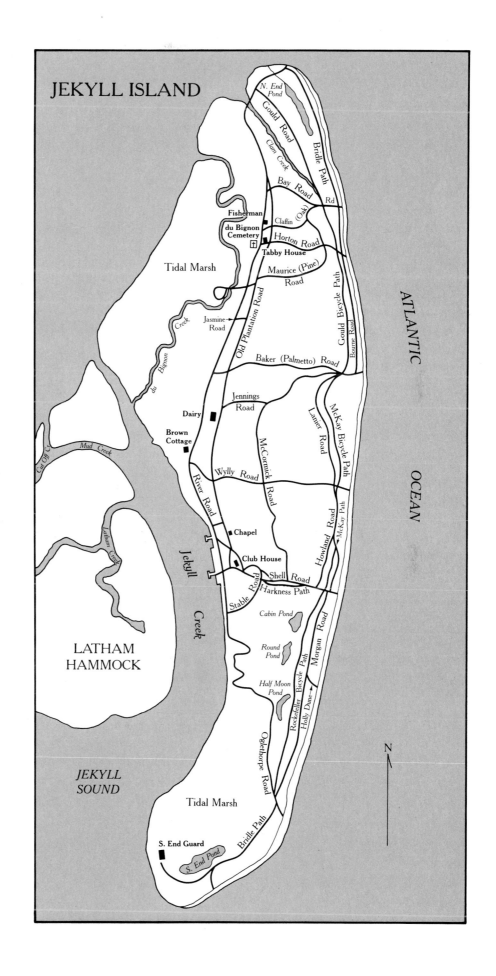

JEKYLL ISLAND

N. End Pond

Gould Road

Clam Creek

Bridle Path

Bay Road

Rd

Fisherman

Claflin (Oak)

du Bignon Cemetery

Horton Road

Tabby House

Maurice (Pine) Road

Tidal Marsh

Gould Bicycle Path

Bourne Road

Creek

Jasmine Road

Old Plantation Road

du Bignon

Baker (Palmetto) Road

Jennings Road

Dairy

McKay Bicycle Path

Lanier Road

Brown Cottage

McCormick Road

Mud Creek

Wylly Road

Cut Off C

Latham Creek

River Road

Howland Road

McKay Path

Chapel

Club House

Shell Road

Harkness Path

Stable Road

Cabin Pond

LATHAM HAMMOCK

Jekyll Creek

Round Pond

Half Moon Pond

Rockefeller Bicycle Path

Holly Dune

Morgan Road

JEKYLL SOUND

Oglethorpe Road

Tidal Marsh

Bridle Path

N

S. End Guard

S. End Pond

ATLANTIC OCEAN

Ernest Gilbert Grob, club superintendent, about the time of his retirement in 1930. In 1931 Grob traveled to Lugano, Switzerland, among other places in Europe. He suffered a stroke in 1940 and spent his remaining years in Brunswick under the care of the George Cowmans. He died in 1945 and was buried in Palmetto Cemetery. (Georgia Department of Archives and History)

To make matters worse, in March 1930 the club had suffered the loss of its experienced superintendent, Ernest Gilbert Grob, who had cordially and efficiently managed the club for forty-two years. One story alleges that he had had a disagreement with President Walter Jennings who had forbidden the tipping of employees, while Grob believed that the loss of tips would work a hardship on his fellow employees in these depression times. Quite probably, however, Ernest Grob, almost seventy years old, was simply tired. To a journalist who inquired what he planned to do in his retirement, he responded that, first, he would go to Europe and then "rest for the remainder of my life." He would eventually return to Brunswick where he lived until his death in 1945.[9]

John C. Etter, who had been hired originally as a bookkeeper and promoted several years later to assistant superintendent, filled Grob's place until a new superintendent could be found. On October 22, 1930, the club announced that Michael L.

De Zutter would succeed not only Grob but also A. L. Berthet as assistant treasurer and assistant secretary. Berthet, who had worked in the New York office for many years, had elected to follow Grob in leaving the club's employment. Jekyll officers saw it as an opportunity to save money by combining the two jobs. The resignations of Captain Clark and J. C. Etter came shortly thereafter. The loss of so many experienced staff members in such a short span of time left Jekyll affairs in some disarray, and, according to Robert Brewster, the "new management being unfamiliar with conditions" made costly mistakes.[10]

But more than that, the club under De Zutter's supervision simply was not the same. Grob's understanding of the graceful and quiet lifestyle required by the members, his good nature, and his tact in difficult circumstances had been a part of Jekyll's atmosphere. When he disappeared from the scene along with so many other familiar faces, a very special world disappeared forever for club members, who could only feel "melancholy" at the "many changes" that Marian Maurice noticed on her arrival in 1931.[11]

De Zutter, who had worked at the Brooklyn Golf Club and the Glenn Island Casino, was a different type of manager, no doubt more up-to-date in his techniques but also less personal. Having absorbed Berthet's job as well as Grob's, he found it essential to spend much of his time at the club's Forty-second Street Office in New York and was never able to develop the personal relationships with and affection of club members and fellow employees that Grob had enjoyed.

Membership as a result continued to decline until by 1933 it had reached sixty-four, having dropped in only two years by

an alarming 34 percent. "The present stress and upheaval of social and business affairs has been fully reflected in the number of recent resignations and withdrawals of our members," lamented club secretary Henry J. Fisher. Attempting to put the best face on matters, he added, "We hope that many of these are of but a temporary nature and that they will mark the end of this difficult phase, throughout which the Club has managed to maintain its activities undiminished in any way." This was wishful thinking. Membership fell again in 1934 to fifty-four, and only one member was added, the first in two years—Jean Pollock Brown Jennings, wife of President Walter Jennings.[12]

On December 30, 1932, the Jenningses were the first people to register for the new season, and a few days later Jean Jennings welcomed the Maurice sisters to the island with a new year's gift of a plant. But the new year quickly turned sour for the Jen-

A number of long-time employees left the club shortly after Grob's retirement. Among them was John C. Etter (right), shown here with his wife (second from right) and other Jekyll workers. (Courtesy of Howard Etter)

Club waiters during the time of Michael L. De Zutter's management of the Jekyll Island Club. (Georgia Department of Archives and History)

ningses. Mrs. Jennings had both her eyes
blackened in an automobile accident on
January 4, and only a few days later her
husband suffered a heart attack. He died
on the island on January 9, despite the
efforts of Dr. Warfield M. Firor, the club
physician, who had been flown from Johns
Hopkins to Jekyll to attend him.[13]

The Jekyll Island Club found itself once
more without a president, yet never in its
history had it been more in need of able
leadership. To cope with the problems it
confronted in 1933, only one man was
perceived to be strong and prestigious
enough—J. P. Morgan. Morgan allowed
himself to be nominated and was elected, to
the delight of everyone, at the annual meeting held at the club house on February 24,
1933. George Brewster, brother of the
club treasurer, and Albert Milbank were
selected vice presidents.

But even having J. P. Morgan for president did not stop the spate of resignations.
At a series of conferences held between
April and November 1933, Morgan and
his officers addressed themselves to the dual
problems of declining membership and the
club's worsening financial condition. Acting
on a proposal outlined at the stockholders'
meeting in February, they took the first
steps toward a complete refinancing of the
club in April. "General conditions now
make it imperative to carry foward this
plan," announced Robert Brewster, as he
called upon the members to exchange their
old bonds for new ones.[14]

The press raised its eyebrows only
slightly at the mortgaging of the wealthy
club for half a million dollars, one newspaper referring to it as a pittance so small
as to "be mere pin money to almost any
one of the club's seventy odd members." In
fact, the club had been mortgaged from the
outset, and this new bond issue was only
one of many in its history. Morgan, it was

J. P. Morgan, Jr., president of the Jekyll Island Club, 1933–38 (second from left), relaxes at the pool with C. S. Brown, Jr. (far right), and Brown's parents. (Everett Collection, Coastal Georgia Historical Society)

Jane Irwin Robeson Henry was decorated by the Belgian government for her work in war relief. Mrs. Henry resigned her regular membership to become an associate member in 1934. (Everett Collection, Coastal Georgia Historical Society)

correctly claimed, "sought to put the club on a more businesslike basis" and believed that the refinancing had "materially improved the financial condition of the Club," but he was also aware that the organization could not rest "upon a secure basis" until something was done to stem the loss of members. [15]

To meet the membership crisis, club leaders revived a plan that Cornelius Lee had pushed for some ten years "to provide for two classes of membership." Each time it had been proposed it had met with stiff opposition from members who felt that such a division might create ill will within the club. Now, however, with the roster so low on names, such drastic action seemed justified. Regular shareholding members would be reclassified as "founders" and could not exceed 100. The second group, non-shareholding annual members, would consist of up to 150 "associates," who, according to the original proposal, could not hold office. Otherwise, they would have the same privileges as the stockholding members but at a fraction of the price. Whereas founders would continue to pay $700 dues, the associates' dues were set at only $150.[16]

Connie Lee was very pleased by the economical level of the dues and wrote to Winthrop Aldrich that it "will put the price within the range of everybody's pocketbook, especially in these hard times." He predicted that the associate memberships would "change entirely the whole picture of the Island" and bring in new members who were "young and active. This will mean that all of the sporting activities will be fully patronized and everyone will be certain of finding a partner for golf, tennis, etc."[17]

By March 2, 1934, sixty-three associates had joined, four of whom were founders who had resigned for the purpose of assuming the less expensive memberships. The plan also brought back seven members who had previously dropped out but who now saw their way clear to become associates. Although Morgan was still worried about the need for "a continued healthy growth" and urged everyone to recommend their "intimate friends" as associates, most officers were pleased with the infusion of new blood into the organization. Vice President George Brewster saw the associates as "a most attractive and agreeable lot" and viewed the matter as a giant step forward: "The Club has taken on a renewed lease on life, and like the National recovery, we hope that it will prove to be permanent and not a flash in the pan. Probably twice as many people have been at the Island as there were a year ago."[18] Unfortunately, exactly like the National Recovery program, the "renewed lease on life" *would* turn out to be "a flash in the

pan." If it helped at all, it was only superficially, for the decline continued; although new members were joining the club, bringing increased activity and enthusiasm, a "substantial number," as Brewster noted, were "Mr. Morgan's partners or associates. . . ."[19]

The feared antagonism between the founders and associates, which had kept the scheme from being implemented earlier, had not materialized, as far as Brewster could tell: "The new members fitted in very nicely and there was no stiffness and it took but a short time for them to feel at home." Everyone, however, did not perceive the situation quite that way, and some years later, Mrs. Reginald Huidekoper, whose husband was an associate from 1936 until 1942, summed up her own experience with the founders: "Oh, we weren't one of the swells." According to Mrs. Huidekoper, some of the members, especially the cottage owners, were "snobs." Despite such reactions, she indicated that her family enjoyed their visits to Jekyll and that they had good friends among the members.[20]

In all probability, the older members of Jekyll were merely trying to continue their lives as they always had, inviting one another to tea or dinner and taking afternoon drives or long walks on the beach. Some of them undoubtedly were quite overwhelmed by the influx of new and younger faces. The Maurice sisters, for example, described by Blanchard Randall as "retiring," could hardly be called snobs, but they were shy and unlikely to go out of their way to befriend the great numbers of new associate members.

As the ranks of the associates swelled, increasing efforts were made to give them a voice in club affairs. On May 8, 1935, when the club constitution was amended to allow associates to serve on the board of governors, five were elected. But as incentives to become founders declined, so did their number. By 1936, the group had fallen below fifty, while associate membership had increased to ninety. The elated new superintendent wrote optimistically to Alfred W. Jones, president of the Cloister at nearby Sea Island, "I am glad to state that Jekyll Island looks as if it were going to have some real business this year. Although it will be a short season, we have quite a few new members of the younger type and I think we are going to be very active. . . ."[21]

Recognizing perhaps that, in comparison to resorts like the Cloister and Palm Beach, the Jekyll Island Club with its Queen Anne facade and Victorian atmosphere must seem dated and a trifle quaint, officers did not let up in their efforts to improve the facilities to attract the members. On January 15, 1936, Lee announced that "The new Skeet Field has been completed and is now in readiness, and, through the courtesy of the Sea Island Beach Company, the members of the Jekyll Island Club and their guests are offered the facilities of the Sea Island hunting preserve [Cabin Bluff] during the open season. . . ."[22]

The relationship with the Cloister, which had opened to guests in 1928, marked a new turn in Jekyll's history, for club officials were turning increasingly to Alfred W. ("Bill") Jones for assistance and advice. The Sea Island landscape architect and

greenskeeper, T. Miesse ("Bummy") Baumgardner, began in the 1930s to work on weekends at the Jekyll Island Club, with full approval and support from Jones, as the landscaper and greenskeeper. Jones believed "the continued successful operation of Jekyll" to be in the best interest of Sea Island and did all that he could to help, even providing lists of his own guests for the club's consideration as possible Jekyll members.[23]

Despite Jones's assistance and their own efforts always to strike a note of optimism in their public statements, as time went on club officers began to express in private their misgivings about the future. Francis Bartow, chairman of the executive committee, declared himself "very discouraged about Jekyll" because of the growing apathy of a majority of its members as well as complaints about De Zutter's extravagance and mismanagement. Bartow, dismayed that he could not even get a quorum of the executive committee, felt an "increasing anxiety" about the lack of cooperation. The superintendent himself noted at the close of the 1936 season that "members get quite enthusiastic during the operating season, but the enthusiasm dies down as soon as the Club is closed and the financial condition of the Club is submitted to them."[24]

Women were moving into the vacuum of leadership in ever-increasing numbers. Even before Morgan became president, they had begun to play an official role in island activities. Under the James administration a welfare committee composed of five women, among them Florence H. Crane, Mary Emma Harkness, and Helen James, had been appointed to oversee the moral and physical needs of club employees and their families. Under their influence an employees' library was constructed in 1927 to discourage gambling, and members' at-

Annie Burr Jennings
(here) and Ruth Lorillard
were the first women to be
elected vice presidents of
the Jekyll Island Club.
(Rockefeller Archive
Center)

tention was directed to "the life on the Island that goes on so inconspicuously that we are barely aware of its existence." They pointed to the wants of the "forty-five colored people in permanent residence . . . as well as several white families" for such things as food and medical care.[25]

Three women, Helen James, Jean Jennings, and Ruth Lorillard, were serving on the board of governors by 1935, and two years later Annie Burr Jennings and Ruth Lorillard were elected to be vice presidents and members of the hallowed executive committee. Women had become by this time a club mainstay, composing almost 25 percent of the founders membership, owning seven cottages, and chairing exactly half of the twelve committees (excluding the executive committee).

Whether the greater involvement of female members at this point was the result of their increasing interest or merely reflected the declining interest of the male members cannot be said for sure. Certainly, if J. P. Morgan's views are any criterion, it did not signal a sudden concern for women's rights on the part of the male members: "woman suffrage," he once remarked, "would only help to complete the ruin of the country already hurt by universal manhood suffrage."[26] But clearly women were asserting themselves in positions of leadership in a club where even the president seemed to be losing interest.

Although he was always generous in his financial support of Jekyll, time was for Morgan another matter. Much of the detail work of his administration seems to have been delegated to such people as Connie Lee, Bernon Prentice, and Francis Bartow. He did not even come to the island

Women as well as men took part in the tennis competitions on Jekyll in the 1930s, as they had in all sports from the beginning of the club era. (Everett Collection, Coastal Georgia Historical Society)

The last two presidents of the Jekyll Island Club, J. P. Morgan, Jr. (1933–38) and New York stockbroker Bernon Prentice (1938–47), on the porch of the club house. (Georgia Department of Archives and History)

during the 1937 season and in July departed for England aboard the *Corsair* with his grandchildren. On the other hand, he was willing to make a $10,000 to $15,000 loan to the club "to tide over the temporary difficulty." Finally, recognizing his own failing interest in Jekyll and the other more pressing matters to which he had to attend, Morgan tendered his resignation as president on February 25, 1938.[27]

That same year the only surviving original member, John Claflin, died. Claflin's death tolled the coming of the end, and although the bell seemed distant and faint, there were club members who could not help but hear.

One of these was Bernon Sheldon Prentice, who was elected to replace Morgan as president. The fifty-five-year-old stockbroker, a partner in the Wall Street firm of Dominick and Dominick, was a Harvard graduate and a sportsman of some celebrity. He had in 1908 married the daughter of club member James W. Ellsworth, whose share he had taken over after Ellsworth's resignation from the club in 1924. Prentice's wife had died in 1929, and, three years before becoming president of the Jekyll Island Club, he had married Josephine McFadden, widow of a prominent Philadelphian. During the Great War he had been deputy commissioner of the American Red Cross in Europe and had organized an ambulance service on the Italian front in 1918, efforts for which he had been decorated by both the French and Italian governments. As an aviation enthusiast, he had served as chairman of the Amundsen-Ellsworth Polar Flight of 1925 as well as of the Amundsen flight over the North Pole in 1926. But it was his love of tennis that most endeared him to Jekyll Is-

Bernon Prentice, an avid tennis player and former chairman of the Davis Cup Committee, on the tennis court with Sylvia Brewster. (Everett Collection, Coastal Georgia Historical Society)

club members, he reflected on the previous season: "The golf course reached a high degree of perfection . . . [and] the new moving picture projector . . . installed in the tea house proved to be a great success. . . . We have the greatest hopes that the next winter season will be a most successful one in every respect."[28]

Prentice's optimism was, however, short-lived. Within a month his confidence had given way to a clear-eyed recognition of the extent Jekyll Island had fallen in the public mind. This less rosy outlook is evident from a telegram he sent to Bill Jones who had asked permission on June 6, 1938, to photograph for *Life* magazine a turtle egg hunt on Jekyll which "is about the only place on the coast you can be sure of finding several turtles each night when the tide is right." He assured Prentice that it would be done with the utmost discretion and promised that Jekyll's name would not be mentioned. Prentice replied promptly that it was "perfectly agreeable" for him to use the name as well as the beach. "My feeling is from now on we will have to have some publicity to show people we are still alive."[29]

It was an astonishing reply from the president of a club that had rarely courted publicity. Although Jekyll Islanders had tried to maintain good relations with the press as early as 1887 when Superintendent Ogden had taken a Brunswick reporter on a tour of the new club house, and although they had allowed an occasional article about the club in newspapers and such magazines as *Munsey's* (1904) and *Cosmopolitan* (1897), they had never actively sought the public eye. Under the Prentice administration, however, the news release became a common feature. The club sponsored exhibition golf matches involving nationally known professionals like

landers. He had held the Seabright (New Jersey) tennis title for twenty-five years and had been 1932 and 1933 chairman of the American Davis Cup Committee. Under his supervision Jekyll invitational golf tournaments, which had begun in 1934, had risen to national prominence by 1936.

Prentice, like others before him, embarked upon his administration with outward optimism, despite the fact that regular membership was the lowest in the club's history, with associates outnumbering founders by more than two to one. But he apparently believed that he could build on what Morgan and others had accomplished and breathe new life into Jekyll. Like his predecessors, he sought to drown out the persistent death knell by loudly proclaiming the positive achievements of the immediate past. In one of his first communications to

A cropped version of this picture, apparently a Jekyll Island Club publicity release, appeared in the *New York Sun* on March 23, 1940, with the caption: "Mr. and Mrs. Bernon Prentice of this city on the terrace of the Tea House on the dunes of the golf course at Jekyll Island." Left to right: Argentine Ambassador Felipe A. Espil, Hugh Dudley Auchincloss, Bernon Prentice, Josephine Prentice. George Brewster donated the brick terrace on which they are sitting in 1930. (Everett Collection, Coastal Georgia Historical Society)

The tea house at the Dunes Course was a popular place to relax after golf, to have refreshments, or simply to watch the ever-changing sea. (Everett Collection, Coastal Georgia Historical Society)

Toward the end of the club era, tournaments were organized and widely publicized. Here a competitor for the C. S. Brown Cup in 1940 prepares to bowl. (Everett Collection, Coastal Georgia Historical Society)

Josephine Prentice awards the C. S. Brown Cup for lawn bowling to stockbroker Cornelius S. Lee, as a photographer snaps their picture for the newspapers. (Everett Collection, Coastal Georgia Historical Society)

Skeet shooting was one of the many pastimes on Jekyll during the 1930s. (Everett Collection, Coastal Georgia Historical Society)

Sam Snead and organized a series of golf, tennis, and lawn bowling tournaments where press photographs were made and duly distributed to newspapers up and down the east coast. Prentice persuaded J. P. Morgan to donate the "Morgan Cup," a reproduction of a George II urn, to be awarded to the winner of the annual invitation golf tournament, while the C. S. Brown Memorial Cup was awarded to the lawn bowling champion. He also worked out an arrangement with the Sea Island Company's director of publicity to handle Jekyll's news releases.

So much news, however, caused the press to scrutinize the club's activities more closely and also brought negative publicity. On January 29, 1941, the *New York World Telegram* announced that the Jekyll Island Club "considered at one time the most exclusive club in America," a phrase clearly suggesting that Jekyll was viewed by the press as a club in decline, had just sent out cards "inviting a carefully selected

list of outsiders to 'use the privileges of the club this winter.' This is letting down the bars of a luxurious institution. . . ." In fact, such cards had been sent out since 1933, when associate memberships were established, but the surge of publicity about the island brought it to the attention of the press.

To keep Jekyll afloat financially, Prentice felt obliged to continue an island timber-cutting project which had begun during the Morgan administration and also sought contributions as needed from wealthy members. J. P. Morgan, who sent him $5,000 on May 8, 1939, received yet another request from Prentice less than a month later, to which he replied with a check and the comment: "I think that the Jekyll Island Club is still sufficiently promising that another $1,000 contribution from me would be worth making."[30]

News of a new contract signed with the American Creosoting Company in 1940 to carry on the timbering had reached the ears of the Maurice sisters, who had come to the island almost every season for fifty-two years. Marian Maurice, arriving on Jekyl on January 4, 1941, recorded that she "lacked courage to investigate lumbering operations on the Island." All around her she saw change and destruction, for on the same day, she observed "Mr. Gould's house being demolished, a sad sight." Edwin Gould had died in 1933, and his cottage had remained unoccupied ever since. Only the pool and the ornamental lions that graced the front entrance would be left. Even the island steamer, "Dear old Jekyll," had not been running when the Maurice sisters had arrived.[31]

Nevertheless, Prentice made every effort to keep Jekyll an up-to-date and active resort. Even in its palmiest days the club had not enjoyed a more varied recreational

Mr. and Mrs. Biggers, lolling on the lawn in front of the tea house on January 24, 1932. Mr. Biggers was the club barber. (Jekyll Island Museum)

After the departure of Captain Clark and boat engineer Courier, the Jekyll Island Club employed a number of different yacht and launch officers, among whom were A. J. Spaulding, commanding the yacht *Jekyll Island,* and Captain Richard (Dick) Backus, shown here on March 20, 1932, in charge of the launch *Sylvia.* (Jekyll Island Museum)

agenda (including golf, tennis, skeet shooting, lawn bowling, movies, swimming, hunting, and speed boat and red bug rides), nor had it been served by a greater abundance of employees.

Yet despite all attempts to amuse members and guests, the club seemed to have lost its old comfortable, tranquil atmosphere and the members' sense of loyalty and commitment to an extended family enterprise. It no longer seemed, as Grob had once described it, like "a large country house" with an amiable superintendent as master host. Instead, it had become like a resort or a country club where people who did not know each other very well came and went, amusing themselves for brief periods of time. The disappearance by the end of 1941 of all but nineteen founder members, many of whom had once spent long periods of time and sometimes the whole winter at Jekyll, was a manifestation of this dismal reality.

The attack on Pearl Harbor on December 7, 1941, and the United States's entry into World War II would be the coup de grâce that finally closed the Jekyll Island Club. A frequently told story with many variations contends that General George S. Patton was dispatched by President Franklin Delano Roosevelt to evacuate the island. German submarines had supposedly been spotted off the Georgia coast and had, according to one version, "thrust a torpedo into the side of a tanker in plain view of Jekyll Islanders on the beach." The president, so the legend goes, fearing the capture of a club allegedly representing one-sixth of the world's wealth, ordered its closing within a matter of hours. The tale is, in fact, pure fantasy. Patton's name does appear under the date of April 3, 1942, as the next to the last entry in the

Transportation to Jekyll Island in 1939 was available on the Atlantic Coast Line Railroad. (Baker Library, Harvard Business School)

Sea Island, Jekyll Island Club
Brunswick, Ga.

QUICKER, BETTER SERVICE
Effective December 15, 1939

FLORIDA SPECIAL (WEST COAST)

Southbound Read Down Nos. 187-119-187		DAILY SCHEDULE (Eastern Standard Time)		Northbound Read Up Nos. 188-136-186
a8:30 A.M.	Lv. Boston	N.Y.N.H.&H.	Ar.	a8:45 P.M.
a b9:30 A.M.	Lv. Providence	"	Ar.	a b7:43 P.M.
a b10:43 A.M.	Lv. New London	"	Ar.	a b6:32 P.M.
c10:15 A.M.	Lv. Springfield	"	Ar.	c7:20 P.M.
a b11:48 A.M.	Lv. New Haven	"	Ar.	a b5:27 P.M.
a5:35 P.M.	Ar. Washington	P.R.R.	Lv.	a11:35 A.M.
d2:05 P.M.	Lv. NEW YORK (Penna. Sta.)	P.R.R.	Ar.	d3:10 P.M.
1:50 P.M.	Lv. New York (Hud. Term.)	"	Ar.	3:11 P.M.
b2:20 P.M.	Lv. Newark	"	Ar.	b2:52 P.M.
b3:09 P.M.	Lv. Trenton	"	Ar.	b2:04 P.M.
b3:39 P.M.	Lv. North Philadelphia	"	Ar.	b1:36 P.M.
b3:49 P.M.	Lv. Penna. Sta. (30th St.)	"	Ar.	b1:27 P.M.
b4:20 P.M.	Lv. Wilmington	"	Ar.	b12:56 P.M.
b5:25 P.M.	Lv. Baltimore	"	Ar.	b11:53 A.M.
6:35 P.M.	Lv. Washington	R.F.&P.	Ar.	10:40 A.M.
9:20 P.M.	Lv. Richmond	A.C.L.	Ar.	7:55 A.M.
d8:09 A.M.	Ar. Nahunta	"	Lv.	d8:43 P.M.
c8:10 A.M.	Lv. Nahunta	A.C.L.	Ar.	c8:35 P.M.
c9:15 A.M.	Ar. BRUNSWICK	"	Lv.	c7:30 P.M.

Reference marks: a—Tuesdays, Thursdays and Saturdays Dec. 16-30; daily effective Jan. 1, 1940. b—Stops only to pick up or let off passengers to or from south of Washington. c—Connecting train. d—Daily.

FLORIDA SPECIAL
(West Coast)

EQUIPMENT

Recreation-Entertainment Car.
  Music, Games, Hostess.
Lounge Car. Dining Car.

Through Sleeping Cars:
  From and to Boston, New York and Washington.

Through De Luxe Coaches:
  From and to New York and Washington.
  Between Boston and Washington.

Modern Steel Coach:
  Between Nahunta and Brunswick.

   All equipment completely
     AIR-CONDITIONED.

GEO. P. JAMES,
General Passenger Agent
Washington, D. C.

ECONOMY

Transfer charges Nahunta to Cloister Hotel, Sea Island, $5.00 per capita and $3.00 per trunk. From Brunswick, $1.75 per capita and $1.50 per trunk. This new service effects a saving of $4.75.

•

CONVENIENCE

Jekyll Island Club boat service is scheduled in direct connection with arrival and departure of FLORIDA SPECIAL (West Coast) patrons. A modern air-conditioned coach train between Nahunta and Brunswick makes close connections with FLORIDA SPECIAL (West Coast).

W. H. HOWARD,
General Passenger Agent
Wilmington, N. C.

ATLANTIC COAST LINE RAILROAD

No. 23—Issued November 25, 1939.

Although commercial air service was available to Savannah, one associate member, David Sinton Ingalls of Cleveland, Ohio, preferred his private plane, which arrived at Jekyll on March 18, 1939. Edwin Gould was reputed to have been the first to bring a plane to the island, where, according to his biographer, Kimball Aamodt, he flew in 1914 "with courageous members of the Jekyl Island colony as nervous passengers." (Georgia Department of Archives and History)

club register, but it is obviously not his signature. Furthermore, army records indicate that on April 3, Patton left Fort Benning for Indio, California, via Mobile, Alabama. His official route did not include Jekyll Island. After the club's closing, the register was temporarily kept by J. D. Compton of Sea Island, who did not recall seeing the Patton signature in the book at that time. Who wrote the Patton name in the register, why, and even when remain a mystery. The truth is far less dramatic.[32]

The club opened as usual for the 1942 season. Nevertheless, Bernon Prentice was worried for a number of reasons. Transportation was becoming increasingly difficult and fuel in short supply, important factors for a club whose guests came primarily from New York; labor was growing both scarce and expensive as workers were being diverted into the war effort. On March 3, Marian and Margaret Maurice invited Mrs. Prentice to tea. As though she were her husband's emissary bringing the bad news, she gave them a "long account of club finances." Three days later the early closing of the club was announced, but despite the announcement, the Jekyll Island Club remained open through Easter with the help of the Sea Island Company.[33]

The Maurice sisters began to make plans to depart. It is obvious from the thoroughness of their packing and from their arrangements to have shipped back to Athens, Pennsylvania, certain family pieces, books, papers, china, and pictures, that they were expecting to be away for longer than usual. Movers came for their furniture on March 15, but they stayed for ten days more, airing blankets and storing teacups. Their slow and deliberate packing belies the theory of a sudden, overnight evacuation.

Finally, on March 26, they left Jekyll on the club's cruiser, the *Sydney*, for a visit to the Hofwyl Plantation. The rain which began about noon and continued throughout the day reflected their mood. Three days later, on Palm Sunday, Ophelia Dent drove them to Saint Mark's in Brunswick for church services and then to the Cloister for lunch. They were welcomed warmly at the splendidly landscaped resort designed, like Jekyll, for the enjoyment of the nation's wealthy. Marian Maurice could fully appreciate the surroundings but felt the lack of what for her had been fifty-four years of family pleasures. She wrote in her diary: "Beautiful plantings good lunch, but oh! the contrast to Jekyll."[34]

12. End of the Club Era

The closing of the club in April 1942 was never intended by its president, Bernon Prentice, to be definitive. When he wrote Bill Jones at Sea Island on April 6 to thank him for helping make it possible to keep the club open through Easter, he expressed uncertainty about the future but clearly held out hopes for a 1943 season. As late as June he asked Jones's advice about operating "on a very limited scale," indicating that he would "hate to close the Club down" after so many years of continuous operation. Jones's response did little to cheer him: "I wish I could be more optimistic over the possibility of a successful operating setup at Jekyll next winter. At present it looks rather difficult, but," he added hopefully, "things may change by fall, and the outlook may be more rosy." But things did not change, and on September 23, Prentice communicated his decision to the Sea Island president: "On account of the difficulty of fuel, transportation, labor and supplies . . . we will not attempt to open Jekyll Island this winter." In fact, the club would not open for the 1943 season or ever again.[1]

Prentice made every effort to hold things together during the war. He needed income to pay a small staff of caretakers and provide at least minimal maintenance of the property. He contemplated leasing the island to the government for military purposes but after discussing this possibility with various resort managers concluded that, instead of making a profit on such a venture, the club would most likely lose money. He decided, therefore, to "let nature take its course." Prentice was never able to find a satisfactory solution to Jekyll's financial problems during the war.

Of necessity he continued the timbering operations and did everything he could to cut costs, but losses were persistent, and he often had to dip into his own pocket to help out.[2]

Other problems plagued him as well. One of the island's boats, the *Sylvia*, burned to the waterline in July 1942. In October 1944 a storm struck the island, eroding the beach, destroying golf holes, and washing out bridges. Finding a reliable resident superintendent to assist M. L. De Zutter and oversee the island during wartime proved difficult. In addition, naval coast patrols did considerable damage to the roads which they failed to repair.[3]

Nevertheless, Prentice was "most anxious to have Jekyll continue as a club after the war." By July 1943 he had come up with a scheme for "forming a syndicate" to buy the island "with all that is on it." Excited about the prospect, he deluged Bill Jones with letters outlining his ideas.

> A few of our members I know would go along, Bert Milbank, Ned Sunderland, Frank Gould, Gerry Milliken, Bob Struthers, Vincent Astor, Emery [Amory] Houghton and myself and I do hope that you could form a group from down your way. . . .
>
> We could make many intelligent changes, perhaps a dock at the north end, a Casino on the beach, a new (additional) diesel engine to do away with coal in the power house and laundry and a helicopter.[4]

Jones was not altogether unreceptive, but he exercised a healthy skepticism about simply trying to restore the past. It was his opinion that a causeway between Jekyll Island and the mainland was essential. He had concluded after talking with aviation experts that helicopters would not be "commercially practical" for at least five

Aerial shot of the Jekyll Island Club on the eve of World War II. (Everett Collection, Coastal Georgia Historical Society)

Alfred W. (Bill) Jones of the Sea Island Company at Cabin Bluff game preserve about 1940. (Sea Island Company)

years or longer. He was also concerned about the erosion of the beaches, the problem of sandflies, the outdated buildings and furnishings, and the need for improvements. And he recognized that "though some of us enjoy the [Victorian] atmosphere we are decidedly in the minority." To implement the syndicate proposal on a sound basis would, in his judgment, require a substantial sum of money. He had concluded, therefore, that "a successful operation of the present club facilities . . . after the war . . . would be practically impossible unless some fairy godfather could make up operating deficits. With the tax situation that confronts us it just doesn't seem to me that there will be enough rich people that will want to foot the bill." And that, of

The launch *Sylvia* at the club house wharf in 1940. The *Sylvia,* allegedly named for Sylvia Brewster, burned to the waterline in July 1942. (Jekyll Island Museum)

course, was the crux of the matter, for even in its heyday the club had been sustained only by the generosity of a few of its wealthiest members.[5]

Despite Jones's pessimism about Jekyll, he was willing to seek ways to overcome the obstacles and was vitally interested in the implications of the project for his own Sea Island resort. Prentice continued to talk up the prospects with well-to-do acquaintances and, at the behest of Jones, sent real estate experts to look over the island.

At the same time he worried about how he could manage even to hold things together until the war was over. Most club members had completely lost interest, and one by one cottage owners were donating their houses to the club. By the end of 1942 only the Maurices, the Goulds, the Jenningses, and the annex association still

retained private ownership of their properties, and the Jennings cottage would be turned over to the club not long thereafter. Although the Sans Souci had ceased to be listed as a separate entity in the tax records as early as 1942, the owners did not officially convey the property to the club until April 4, 1944, when they held a special meeting in New York to "sell" the property to the Jekyll Island Club "for a consideration of $1.00."[6]

The timbering contract with the American Creosoting Company, which had brought in almost $44,000 from 1941 until 1944, was the only thing keeping the club afloat financially. Dues had not been collected since the closing. Taxes were piling

Club employees take the launch *Kermath* on a picnic to Cypress Lumber Mill. The sale of timber by the Jekyll Island Club provided a needed source of income during the depression and war years. (Jekyll Island Museum)

up or, at best, paid sporadically. Interest had not been paid on the club's income bonds since April 1, 1940. And club officials feared foreclosure on its mortgage. It was clear that something had to be done.[7]

Although Prentice had not entirely given up the idea of reopening after the war as a private club, the soundest solution seemed to be either to incorporate on an independent, commercial basis as a resort modeled after the Cloister or to sell Jekyll to the Sea Island Company to be run as an adjunct to its present facilities. Either way, the first order of business was to acquire the outstanding stocks and bonds to give the partners a free hand in doing whatever they wanted with the island. On June 8 and again on August 1, 1944, letters were sent to all Jekyll Island bondholders from the

vice president of the National Bank of Brunswick. Serving as an agent for Bill Jones and Frank Miller Gould, he offered ten cents on the dollar for the outstanding first and refunding mortgage bonds, which had been issued under the refinancing plan of 1933. Prentice, perhaps because he felt that any personal involvement in the syndicate would appear to be a conflict of interest with his position as club president, did not participate in the effort to buy up the bonds. In fact, he sold $16,000 of his own bonds to the syndicate.[8]

The syndicate's plan seemed to be working well, and efforts were begun to get all records in order, determine tax liabilities, obtain accurate descriptions of the property, secure appraisals, and do title searches—all necessary whether they reincorporated on an independent basis or decided to sell.[9] All activity came to an abrupt end, however, with the sudden

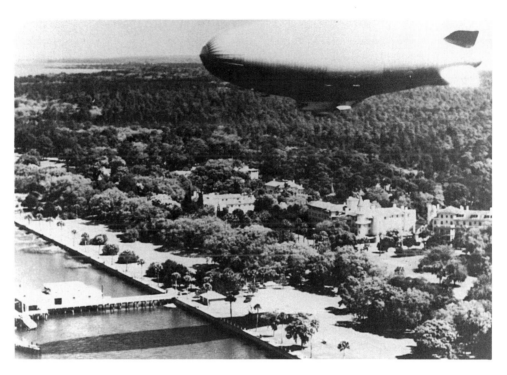

Navy blimp crossing Jekyll Island on a routine submarine patrol during World War II. (Official photograph of U. S. Navy, Coastal Georgia Historical Society)

death from a heart attack of forty-five-year-old Frank Gould on January 13, 1945. Gould had been the only club member left with sufficient expendable funds to construct the causeway between Brunswick and Jekyll, which Jones believed essential if their plan was to succeed.

At this point Jones began to consider seriously the possibility of the Sea Island Company's purchasing the Jekyll property. A New York law firm prepared for him lengthy memoranda outlining the various pros and cons of the Jekyll Island acquisition and reflecting one of his major concerns, that "If Jekyll Island by reason of foreclosure of the mortgage or otherwise should fall into the hands of strangers, the character of operation and development would be unpredictable and might indeed be highly undesirable and even damaging to the Sea Island Company." The matter was still being deliberated in late March when J. D. Compton, by then president of the

Sea Island Company, submitted to Jones, who had been made chairman of the board in October 1944, a detailed feasibility study which indicated that the costs of putting the island into shape would exceed $130,000, while the first-season profits would be less than $9,000. It hardly seemed at the time a sound business venture, so Jones's final decision was not to make the investment. [10]

He would, nonetheless, remain very much a part of the picture. By the summer of 1946 Jekyll Island was being overseen entirely by the Sea Island Company, and on August 1 of that year, Jones was officially elected a stockholding member of the club, paying one dollar for his share. Another postwar member elected to the club was Lawrence Condon, the New York attorney who, in helping Mrs. Frank Gould settle the estate of her husband, had ac-

J. D. Compton (pictured), president of the Sea Island Company, and Bill Jones oversaw Jekyll Island during the war years. (Sea Island Company)

Governor Melvin E. Thompson. In 1946, as commissioner of revenue, Thompson initiated action that would eventually lead to state condemnation of Jekyll Island during his gubernatorial administration. (Georgia Department of Archives and History)

quired Gould's Jekyll Island property for himself. Condon, who had been active in revitalizing several New York clubs, still believed that it could be reopened on its prewar basis, but both Jones and Compton remained convinced that this was not practicable. As for Prentice, he was only sure that something had to be done—and soon. "There is no way that I know of," he concluded, "for the Club to go on as it has been. . . ." None of them foresaw what finally happened.[11]

The State of Georgia entered the picture in August 1946. Revenue Commissioner Melvin E. Thompson decided at the conclusion of World War II that he would like to see the state purchase one of the Georgia sea islands for use as a public park and persuaded Governor Ellis Arnall to appoint him to head up a special state beach park committee. The committee considered and ruled out, for a variety of reasons, such sites as Blackbeard Island, Saint Simons, and Ossabaw. They might have obtained Ossabaw for three-quarters of a million dollars, but, as committeeman and Brunswick attorney Charles Gowen remarked, "if the State was going to spend anything like that kind of money," it might as well buy Jekyll, an island synonymous with unlimited wealth. In Brunswick there was an expression, "Settin' on Jekyll," which had for years carried the connotation of absolute well-being, just this side of heaven.[12]

The seed was planted. On August 19, 1946, Gowen, speaking for the state, for the first time broached the idea of buying Jekyll in a telephone conversation with J. D. Compton. Was it available? he wanted to know. And if so, at what price? Compton suggested that a million dollars or so would probably be a fair assessment of the value. "Do you think it could be bought for $750,000?" Gowen asked. "Charlie," came the reply, "I don't know if it can be bought at all and am doubtful if it can, but I am quite sure it couldn't be bought for $750,000."[13]

Not in the least discouraged by Compton's comments, committee members organized a party of state officials and other interested persons, including Thompson and a reporter from the *Atlanta Constitution,* to tour the island ten days later. They liked what they saw, and at that point matters began to move rapidly. The following day, September 19, the first public announcement of the state's intentions appeared in the Atlanta newspapers. According to the press, Thompson's committee had recommended that Georgia "take such steps immediately as are necessary for the acquisition of Jekyll Island for state park purposes." Buried deep in the article was the prediction: "Purchase of the island would probably have to be through condemnation."[14]

Up to this point, Prentice appears to have been left in the dark concerning the state's design on Jekyll and especially its possible intent to condemn. In a conversation with Thompson on September 5, Compton had stated, "I am not at all sure . . . of how Prentice is going to react to this. He has a great desire to resume the operation of the Club on its old basis, with this group of people who have owned the Club property . . . since the late 1800's."[15]

When he finally did learn of developments, Prentice authorized Brunswick attorney John Gilbert to issue a statement to the press which declared that "the island has never been offered for sale at any time since its purchase by the club in 1886, and is not for sale today." The statement went on to indicate, however, that "in view of the agitation for acquisition . . . and with the full knowledge that the state . . . has the right to condemn the property, the club does not expect to proceed any further with its plans until the state's position is clarified. . . ." But, it concluded, if condemnation became a reality "the club will cooperate . . . in order to provide a public beach park for the people of Georgia." Whatever was to be done, Prentice was eager for a prompt decision. His first official contact with the state came on September 30 in the form of a letter from Governor Arnall, which stated:

> Some of Georgia's officials are most anxious to secure Jekyll Island for utilization as a State Park. . . .
>
> Before giving any consideration to the possible condemnation of any coastal property for State use, I am addressing this communication to you with the request that you advise whether the Jekyll Island Club would be interested in selling its holdings to the State of Georgia and, if so, under what terms and conditions and at what price.[16]

Prentice replied on October 3, reiterating the public statement that the island was "not for sale" but that the club would cooperate "as far as its interests will permit." Although he would await the state's decision, he contended once more that he had "planned to open the Club in a limited way this winter." He must have known that there was little chance for reopening, for he was already disposing of club property. In early October the majority of the red bugs were sold, and he discussed with De Zutter the possibility of closing the New York office.[17]

Then unexpectedly that same month Prentice received a second letter from Governor Arnall calling a halt to plans for state acquisition of the island. This change meant for the Jekyll Island Club further indecision, delay, and expense.[18]

The confusion was compounded by the November gubernatorial election which introduced a note of partisan politics into an already murky situation. It turned out to be one of the most controversial political contests in Georgia history. Eugene Talmadge won the election in a field of three candidates but died the following December before he could be inaugurated. The squabble over the gubernatorial succession boiled down to M. E. Thompson, who had been elected lieutenant governor, and Talmadge's son, Herman, who was claiming victory through write-in ballots. When Governor Arnall refused to give up the governor's office to anyone but Thompson, Talmadge had him bodily carried out and seized both the office and the executive mansion. Arnall then surrendered the governorship to Thompson who set himself up as governor-in-exile in a building in downtown Atlanta.

Thompson, unlike Arnall, had not lost interest in procuring Jekyll for the people of Georgia. Once appointed acting governor by the Georgia Supreme Court, he notified Prentice on April 2, 1947, that the state was prepared to proceed "by condemnation or otherwise" to acquire the island. An informal meeting was held in Brunswick on April 7 to discuss the terms. Prentice was unable to attend because his wife was ill, but Bill Jones represented Jekyll interests. When Gowen indicated that the state might be willing to pay $750,000 to $800,000, Jones retorted that Prentice would not "consider less than a million dollars." The conference dissolved with nothing decided except to meet again in New York. Between this second meeting on April 28 and a third in Atlanta on May 19, the state lowered the price it was prepared to pay.[19]

Thompson, now confidently signing his letters as "governor," made an offer on May 19 of only $600,000 as "fair compensation" for the island with all improvements. Prentice judged the offer to be "quite inadequate" and reiterated that the island "is not for sale."[20]

On June 3, less than a week after receiving Prentice's reply, Thompson had the condemnation proceedings drawn up. Herman Talmadge was vitriolic in his attacks on "M. E. too" Thompson, as he persisted in calling the governor. He contended that Jekyll Island was sinking and that his political enemies merely wanted an island "where they can go to hide from the people and plan and scheme to spend the state's money for the favored few." Despite his protests and a few scattered editorials such as one from the *Savannah News* on June 6, 1947, which condemned the takeover as "unjust, confiscatory, undemocratic, and unAmerican," the acquisition of Jekyll by the state seemed to be a popular move and was well covered in the press, which repeated and embellished myths about the origins and history of the Jekyll Island Club.[21]

In this atmosphere the legal battle began on June 26, 1947, in Glynn County Superior Court, with Judge Gordon Knox presiding. As events would show, it was not much of a battle from the point of view of the Jekyll Island Club. Despite the fact that club officials considered the price too low, they refused to permit their attorney to take action which, in his opinion, might

Governor Ellis Arnall
hoped to acquire Jekyll
Island but gave up the plan
before he left office.
(Georgia Department of
Archives and History)

have prevented the takeover. Indeed, they encouraged him to use "every fair and legitimate persuasion" to keep the condemnation from being voluntarily dismissed by the state when, from time to time, state officials seemed on the verge of so doing. For Prentice and Jones, who were bearing the major expense in maintaining the island, the situation was becoming critical. They were no longer willing to tolerate the on-again off-again position of the state. The matter needed to be settled once and for all, and while they had hoped to get more for the island, $600,000 at this point was better than nothing.[22]

Only Condon and the Maurice sisters seemed sincere in wanting to block the state action. Condon indicated that he was "very unhappy about the State taking the property and have requested my counsel in Brunswick to see if it is not possible for me to retain my property. I really love the place and I am sure I would not be troublesome to any neighbors I might have on

Jekyll Island." If he loved the island after such a short attachment to it, how much more the Maurice sisters must have felt the pain of separation after a sixty-year association. They were, however, reconciled to the fact that little could be done if the state was determined. When the takeover seemed imminent in late June, they began making plans to go to Jekyll and remove their remaining possessions from Hollybourne. Like all other Jekyll Islanders at this point, they turned to Jones for help. And, as always, he was ready to do whatever he could, arranging for boat transportation to the island, lighters to move the furniture, and a moving van to take it north.[23]

Then in July another unexpected event further delayed any action by the state. A suit had been filed not by a Jekyll Islander but by a Talmadge supporter, a state legislator and Dublin banker named Herschel Lovett, to "enjoin the State Parks Department from issuing . . . revenue bonds for the purchase of Jekyll Island," which, he contended, was "a poor investment for the state of Georgia." The Lovett injunction was viewed generally as pure politics and a mere nuisance suit. The debate over Jekyll Island promised to be a major political issue in the 1948 special gubernatorial election if the matter could not be cleared up prior to voting time. Nothing further could be done until Lawrence Condon's and Representative Lovett's suits were settled.[24]

The Condon matter was quickly dismissed when the state refused to hear a separate petition, forcing Condon to become a party to the general condemnation proceedings. The Lovett suit also met with a ruling in favor of the state in late July,

and the date was set for the condemnation hearing. The only unsettled matter that remained was what the state would pay. Both the Jekyll Island appraiser and an independent appraiser had valued the property at $850,000, while the state's appraiser had set its worth at $675,000.

On October 4, Judge Knox finally handed down the decree that gave the State of Georgia the right to condemn Jekyll Island for a compensation to its owners of $675,000. Court records in Brunswick revealed that the club received only $153,353.19, to be split among the remaining stockholders. The rest was divided among Lawrence Condon ($60,000), Margaret Maurice ($20,000), Bernon Prentice ($14,590.56 for tax liens he held against the Jekyll property), the Bankers Trust Company ($11,306.25), The New York Trust Company ($396,750), The Jekyll Annex Association ($18,000), and

two Brunswickians who claimed title rights to a part of Latham Hammock ($500 each). On October 7, 1947, the state took possession of the island, "a playground," according to M. E. Thompson, "that now belongs to every Georgian." It had been a bargain for the state, in spite of Talmadge's objections, and for the Jekyll Island stockholders, it had, Jones judged, been "a good solution to a difficult problem."[25]

Governor Thompson had to move quickly to prove the worth of his purchase before election time. Within a matter of weeks hundreds of convicts had been brought to the island to begin the process of preparing it for state use. Although the target date for opening the island as a state park was January 15, 1948, club members were given until January 1 to remove their belongings. The Maurice sisters came to Sea Island in October to arrange transportation of their effects back to Athens, Pennsylvania.

For the aging sisters the task of "dismantling our dearly loved house" was "heartrending." Compton did what he could to make them comfortable and to provide assistance from the Cloister. Marian Maurice expressed her appreciation for the help: "I am wondering to whom our thanks should go for the beautiful packing of the shells which insured their safe arrival. . . . They will be a lovely memory of Jekyll and I know that I will never look at them without a grateful thought for their respite of peace and comfort afforded us . . . in the old cottage of which we have many memories of past days of happiness on Jekyll." She thanked him also for the accommodations he had provided them at the Cloister and for "the comfort and beauty of the place . . . the friendly atmosphere . . . and . . . courteous attention. The combination will take us back there some day I know, in

Margaret Maurice (center) and guests on the front porch of Hollybourne during one of her last years on Jekyll Island. (Southern Historical Collection, University of North Carolina)

spite of the fact that many times we have asserted that when Jekyll was lost to us we never wanted to see the coast of Georgia again."[26]

There remained only the legal technicalities, the final settlement of accounts, and the disposition of club furnishings and other property. Many of the club house and cottage contents were sold to Lawrence Condon, the Cloister, an antique dealer in Atlanta, and various other individuals. Additional matters were resolved at a final stockholders' meeting on November 5 in the New York office of Davis, Polk, Wardwell, Sunderland & Kiendl, Edwin (Ned) S. S. Sunderland having been a member of the club. At that time, Prentice presented the various club obligations, which included compensation for services rendered by the Sea Island Company, sundry legal fees, outstanding notes, and taxes.

A claim of $36,000 had been submitted by Superintendent De Zutter, who had agreed to work for no compensation from 1939 until 1947, years in which Jekyll was

running a large deficit. Now that the club had received final payment from the state, however, he expected compensation for back services. The claim was ultimately settled for $15,000.

At the same meeting, club officials voted to donate to the State of Georgia most of the furnishings of Faith Chapel (with the exception of the communion service and altar cloth, which went to Saint Marks in Brunswick), the contents of the infirmary and the library, and two paintings of historical interest, one a portrait of Sir Joseph Jekyll, the other a depiction of the slaveship *Wanderer*.

Finally, the stockholders made a provision for an annuity of $30 a month for Ophelia Polite, a seventy-one-year-old black employee who had lived her entire life on the island. She was "the only employee of the Club of such long standing . . . and in view of her long and faithful service," the stockholders concluded that "it was only fair, appropriate and proper that [such] provision should be made. . . ." The Maurice sisters had privately provided an annuity for their caretaker, Charlie Hill.[27]

The Jekyll corporation was formally dissolved on January 31, 1948, but final assets were not distributed to the remaining stockholders until December 30 of that year, after all claims had been settled. In the end, each of the nine remaining stockholders received a cash distribution of $10,590.18. Bill Jones donated his share to the Thomas and Jones Educational Foundation and, hence, made no personal profit for all his efforts.

The Jekyll Island Club's last president, Bernon Prentice, died on June 13, 1948, less than five months after the dissolution of the organization. Most of the records of the Jekyll Island Club were subsequently scattered, some apparently destroyed in the

"cleanup" of the island in preparation for the influx of eager Georgians, and others were simply lost to time and neglect. The "era of splendid isolation," as one newspaperman referred to it later, had forever ended on Jekyll Island.

During the club's active years, the island had been not only a seasonal haven for millionaires but also a home for many island workers, white and black, who had been an integral part of its history. Jekyll society, stratified though it was, had been composed not just of Rockefellers, Vanderbilts, and Goulds, but of Cowmans, Etters, and Clarks, of Denegals, Polites, and Hills as well. With the closing of the club a way of life had come to an end for them all.

Before his death and in a final gesture as club president, Prentice had sent a check to Captain Clark's widow for the amount that had been reduced from his pension when the club had gotten into financial difficulty. She wrote her thanks, with a touch of nostalgia: "I am only sorry that Captain is not here to enjoy it with me. . . . Jekyll was home to us and he loved it." She had many "pleasant memories of the years—seeing the club grow and sad thoughts seeing it go down."[28]

Her daughter, Catherine, had closely followed the state's takeover of Jekyll, for she was now employed as secretary to Bill Jones at Sea Island. Many years later, in 1978, Nancy Albright Hurd, the daughter of John J. Albright, recalled in a newspaper interview the delights of her young life on Jekyll Island, remembering her Christmases there and her happy rides on the upper deck of the Jekyll launch. Catherine Clark, now in her seventies, saw the article and wrote to her: "I am Catherine Clark, the daughter of Captain Clark who let you sit on the upper deck of the *Jekyll*—and maybe in the pilot house where he always let me sit. Those were happy days on Jekyll and I am glad there is someone else who remembers them too."[29]

The memories of the two women had merged, weaving their bright skeins of childhood joys into the fabric of this unique club which had endured for sixty-two years. As a visitor once said, it had been "the only place of its kind in the world—and will never be again."[30]

Members of the Jekyl Island Club, 1886–1947

NAME	DATES OF MEMBERSHIP
Albright, John Joseph	1890–1931
Aldrich, Nelson Wilmarth	1912–1915-E-1927*
Aldrich, Winthrop Williams	1927–1939
Allerton, Samuel Waters	1893–1893
Anderson, William Pope	1888–1897-E-1912
Andrews, Avery DeLano	1929–1931
Arnold, Benjamin Walworth	1908–1911
Aspinwall, Lloyd	1886–1886
Aspinwall, Lloyd, Jr.	1886–1892
Astor, Vincent	1916–1945
Atkinson, Henry Morrell	1906–1915
Auchincloss, Gordon	1929–1931
Auchincloss, Emma Burr Jennings**	1932–1942
(Mrs. Hugh Dudley Auchincloss)	
Austin, William	1888–1897
Bacon, Hope Norman	1930–1937
(Mrs. Elliott Cowdin Bacon)	
(Mrs. Paul E. Gardner)	
Bacon, Martha Waldron Cowdin	1926–1940-E-1941
(Mrs. Robert Bacon)	
Baker, Frances Emma Steers (Lake)	1897–1905
(Mrs. Frederic Baker)	rejoined
	1913–1919
Baker, Frederic	1888–1913
Baker, George Fisher	1901–1931
[Baldwin, William B.]	1886†
Ballantine, John Herbert	1895–1906
Barber, Amzi Lorenzo	1901–1903
Baring, Alexander	1888–1898
Barker, Lewellys Franklin	1924–1931
Barnes, John Sanford	1896–1899
Barron, John Connor	1886–1899
Bartlett, Francis	1886–1911
Bartow, Francis Dwight	1931–1945
Beale, William Gerrish	1918–1923
Beard, Anson McCook	1927–1929-E-1931
Bellamy, Frederick Wilder	1930–1934
Bertron, Samuel Reading	1904–1917

*"E" denotes that the member's estate continued to own stock in the club for a number of years.

**Female members are listed by their names as they appeared at the time of membership. If married one or more times, their married names are given in parentheses.

†Designates individuals who, though elected to the club, never became members because of non-payment of dues, initiation fees, or stock subscriptions.

Biddle, Lynford	1928–1933
Billings, Cornelius K. G.	1904–1919
Blair, Clinton Ledyard	1902–1910
Blair, John Insley	1928–1939
Blake, John Amory Lowell	1929–1931
Bleistein, George	1892–1915
Bliss, Cornelius Newton	1886–1911
Bliss, Cornelius Newton, Jr.	1912–1921
Bliss, Jeannette Atwater Dwight	1919–1923
(Mrs. George Theodore Bliss)	
Bliss, Lillian Plummer	1911–1912
Boeckmann, Egil	1921–1947
Bond, Frank Stuart	1900–1912
Borden, Matthew Chaloner Durfee	1892–1912
Bourne, Frederick Gilbert	1901–1919
Bourne, Marian C.	1919–1937
(Mrs. Robert George Elbert)	
Bourne, Marjorie	1920–1929
(Mrs. Alexander Dallas Thayer)	
Brewster, George Stephenson	1919–1936-E-1940
Brewster, Robert Stanton	1912–1939-E-1940
Brice, Calvin Stewart	1887–1898-E-1902
Brinton, Jacob Percy	1898–1902
Brown, Charles Stelle	1924–1935
Brown, McEvers Bayard	1886–1926
Burrill, Edward Livingston, Jr.	1927–1931
Butler, Cornelia Stewart	1909–1915
(Mrs. Prescott Hall Butler)	
Butler, Prescott Hall	1895–1901-E-1909
Byrne, James	1919–1930
Cannon, LeGrand Bouton	1901–1906-E-1909
Carhart, Amory	1926–1928
Choate, Arthur Osgood	1929–1935
Claflin, Arthur Brigham	1889–1904
Claflin, John	1886–1912
	rejoined
	1921–1938-E-1940
Clark, Edward White	1899–1904-E-1909
Clark, Herbert Lincoln	1909–1915
Clark, Stephen Carlton	1916–1939
Clarke, Thomas Curtis	1886–1896
Clowry, Robert Charles	1912–1917
Cochrane, Alexander	1886–1895
Coe, Henry Edward	1925–1934-E-1935
Condon, Lawrence M.	1946–1947‡

‡Elected after the club had ceased to operate.

Converse, Edmund Cogswell	1911–1915
Coppell, George	1900–1901-E-1902
Corning, Erastus	1886–1893
Coykendall, Robert Bayard	1903–1911
Crane, Charles Richard	1916–1924
Crane, Florence Higinbotham	1919–1940
(Mrs. Richard Teller Crane, Jr.)	
Crane, Richard Teller, Jr.	1912–1931-E-1932
Crosby, Franklin Muzzy	1914–1925
Cross, Eliot	1928–1931
Crouch, Herbert Edwin	1915–1921
Cunningham, Briggs Swift	1893–1899
Cutting, Robert Fulton	1923–1934-E-1940
Cutting, William Bayard	1886–1912-E-1915
Dabney, Charles William	1911–1915
Dana, Richard Henry	1926–1928
Daniels, Charles Meldrum	1924–1932
Davis, John Tilden	1922–1926
Davison, Henry Pomeroy	1912–1917
Deering, Charles	1887–1902
de Forest, Robert Weeks	1898–1931
De Koven, John	1886–1898-E-1899
Delano, Eugene	1910–1920
Dexter, Josephine Moore	1896–1901
Dexter, Samuel	1893–1894-E-1896
Dexter, Wirt	1886–1890-E-1893
Dick, John Henry	1916–1925-E-1926
Dick, William Kingsland	1926–1931
Dickerman, Watson Bradley	1886–1892
Doane, John Wesley	1887–1896
Dows, Tracy	1915–1919
du Bignon, John Eugene	1886–1896
Duncan, Stuart	1909–1911
D'Wolf, William Bradford	1886–1891
Eames, Edward Everett	1886–1901
Edwards, Lewis	1886–1895
Elbert, Robert George	1926–1929
Elliott, Howard	1921–1928
Ellis, Rudolph	1886–1915
Ellsworth, Duncan Stuart	1895–1908
Ellsworth, James William	1915–1924
Eno, Amos F.	1904–1915-E-1919

Fabyan, George Francis	1891–1907-E-1908
Fairbank, Nathaniel Kellogg	1886–1903-E-1905
Ferguson, Henry	1906–1917-E-1923
Ferguson, Walton	1887–1922
Ferguson, Walton, Jr.	1902–1906
Field, George Spencer	1891–1897
Field, Henry	1886–1890-E-1908
Field, Marshall	1886–1906-E-1909
Finney, Newton Sobieski	1886–1897
Fish, Latham Avery	1886–1908
Fisher, Henry Johnson	1917–1943
Fisk, Pliny	1915–1923
Forrest, Charles Robert	1889–1902
Foulke, William Dudley	1895–1908
Frick, Childs	1927–1947
Furness, Walter Rogers	1886–1901
Gary, Edward Stanley	1921–1926
Gavin, Michael	1924–1933
Goelet, Ogden	1886–1897-E-1903
Goelet, Robert	1886–1899-E-1901
Goelet, Robert II	1901–1902
Goelet, Robert Walton	1901–1934
Goodyear, Frank Henry	1902–1907-E-1909
Goodyear, Frank Henry, Jr.	1916–1930-E-1932
Goodyear, Josephine Looney	1909–1915-E-1916
(Mrs. Frank Henry Goodyear)	
Gould, Edwin	1899–1933-E-1940
Gould, Edwin, Jr.	1914–1917
Gould, Frank Miller	1924–1945-E-1946
Gould, George Jay	1895–1916
Grant, Hugh John	1909–1910-E-1912
Grant, Julie M. Murphy	1912–1919
(Mrs. Hugh John Grant)	
Gray, George Edward	1886–1886
Grosvenor, James Brown Mason	1886–1905-E-1915
Gurnee, Walter Suffern	1886–1904
Guthrie, William Dameron	1926–1928
Hadden, Hamilton	1929–1934
Hall, John Loomer	1929–1936
Hammond, John Henry	1917–1939
Harding, Dorothea Barney	1930–1934
(Mrs. James Horace Harding)	

Harding, James Horace	1916–1929-E-1930
Harkness, Edward Stephen	1911–1923
Harris, Dwight Miller	1900–1903-E-1904
Harrison, Thomas Skelton	1906–1909
Hawley, Edwin	1910–1912-E-1915
Hayes, Edmund	1886–1921
Henry, Bayard	1926-1926-E-1931
Henry, Jane Irwin Robeson (Mrs. Bayard Henry)	1931–1934
Herrick, Parmely Webb	1928–1931
Herter, Christian Archibald	1905–1910-E-1911
Higgins, Andrew Foster	1886–1904
Higgins, Eugene	1891–1947
Hill, James Jerome	1888–1916
Hill, Mary Theresa Mehegan (Mrs. James Jerome Hill)	1916–1921-E-1924
Hoadley, Mary Eliot Betts (Mrs. Russell H. Hoadley)	1926–1930
Hoffman, Charles Frederick	1895–1897-E-1912
Hoffman, Eugene Augustus	1892–1902-E-1912
Hoffman, William Mitchell Vail	1928–1932
Holter, Edwin Olaf	1925–1931
Hooker, Elon Huntington	1919–1932
Hope, Walter Ewing	1925–1931
Hopkins, Amos Lawrence	1886–1912
Hoppin, Bayard Cushing	1925–1931
Hoppin, Gerard Beekman	1923–1938
Houghton, Alanson Bigelow	1919–1941-E-1942
[Houston, James Buchanan]	1887†
Howland, Henry Elias	1886–1901
Hubbard, Elijah Kent	1886–1888 rejoined 1899–1909
Hubbard, Thomas Hamlin	1904–1915
Hyde, Charles Livingston	1902–1905
Hyde, Henry Baldwin	1886–1899-E-1901
Inman, John Hamilton	1886–1889
Isham, William Bradley	1894–1909-E-1912
James, Helen Goodsell Jennings (Mrs. Walter Belknap James)	1926–1942
James, Henry Ammon	1924–1929-E-1930
James, Lucy Wortham (Mrs. Huntington Wilson)	1925–1929
James, Norman	1918–1931
James, Walter Belknap	1917–1927
Jarvie, James Newbegin	1910–1929

Jenkins, Helen Hartley	1909–1934-E-1935
Jennings, Annie Burr	1938–1939-E-1940
Jennings, Jean Pollock Brown	1934–1941
(Mrs. Walter Jennings)	
Jennings, Lila Hall Park	1920–1924
(Mrs. Frederick Beach Jennings)	
Jennings, Walter	1926–1933-E-1934
Jesup, Maria Van Antwerp DeWitt	1909–1910
(Mrs. Morris Ketchum Jesup)	
Jesup, Morris Ketchum	1888–1908-E-1909
Jewett, Augustine David Lawrence	1886–1898
Johnstone, Hugo Richards	1899–1907
Jones, Alfred William	1946–1947‡
Jones, Nathaniel Scammon	1887–1891
Keep, Frederic Augustus	1888–1891
Kellogg, Frederic Rogers	1923–1932
Kennedy, Emma Baker	1910–1919
(Mrs. John Stewart Kennedy)	
Kennedy, John Stewart	1898–1909-E-1910
Kernochan, Marshall Rutgers	1926–1934
Ketchum, Franklin M.	1886–1888
King, David H., Jr.	1889–1903
King, Henry William	1888–1898
King, Oliver Kane	1886–1886
Krech, Alvin William	1916–1928-E-1931
Lake, Henry Steers	1912–1917
Lanier, Charles	1889–1926
Lawson, Leonidas Moreau	1886–1895
Lawson, William Thornton	1887–1888
Ledyard, Lewis Cass	1902–1916
Lee, Cornelius Smith	1919–1947
Lee, Elliot Cabot	1915–1920
Lester, John Threadgold	1888–1890-E-1893
Lindley, Erasmus Christopher	1922–1940
Longstreth, Charles	1906–1915
Loomis, Edward Eugene	1926–1937
Loomis, John Mason	1886–1900-E-1910
Lorillard, Pierre	1886–1886
	rejoined
	1888–1891
Lorillard, Ruth Hill	1931–1947
(Mrs. Pierre Lorillard)	
(Mrs. Anson McCook Beard)	
(Mrs. Emile John Heidsieck)	

Macy, George Henry	1902–1918-E-1921
Macy, Valentine Everit	1909–1927
Macy, William Kingsland	1921–1930
Magee, John	1893–1908
Masten, Arthur Haynesworth	1928–1935-E-1938
Maurice, Archibald Stewart	1924–1928
Maurice, Charles Stewart	1886–1924
Maurice, Margaret Stewart	1924–1947
McCagg, Ezra Butler	1886–1902
McClave, Edmund Wilkes	1886–1895
McCormick, Cyrus Hall, Jr.	1891–1936
McCrea, Willey Solon	1893–1927
McHarg, Henry King	1906–1911
McKay, Gordon	1891–1903-E-1905
McLane, Allan	1924–1928
McVeigh, Charles Senff	1929–1931
Medill, Joseph	1888–1893
Milbank, Albert Goodsell	1922–1943
Milliken, Gerrish Hill	1924–1947
Moore, John Godfrey	1892–1899
Morawetz, Victor	1912–1918
Morgan, John Hill	1930–1942
Morgan, John Pierpont	1886–1913
Morgan, John Pierpont, Jr.	1913–1943
Morgan, William Fellowes	1925–1934
Morris, Ray	1929–1931
Mortimer, Stanley Grafton	1926–1928
Nelson, Murry	1888–1899
Newcomb, Horatio Victor	1886–1888
Nickerson, Hoffman	1912–1919
Ogden, Richard Livingston	1886–1892
Ogilvie, Helen Slade	1917–1925
(Mrs. Clinton Ogilvie)	
O'Shaughnessy, James Francis	1887–1894
	rejoined
	1899–1914
Palmer, Edgar	1914–1939
Palmer, Stephen Squires	1911–1913-E-1914
Papin, Kate Rennett Allerton	1893–1899
(Mrs. Francis Sidney Papin)	rejoined
(Mrs. Hugo Richards Johnstone)	1907–1937-E-1940
Parkhurst, Charles Henry (Honorary)	1894–1909
Parks, George Elton	1930–1934
Parmly, Duncan Dunbar	1897–1898
Parrish, James Cresson	1888–1893

Paterson, Robert Warden	1902–1910
Paul, Anthony Joseph Drexel	1927–1933
Pearsall, Thomas Willits	1886–1896
Pell, Alfred	1898–1901-E-1902
Pelton, Franklin Dwight	1902–1906
Phoenix, Phillips	1905–1921
Pierson, John Fred	1888–1892
Porter, Henry Kirke	1891–1921-E-1924
Pratt, Harold Irving	1924–1939
Prentice, Bernon Sheldon	1924–1947
[Price, Dunbar]	1886†
Procter, Harley Thomas	1902–1910
Procter, William Alexander	1895–1898
Procter, William Cooper	1898–1902
Pruyn, Robert Clarence	1897–1931
Pulitzer, Joseph	1886–1911-E-1912
Pulitzer, Ralph	1912–1914
[Pullman, George Mortimer]	1888†
Pyne, Moses Taylor	1915–1921-E-1931
Randall, Blanchard	1921–1931
Ream, Norman Bruce	1886–1902
Reed, Lansing Parmalee	1926–1937-E-1938
Renwick, James	1887–1895
Richardson, William King	1922–1929
Roche, Francis George Burke	1915–1919
Rockefeller, William	1886–1922
Rogers, Edmund Pendleton	1932–1941
Rogers, Fairman	1886–1897
Rumsey, Dexter Phelps	1895–1901
Sampson, Charles E.	1929–1931
Sard, Grange	1886–1886
Sawyer, James Denison	1930–1931
Schley, Grant Barney	1903–1917-E-1919
Schwab, Gustav Henry	1907–1912-E-1915
Scrymser, James Alexander	1894–1918-E-1920
Sears, Henry Francis	1905–1910
Shattuck, Frederick Cheever	1912–1929
Sheldon, Edwin Bernon	1901–1907
Shrady, George Frederick	1904-1907-E-1908
Shrady, Hester Ellen Cantine (Mrs. George Frederick Shrady)	1908–1916
Slade, George Theron	1909–1913 rejoined 1916–1937

Sloane, John	1897–1897
Sloane, John	1919–1934
Smith, James Hopkins	1897–1900
Smith, Robert Dickson	1886–1888
Snow, Frederick Augustus	1915–1918
	rejoined
	1925–1929
Spencer, Louisa Vivian Benning	1909–1919-E-1938
(Mrs. Samuel Spencer)	
Spencer, Samuel	1898–1906-E-1909
Spoor, John Alden	1916–1926
St. George, George Baker	1926–1928
Stackpole, Joseph Lewis	1886–1888
Steward, John	1921–1923
Stewart, George David	1925–1933-E-1934
Stewart, John Aikman	1886–1907
Stewart, William Adams Walker	1911–1918
Stickney, Carolyn Foster	1904–1909
(Mrs. Joseph Stickney)	
Stickney, Joseph	1886–1903-E-1904
Stillman, James	1892–1918-E-1919
Stotesbury, Edward Townsend	1909–1919
Strassburger, Ralph Beaver	1919–1924
Struthers, William	1887–1890
	rejoined
	1895–1911-E-1912
Talmadge, Edward Taylor Hunt	1902–1908
Taylor, William Hickok	1901–1914
Terry, John Taylor	1924–1929
Thayer, Alexander Dallas	1929–1937
Thomas, Samuel	1901–1903-E-1905
Thompson, Henry Burling	1927–1931
Thorne, Edwin	1888–1889-E-1894
Thorne, Jonathan	1888–1900
Thorne, Oakleigh	1900–1902
Thorne, Samuel	1886–1895
Thorne, William	1888–1896
Touzalin, Albert Edward	1886–1889-E-1891
Turnure, George Evans	1925–1931
Tyler, Alfred Lee	1888–1891
Vail, Henry Hobart	1897–1925-E-1926
Vail, Theodore Newton	1912–1920
Vanderbilt, William Kissam	1886–1902
Van Santvoord, Alfred	1900–1901-E-1902
Van Wickle, Augustus Stout	1895–1898-E-1900
Vaughan, William Warren	1919–1931

Walters, Henry	1901–1931
Wardwell, Allen	1924–1942
Waterbury, John Isaac	1902–1915
Watmough, John Goddard	1896–1897
Welsh, Charles Newbold	1909–1911
Wetherill, Samuel Price	1905–1914
Whipple, William Denison	1886–1899
Whitney, George	1928–1941
Willard, Edward Kirk	1886–1888
Willard, Joseph Edward	1907–1913
Willets, Howard	1909–1911
Williams, Thomas	1921–1935-E-1936
Woodruff, Samuel DeVeaux	1887–1902
Woodruff, Welland DeVeaux	1904–1920
Woodward, George	1926–1936
Wyeth, John	1886–1907-E-1908

Associate Members

(This class of membership was adopted in 1933.)

Aldrich, William Truman
Allen, George Garland
Allen, Robert Eugene
Alston, Robert Cotton
Amory, John Singleton
Armour, Lester
Auchincloss, Reginald
Audibert, Xavier M.

Bailie, Earle
Baker, John Stewart
Bartholomew, George H.
Bellamy, Frederick Wilder*
Benton, Charles V.
Biddle, Lynford*
Blanchard, Archibald
Bliss, Cornelius Newton, Jr.*
Bodman, George M.
Bodman, Henry Edward
Bogue, Morton Griswold
Booker, Neville Jay
Booth, Willis H.
Bradford, Lindsay
Bradley, Albert
Brady, William Gage, Jr.
Brown, Lewis Howland
Buckner, Mortimer N.

Callaway, Merrel Price
Campbell, H. Donald
Cannon, William Cornelius
Carpenter, George W.
Catlin, Randolph
Chace, Mrs. Franklin
Cochrane, Thomas
Coe, George V.
Crawford, David A.
Cummings, Wilbur Love
Cushman, Paul
Cutler, John W.

Davis, John William
Davison, Henry Pomeroy*
Dick, William Kingsland*

Dorrance, Arthur Galbraith
Dulles, John Foster
Duncan, Stuart*
Dunlap, Charles Edward

Edmonds, Dean Stockett
Engelsted, Knud
Eppley, Marion
Erminger, Howell B., Jr.
Ewing, William

Ferry, Mansfield

Gardner, Robert Abbe
Gates, Arthemis L.
Gerdes, John
Gibbons, Douglas
Gibson, Harvey Dow
Gilbert, S. Parker
Gordon, Richard H.
Graham, Albert D.
Groesbeck, Clarence Edward

Hadden, Hamilton*
Hadley, Morris
Haggerson, Fred H.
Hall, Perry E.
Hammond, John Henry*
Harrison, George Leslie
Heinz, Howard
Henry, Jane Irwin Robeson*
Hite, George E., Jr.
Hope, Walter Ewing*
Houghton, Amory
Howard, George H.
Huidekoper, Reginald S.
Hunt, Richard Carley

Ingalls, David Sinton
Ingalls, Fay

Jackson, Donald E.
Jackson, John Gillespie
Jameson, Jeanetta
Jennings, Annie Burr*

*Denotes regular members who were also associates.

Kernochan, Marshall Rutgers*
Kiendl, Theodore
King, Herbert Thorn
Kinney, Gilbert

Lamb, John R.
Lamont, Thomas William
Leeds, William B.
Lloyd-Smith, Wilton
Loew, E. Victor
Lord, J. Couper
Lovett, Robert Abercrombie
Lyon, George Armstrong

Macy, William Kingsland*
Manville, Hiram Edward
Marshall, James A. K.
McGarrah, Gates W.
McInnerney, Thomas Henry
McLucas, Walter Scott
Mills, Dudley Holbrook
Mitchell, William DeWitt
Moorhead, William S.
Morgan, Henry Sturgis
Morgan, Junius Spencer
Morgan, Shepard Ashman
Morgan, William Fellowes*
Morris, Caspar W.
Morrow, Frederick Keenan
Murphy, James Bumgardner
Myrick, Julian S.

Paul, Anthony Joseph Drexel*
Place, Hermann Gauntlett

Ranolphy, Francis Fitz
Rentschler, Gordon S.
Richardson, Franklin S.
Richardson, Henry Smith
Ripley, Joseph Pierce

Robinson, James Dixon
Rogers, H. Pendleton
Rogers, Mrs. H. Pendleton
Ross, Leland H.
Russell, Faris R.
Rutgers, Nicholas G., Jr.

Sampson, Charles E.*
Savage, Ernest C.
Schley, Reeve
Sloan, Alfred Pritchard, Jr.
Spaulding, Vaughan C.
Spencer, Henry Benning
Springs, Eli B.
Steers, J. Rich
Stetson, Eugene William
Stockton, Phillip
Strawn, Silas Hardy
Struthers, Robert
Stuart, Robert Douglas
Sunderland, Edwin S. S.

Taft, Walbridge S.
Taylor, Irving H.
Taylor, Myron Charles

Wagner, Ernest C.
Waldon, Sidney D.
Walker, George H.
Ward, Harry Edwin
Watson, Thomas John
Wheeler, Wilmot Fitch
White, Robert H.
Williams, Andrew Murray
Winston, Garrard Bigelow
Woodruff, Robert Winship

York, Edward Howard
Young, John M.

Notes

Abbreviations Used in Notes

AC   *Atlanta Constitution*

BAA   *Brunswick Advertiser and Appeal*

BC   *Brunswick Call*

BJ   *Brunswick Journal*

BN   *Brunswick News*

BTA   *Brunswick Times-Advertiser*

BTC   *Brunswick Times-Call*

BRP   Brune-Randall Papers, MS. 2004, Manuscripts Division, Maryland Historical Society Library, Baltimore, Maryland

CMP   Cyrus Hall McCormick, Jr., Papers, State Historical Society of Wisconsin, Madison, Wisconsin

FP   William D. Foulke Papers, Library of Congress

GCP   George Cowman Papers, Jekyll Island Museum, Jekyll Island, Georgia

HP   Henry B. Hyde Papers, Baker Library, Harvard University Graduate School of Business Administration, Boston, Massachusetts

JIM   Jekyll Island Museum, Jekyll Island, Georgia

JPMP   J. P. Morgan, Jr., Papers, Pierpont Morgan Library, New York, New York

JPP   Joseph Pulitzer Papers, Rare Book and Manuscripts Library, Columbia University, New York, New York

MP   Maurice Family Papers, Southern Historical Collection, Library of the University of North Carolina, Chapel Hill

NYT   *New York Times*

SICR   Sea Island Company Records, Sea Island, Georgia

WAP   Winthrop Aldrich Papers, Baker Library, Harvard University

WMP   William McKinley Papers, Library of Congress

WRP   William Rockefeller Family Papers, Rockefeller Archive Center, North Tarrytown, New York

1. Formation of the Club

1. J. Bryan III, "Privacy Unlimited: Island Refuge for the Harried Rich," *Saturday Evening Post*, 8 March 1941, 16–17, 93. The myth has been perpetuated by Tallu Fish, *Once Upon an Island: The Story of Fabulous Jekyll. Historical, Pictorial, Legends, Anecdotes* (Darien, Ga.: *Darien News*, 1959), p. 17, and by Cleveland Amory, *The Last Resorts* (New York: Harper & Brothers, 1948), p. 153.

2. Finney's West Point career is documented in United States Military Academy Application Papers, 1805–1866, Record Group 94, Records of the Adjutant General's Office, Microcopy 688, file 90, roll 185, National Archives, Washington, D.C.; card file, United States Military Academy Archives, West Point, N.Y.; N. S. Finney to Aunt, 20 November 1854, copy in Finney file, JIM, original in possession of Mrs. Lawrence C. Liebrecht.

3. For information on the du Bignon family, see du Bignon file, JIM; Tom Henderson Wells, *The Slave Ship Wanderer* (Athens, Ga.: University of Georgia Press, 1967), pp. 24–27, 34–35, 41, 45, 58–59, 85–86. Finney's work in the coast survey is recorded in the Reports of the Superintendent of the U.S. Coast Survey, 1856–1861, Washington, D.C.

4. Newton Finney to Edwin Finney, 16 March 1866, copy in Finney file, JIM, original in possession of Mrs. Lawrence C. Liebrecht.

5. *Brunswick—The City By The Sea. A Pamphlet Descriptive of Brunswick and Glynn County Georgia* (Brunswick, Ga.: *BAA*, 1885), p. 13; Prospectus of the Jekyl Island Club, April 1, 1887, pp. 8–9, JIM (hereafter cited as Prospectus); *BAA*, 22 August 1885; John E. du Bignon, "Abstract of titles to Jekyl Island, Ga.," in possession of Mrs. Lawrence C. Liebrecht; Glynn County, State of Georgia, Superior Court, Deeds and Mortgages, book Y, 1885, pp. 302–3 (hereafter cited as

Glynn County Deeds); Charlotte Marshall Maurice and Charles Stewart Maurice, *Jekyl Island: Some Historic Notes and Some Legends and a Brief Outline of the Early Days of the Jekyl Island Club* (n.p.; n.d.), p. 9 (hereafter cited as Maurice, *Jekyl Island*).

6. For transactions regarding the acquisition of Jekyl by du Bignon see *BAA*, 18, 25 April, 20 June 1885; Glynn County Deeds, book Y, 1885, pp. 303–6; Maurice, *Jekyl Island; Brunswick—The City By The Sea*, pp. 9, 21. Sketches of Claflin are in *The National Cyclopaedia of American Biography* (New York: James T. White & Company, 1893), 3:729; John H. Ingham, ed., *Biographical Directory of American Business Leaders* (Westport, Ct.: Greenwood Press, 1983), 1:161–62.

7. William Von Rensselaer Miller, ed., *Select Organizations in the United States* (New York: Knickerbocker Publishing Company, 1896), p. 302.

8. Glynn County Deeds, book AA, 1886–87, pp. 672, 675; Jekyl Island Club subscription list, February 17, 1886, copy in JIM, original in possession of Mrs. Lawrence C. Liebrecht.

9. Henry B. Hyde to David H. King, Jr., 16 December 1885, Letterpress book A-22, HP.

10. The Jekyl Island Club record of shares, JIM. Unless otherwise specified, all subsequent references to the exchange of club shares will be based on this source.

11. Glynn County Deeds, book AA, 1886–87, p. 388; Prospectus, p. 11; extracts from the reports of officials made to the shareholders at their meeting, 25 May 1887, HP.

12. Jekyl Island Club charter, constitution, by-laws, officers, and members for the year 1886, JIM.

13. All officers served on the board of directors (or board of governors as it was later called).

2. The Early Seasons

1. Prospectus, pp. 16–17.

2. Executive committee meetings, 1886–1919, Minutes, 6 December 1886, JIM (hereafter cited as Minutes).

3. Laura Wood Roper, *FLO: A Biography of Frederick Law Olmsted* (Baltimore: Johns Hopkins University Press, 1973), pp. 327, 333–34, 339, 376, 407; Elizabeth Stevenson, *Park Maker: The Life of Frederick Law Olmsted* (New York: MacMillan Publishing Company, 1977), pp. 162, 307, 315, 396.

4. Quoted in Theodora Kimball Hubbard, "H. W. S. Cleveland: An American Pioneer in Landscape Architecture and City Planning," *Landscape Architecture* 20 (January 1930):108.

5. "Extract from the Report of H. W. S. Cleveland," in Prospectus, pp. 18–30.

6. Charles A. Alexander to Wirt Dexter, 1 May 1887, copy in Richard A. Everett Collection, used by permission of Mrs. Richard Everett (hereafter cited as Everett Collection). This collection has subsequently been deposited with the Coastal Georgia Historical Society, Saint Simons Island, Ga.

7. Minutes, 16 June 1886; *San Francisco Call*, 7 October 1900; *Forest and Stream*, 20 October 1900.

8. Report of R. L. Ogden, Supt., for the 2nd Fiscal Year, ending April 30, 1888, MP (hereafter cited as Ogden Report). See also *BAA*, 12 March, 7 October 1888; *BC*, 22 June 1899.

9. *Saturday Evening Post*, 8 March 1941; Lloyd C. Griscom, *Diplomatically Speaking* (Boston: Little, Brown and Company, 1940), pp. 323–24; circular from George H. Macy to Jekyl Island Club members, 11 December 1913, CMP.

10. Jekyl Island Club register, 1888, JIM; *BAA*, 23 February, 15, 16, 27, 30 March, 1888.

11. Ogden Report.

12. Minutes, 31 May 1888.

13. Hyde to Finney, 23 January 1889; Finney to Hyde, 24 January 1889, HP.

14. Financial statement of the Jekyl Island Club from 1 May 1888 to 1 May 1889, Everett Collection; memorandum in regard to . . . club house profits and losses, 30 May 1895, HP.

3. A Life of Elegant Leisure

1. Falk to Leland, 17 October 1898, Ernest G. Grob, Letterbook 1, JIM. All Grob letterbooks are in JIM (hereafter cited Letterbook).

2. Hyde to Frederick Baker, 12 October 1897, Letterpress book A-37, HP.

3. Falk to Tamagin, 17 September 1898, Letterbook 1.

4. Grob to Lyman Fuller, 23 October 1899; Grob to Charles Lanier, 17 January 1900, Letterbook 2.

5. Minutes, 3 December 1915.

6. Ibid., 28 November 1888; *BC*, 28 February 1900. See also Grob to H. S. McCrary, 11 February 1900, Letterbook 2.

7. Grob to Eiscene Supply & Construction Co., 21 January 1898, Letterbook 1.

8. Grob to Charles Lanier, 20 December 1898, ibid.; Grob to Lanier, 9 December, 1899, Letterbook 2.

9. Grob to Ballantine, 6 February 1898, Letterbook 1.

10. *NYT*, 9 April 1892; Hyde to Grob, 28 June 1897, Letterpress book A-37, HP; Grob to E. Peterson, 7 December 1897, Grob to H. B. Rowe, 13 January 1898, Letterbook 1; Grob to Franklin Creamery, 18 December 1900, Letterbook 2; *BJ*, 8 April 1908.

11. Charlotte Maurice Diary, 1899–1909, Daily Record of Menus and Guests from Christmas through March each Year, 17 February 1902, 22 March 1903 (hereafter cited as Maurice Menu Diary).

12. Frederick Baker to Henry Hyde, 10 October 1897, carton P-1, HP; Grob to Charles Lanier, 27 January, 1 February 1900, Grob to E. Der Verner, 11 February 1900, Letterbook 2; Grob to J. Herbert Ballantine, 9 March 1898, Letterbook 1.

13. Minutes, 9 May 1917.

14. Baker to Hyde, 20 July 1896, carton P-1, HP.

15. John S. Sturges to Joseph Pulitzer, 30 August 1899, JPP; Hyde to David H. King, 3 April 1895, Letterpress book A-33, HP; *NYT*, 4 October 1896.

16. Grob to George Coppell, 20 January 1900, Letterbook 2; Grob to Mrs. A. A. Preston, 6 March 1898, Letterbook 1.

17. Grob to Mrs. John G. Moore, 28 February 1899, Letterbook 2.

18. Baker to Hyde, 15 March 1898, carton P-1, HP.

19. Hyde to Caleb [James Hazen Hyde], n.d. 1897, HP. See also Mrs. Ray Lincoln to William McIntyre, 12 December 1898, carton P-6, HP; Julius Falk to Mrs. William Struthers, 2 July 1900, Letterbook 2.

20. *NYT*, 12 January 1898.

21. Minutes, 27 January 1897.

22. Ibid., 28 November 1888, 27 January 1897; rules and regulations for the government of the game department for the season of 1891–92, carton P-5, HP. Unless otherwise indicated, all further references to game rules are based on the above sources.

23. Game Book, JIM.

24. Baker to Hyde, 10, 20 October 1897, carton P-1, HP; Falk to Struthers, 3 August 1898, Letterbook 1.

25. Hoffman to Frederick Baker, 15 January 1898, Letterbook 1.

26. Minutes, 12 April 1905; Maurice to McCormick, 18 March 1904, CMP; Jekyll Island Club announcement, 22 October 1930, WAP.

27. Grob to A. B. Claflin, 1 April 1898, Falk to Charles Lanier, 24 October 1898, Falk to A. B. Claflin, 24 October 1898, Grob to A. B. Claflin, 30 December 1898, Letterbook 1. See also Frederick Baker to Hyde, 17 March 1898, carton P-1, HP.

28. The correspondence relating to the new golf course is voluminous, but see McCormick to George Macy, 9 March 1909, Macy to McCormick, 11 March, 22 October, 10, 24 November 1909, Grob to McCormick, 10 April 1909, Grob to F. A. Stewart, 9, 26 April, 11 May 1909, Macy to Robert Pruyn, 18 January 1910, CMP.

29. Fred C. Kelly, "The Great Bicycle Craze," *American Heritage: The Magazine of History* 8 (December 1956): 69–73; William Rockefeller to Emma Rockefeller, 19 March 1895, WRP; *BTA*, 21 February, 29 April 1896.

30. Grob to Charles Lanier, 7 January 1899, Grob to G. W. Evans, 8 January 1899, Letterbook 1.

31. William McIntyre to Grob, 16 January 1897, Letterpress book A-36, HP; Grob to William Rockefeller, 5 April 1898, Letterbook 1; Minutes, 13 May 1901.

32. Hyde to Caleb, 18 February 1898, carton P-5, HP.

33. Grob to J. H. Nelson, 8 February 1899, Letterbook 2.

4. The Early Cottage Colony

1. Clarke to Maurice, 22 February 1888, MP.

2. Frederick Baker to Charles Maurice, 20 April 1904, MP; Almira Rockefeller to Emma Rockefeller McAlpin, 14 January 1920, Emma Rockefeller McAlpin Correspondence, WRP.

3. On Brown and his cottage, see *NYT*, 9–10 April, 2, 5, 25 May 1926; *Times of London*, 9 April 1926; *Essex County Telegraph* (England) 17, 20 April 1926; Glynn County, Ga., Tax Digests, 1889–1929 (hereafter cited as Tax Digests); Grob to Lyman Rhoades, 11 May 1898, Letterbook 1.

4. On Fairbank see *NYT*, 23 May 1889, 26 June 1896; Lady Helen de Frietas, *Nathaniel Kellogg Fairbank* (n. p., privately printed, n. d.), pp. 75–86; Craig Timberlake, *The Life and Work of David Belasco: The Bishop of Broadway* (New York: Library Publishers, 1954), p. 188; Helen L. Horowitz, *Culture of the City: Cultural Philanthropy in Chicago from the 1800s to 1917* (Lexington: University of Kentucky Press, 1976), pp. 39, 41, 58, 74, 231; Tax Digests, 1890–1904.

5. Touzalin to Maurice, 25 July 1888, MP.

6. Memorandum, Burr Winston to Crovatt and Whitfield, 9 March 1892, and receipt, Crovatt and Whitfield to Winston, 11 April 1892, MP; Tax Digests, 1891–1947.

7. Minutes, 3 March 1889; *New York City Directory*, 1879–99.

8. Baker to Hyde, 2 February 1891, carton P-1, HP; Tax Digest, 1891.

9. Grob to Furness, 28 January 1901, Letterbook 2; *Philadelphia City Directory*, 1898–99; Tax Digests, 1891–97.

10. Tax Digests, 1892–1904. For sketches of McKay, see Ingham, ed., *Biographical Directory*, 2: 907–8; *Dictionary of American Biography*, s.v. "Gordon McKay."

11. Baker to Hyde, 14 January 1895, carton P-1, HP; Charles Gifford to Alfred Butes, 25 September 1899, JPP. For Pulitzer's illnesses, see W. A. Swanberg, *Pulitzer* (New York: Charles Scribner's Sons, 1967), pp. 145–46, 178. The tale "Pulitzer and the River Captain" is recounted in Fish, *Once Upon an Island*, p. 20.

12. Arthur H. Billings to Alfred Butes, 28 February 1901, JPP. See also *BTC*, 27 February 1901.

13. Hyde to Caleb, 26 January 1898, carton P-4, HP.

14. Baker to Hyde, 25 March 1898, carton P-1, Hyde to Baker, 29 March 1898, Letterpress book A-38, HP.

15. Hyde to Baker, 8 August 1897, Letterpress book A-37, HP; Tax Digests, 1898–1900; *NYT*, 21 April 1916.

5. The Czar of Jekyl Island

1. Minutes of members' meeting, 11 March 1892, carton P-5, Hyde to Baker, 24 May 1892, Letterpress book A-31, HP.

2. Charlotte Maurice to Archibald Maurice, 17 November 1893, MP.

3. Grob to C. S. Maurice, 25 August 1893, MP.

4. William T. Jenkins to Hyde, 27 September 1893, carton P-5, HP.

5. Marian Maurice to Archibald Maurice, 29 June 1893, Charlotte Maurice to Archibald Maurice, 5 December 1893, MP.

6. Swanberg, *Pulitzer*, pp. 211–14; Baker to Hyde, 17 July 1896, carton P-1, HP. See also William D. Foulke to Carl Schurz, 7 May 1897, FP.

7. Hyde to Caleb, 9 January 1895, carton P-4, Hyde to Baker, 5 February 1895, Hyde to David H. King, Jr., 3 April 1895, Letterpress book A-33, HP.

8. Baker to Hyde, 10 April 1895, carton P-1, HP.

9. Hyde to King, 3 April, 22 May 1895, Letterpress book A-33, HP.

10. Baker to Hyde, 10 April 1895, carton P-1, Hyde to Baker, 3 May 1895, Letterpress book A-33, HP.

11. Hyde to King, 31 January 1896, Letterpress book A-35, Hyde to Baker, 7 July 1897, Letterpress book A-37, HP.

12. McIntyre to Rockefeller, 15 May 1896, Hyde to Baker, 22 July 1896, Letterpress book A-35, HP.

13. Hyde to William P. Anderson, 27 July 1896, HP.

14. Hyde to Baker, 29 July 1896, HP.

15. Hyde to Stewart Contracting Company, 24 August 1896, Letterpress book A-35, A. R. Stewart to Hyde, 27 August 1896, carton P-8, HP; *BTA*, 20 September 1896.

16. Hyde to Stewart Contracting Company, 24 August 1896, Hyde to James F. Wilson, 30 July 1896, Hyde to Charles Gifford, 24 August 1896, Hyde to Baker, 26 August 1896, McIntyre to Gifford, 28 August 1896, Letterpress book A-35, McIntyre to A. W. Conover, 28 December 1896, Letterpress book A-36, HP.

17. Hyde to Baker, 18 September 1896, William McIntyre to Baker, 29 September 1896, Letterpress book A-35, HP.

18. McIntyre to Gifford, 5 October 1896, HP.

19. Hyde to Frederick Baker, 13 October 1896, HP; *BTA*, 30 September, 25 October 1896; *NYT*, 4 October 1896.

20. Hyde to Baker, 13 November 1896, William McIntyre to Charles Gifford, 18 November 1896, McIntyre to Torrey, Bright, & Capen Co., 23 November 1896, Letterpress book A-36, HP.

21. Glynn County Deeds, book SS, 1899–1900, p. 96; Hyde to William P. Anderson, 7 November 1896, Hyde to Baker, 29 July 1896, Letterpress book A-35, Baker to Hyde, 3 April, 24 December 1896, carton P-1, HP.

22. William McIntyre to Charles Gifford, 9 November 1896, Letterpress book A-36, HP.

23. Hyde to Annie Hyde, 22 January 1897, carton P-5, HP.

24. Hyde to Gifford, 8 February 1897, carton P-3, Hyde to King, 10 February 1897, Letterpress book A-36, HP.

25. Hyde to Baker, 18 March 1897, Letterpress book A-36, HP.

26. Hyde to Baker, 12 June 1897, carton P-1, King to Grob, 2 June 1897, carton P-5, Baker to Hyde, 1 July 1897, carton P-1, HP.

27. Hyde to King, 10 June 1897, Letterpress book A-37, Hyde to Baker, 2 July 1897, carton P-1, Hyde to King, 16 June 1897, Letterpress book A-36, HP.

28. Hyde to James A. Scrymser, 13 January 1898, carton P-7, HP.

29. Hyde to McIntyre, 24 September 1898, carton P-6, McIntyre to Grob, 9 March, 8 April 1899, Letterpress book A-39, HP.

30. Hyde to Baker, 15 March 1897, Constable to Hyde, 18 June 1897, Letterpress book A-36, HP.

31. Baker to Hyde, 14 June, 20 August 1897, carton P-1, HP.

32. Hyde to Baker, 24 August 1897, Letterpress book A-37, HP.

33. Hyde to Baker, 18 September 1897, Letterpress book A-37, HP.

34. Hyde to Torrey, Bright & Capen, 13 January 1898, carton P-8, HP.

35. Hyde to Grob, 24 December 1897, Letterpress book A-38, HP.

36. Hyde to A. M. Shields, 14 January 1898, carton P-7, HP.

37. McIntyre to Stickney, 3 January 1899, McIntyre to Grob, 4 January 1899, Hyde to Grob, 27 January 1899, Letterpress book A-39, HP.

38. *NYT*, 3 May 1899.

6. The President's Visit

1. Robert de Forest to William D. Foulke, 16 May 1899, FP. After resigning as president, Howland served as secretary until 1902, when he was replaced by a paid club employee named J. C. Purdy. Hyde to Baker, 13 May 1897, Letterpress book A-36, HP.

2. Hyde to Baker, 29 July 1897, Letterpress book A-37, HP.

3. Grob to C. S. Maurice, 2 May 1898, Letterbook 1.

4. Grob to Frederick Baker, 29 April 1898, Grob to Cassius E. Gillette, 9 May 1898, ibid.

5. Grob to William Struthers, 2 May 1898, Grob to William McIntyre, 9 May 1898, Grob to B. S. Cunningham, 6 May 1898, ibid.

6. Grob to Joseph Stickney, 11 May 1898, ibid.

7. The hurricane damage is described in Julius Falk to Charles Lanier, 3 October 1898, Grob to John Mason Loomis, 18 December 1898, Falk to David H. King, 3 October 1898, ibid.

8. Grob to John Mason Loomis, 28 December 1898, ibid.

9. Cornelius N. Bliss to Pres. William McKinley, 9 March 1899, WMP; *BC*, 8 March 1899.

10. G. J. Orr to McKinley, 15 March 1899, WMP.

11. Margaret Leech, *In the Days of McKinley* (New York: Harper, 1959), pp. 455, 458. Details of McKinley's visit are recounted in *BC*, 19–20 March 1899; *NYT*, 21 March 1899; William A. Robinson, *Thomas B. Reed: Parliamentarian* (New York: Dodd, Mead & Company, 1930), pp. 377–78.

7. The New Century

1. Jekyl Island Club officers, members, constitution, by-laws, and charter, 1901, JIM.

2. De Forest to William D. Foulke, 16 May 1899, FP; Grob to Frederick Baker, 13 January 1900, Letterbook 2; *BC*, 13 January, 28 February, 1, 3, 10 March 1900.

3. Grob to Charles Lanier, 26 December 1900, 9 January 1901, Letterbook 2; Minutes, 10 January 1901.

4. Grob to D. A. Tompkins, 22 October 1900, Grob to Charles Lanier, 21 November 1900, Letterbook 2; Minutes, 13 November 1902; Joseph Pulitzer to Charles Lanier, 17 March 1903, JPP.

5. Charles Lanier to Pulitzer, 8 January 1903, Grob to George Ledlie, 11 January 1903, JPP; Tax Digests, 1903.

6. Bliss to Hayes, 26 February 1901, Letterbook 2; Minutes, 25 February 1901; Hyde to Baker, 18 March 1897, Letterpress book A-36, Hyde to Baker, 29 July 1897, Letterpress book A-37, HP.

7. Spencer to Louisa Spencer, 21 October 1901, Samuel Spencer Papers, Southern Historical Collection, University of North Carolina Library.

8. *National Cyclopaedia*, 29:503; Julius Falk to Charles Gifford, 22, 30 June 1900, Grob to Porter, 16 November, 17 December 1900, Letterbook 2.

9. George F. Goodyear, *Goodyear Family History*, 4 vols. (Buffalo: privately printed, 1976), 3:45–61; Minutes, 29 April 1903; Tax Digest, 1907.

10. Maury Klein, *The Life and Legend of Jay Gould* (Baltimore: Johns Hopkins University Press, 1986), p. 486; [Kimball Aamodt], *Edwin Gould: The Man and His Legacy* (New York: Edwin Gould Foundation for Children, 1986), p. 6.

11. Marquis Boni de Castellane, *How I Discovered America: Confessions of the Marquis Boni de Castellane* (New York: Alfred A. Knopf, 1924), p. 15.

12. Grob to Cornelius Bliss, 25 March 1900, Letterbook 2.

13. Ernest Van R. Stires to Richard Everett [ca. 1966], Everett Collection.

14. *BTC*, 21 January 1901; Tax Digest, 1903; Walter Blair to George Cowman, 15 July 1913; estimate of labor and materials for the Gould Court, 21 July 1913, GCP; *BN*, 16 March 1915.

15. Minutes, 23 May 1904; *National Cyclopaedia* 7:271–72; Tax Digest, 1905.

16. Kate Brown to family, [?] February 1917, Kate Brown Letters, copies in JIM, originals in possession of Katherine G. Owens.

17. *BN*, 7, 11, 13 January 1914.

18. On the death of Edwin Gould, Jr., see Kate Brown to family, 25 February 1917, Kate Brown Letters; *BN*, 26–27 February 1917; *NYT*, 26 February 1917.

19. Lydia French to Marian Maurice, 16 February 1924, MP.

8. A Paradise Imperfect

1. Bishop of Georgia to Charlotte Maurice, 23 March 1898, 16 March 1899, 23 March 1900, MP.

2. For Charlotte Maurice's hospitality and good works, see P. J. Luckie to Charlotte Maurice, 7 February 1905; Charlotte Maurice Diary, 1 January, 21 March 1908, 23 February 1909, Maurice Menu Diary, 21 March 1908, 10 February 1909, MP.

3. Nina Maurice to Grandmother, 1 February 1899, Maurice Menu Diary, 23 March 1901, MP.

4. Nina Maurice to Grandma, 28 December 1898, MP.

5. Ibid.

6. *National Cyclopaedia* 7:201–2; Frederick Baker to Henry Hyde, 21 March 1897, 4 October 1897, carton P-1, HP; Grob to Charles Lanier, 15 January 1898, Letterbook 1.

7. Merrill to Henry Hyde, 22 April 1898, carton P-6, Edmund D. Chesbro to Hyde, 8 September 1898, carton P-2, HP; Grob to Merrill, 15 February, 18 November 1899, Letterbook 2.

8. Hyde to Jekyl Island Club, 14 February 1896, Letterpress book A-35, HP.

9. Minutes, 12 April 1905; Grob to Miss Maurice, 28 April 1909, William Merrill to Miss Maurice, 28 April 1909, MP.

10. Dent to Charlotte Maurice, 2 September 1909, MP.

11. Grob to Marian Maurice, 8 September 1909, MP.

12. Report on typhoid fever outbreak made by Dr. Charles Bolduan, James J. Hill Papers, James J. Hill Reference Library, Saint Paul, Minn.

13. Minutes, 7 February 1913.

14. Grace Meeker to Cyrus McCormick, 20 January 1910, CMP.

15. Claflin to Maurice, 27 January 1908, MP; "A [printed] Letter of John Claflin to His Children," 14 July 1918, JIM.

16. For details concerning the meeting on Jekyl see Nathaniel W. Stephenson, *Nelson W. Aldrich: A Leader in American Politics* (1930; reprint, New York: Kennikat Press, 1971), pp. 384–87; John K. Winkler, *The First Billion: The Stillmans and the National City Bank* (New York: Vanguard Press, 1934), p. 202; Frank A. Vanderlip, *From Farm Boy to Financier* (New York, D. Appleton-Century Company, 1935), pp. 211, 213–16; Paul M. Warburg, *The Federal Reserve System: Its Origins and Growth*, 2 vols. (1930; reprint, New York: Arno Press, 1975), 1:260.

17. Vincent P. Carosso, *Investment Banking in America: A History* (Cambridge, Mass.: Harvard University Press, 1970), pp. 139, 145.

18. Emily Maurice to children, 6 January 1913, MP.

19. For mention of Rockefeller's throat problems, see *NYT*, 21 March 1906, 15 October 1911; Almira Rockefeller to Emma Rockefeller, 28 February 1895, WRP. The pursuit of Rockefeller is chronicled in *NYT*, 20 October, 28, 31 December 1912, 3, 8, 9, 12–14, 16, 22–24 January, 4 February 1913; *BN*, 4–5 January 1913. Rockefeller's testimony is described in *NYT*, 8–9 February 1913.

20. Carosso, *Investment Banking*, pp. 151, 153.

21. Quoted in John Douglas Forbes, *J. P. Morgan, Jr., 1867–1943* (Charlottesville, Va.: University Press of Virginia, 1981), p. 73.

9. The Great War

1. For information on Bourne's life and business career, see *NYT*, 10 March 1919; Robert Bruce Davies, *Peacefully Working to Conquer the World: Singer Sewing Machines in Foreign Markets, 1854–1920* (New York: Arno Press, 1976), chapter 4.

2. Minutes, 28 April 1914; annual report of the president of the Georgia State College of Agriculture, minutes of the board of trustees of the Georgia State College of Agriculture, pp. 6–7, in the University of Georgia Archives, University of Georgia Libraries, Athens, Ga. Julius Falk, who had been the assistant superintendent during most of Grob's tenure, had assumed the joint duties of secretary and assistant treasurer of the club in 1909 with an office in New York. Captain Clark replaced him as assistant superintendent until Hart was employed.

3. Reports of the shooting are in the *Savannah Morning News*, 31 May 1914; *Atlanta Georgian*, 30 May 1914; *Athens Daily Herald*, 1 June 1914.

4. For the circumstances surrounding the acquittal of Thompson, see *BN*, 2, 4 June 1914; *Savannah Morning News*, 30 June, 1 July 1914; *Athens Daily Herald*, 2 June 1914; *Athens Weekly Banner*, 3 July 1914; Criminal Minutes, Superior Court of Glynn County, May Term, 3 July 1914, pp. 545–46. For references to Thompson's family see *BN*, 15 April 1914; *Brunswick City Directory*, 1917–23.

5. George H. Macy to Club Members, 2 November 1914, Nelson W. Aldrich Papers, Library of Congress; *BN*, 25, 30 October, 24 November 1914; club register, 1–2 November 1914, JIM.

6. Minutes, 1 February 1915.

7. *BN*, 2 February 1916; Grob to J. D. Essterles, 21 December 1899, Letterbook 2.

8. Recollections of Sydney Hogerton, 1964, Everett Collection.

9. Detailed report of transcontinental demonstration, 25 January 1915, American Telephone and Telegraph Archives, New York, N.Y.

10. Ibid.; John Brooks, *Telephone: The First Hundred Years* (New York: Harper & Row, 1975), p. 139.

11. Forbes, *J. P. Morgan*, pp. 87, 94.

12. Anna R. Burr, *The Portrait of a Banker, James Stillman* (1927; reprint, New York: Arno Press, 1970), pp. 340–41; Al-

bro Martin, *James J. Hill and the Opening of the Northwest* (New York: Oxford University Press, 1976), pp. 601–4.

13. *BN*, 31 October 1916.

14. All references to Kate Brown are from these letters to her family during February and March 1917.

15. *BN*, 1, 7 April 1916.

16. Forbes, *J. P. Morgan*, p. 99.

17. For club construction see Minutes, 14 June 1917; Frederick G. Bourne to J. P. Morgan, [June 1917], Grob to Morgan, 20 June 1917, Morgan to Bourne, 25 June 1917, JPMP; George Cowman to G. A. Kay, 4 August 1917, Cowman to Grob, 11, 15, 22 August, 17 September 1917, GCP.

18. Crane to McCormick, 14 March 1912, CMP.

19. *BN*, 10 March 1914.

20. For the Crane house see *BN*, 17, 28 August 1917; Cowman to G. A. Kay, 4 August 1917, GCP; Richard Pratt, *David Adler* (New York: M. Evans and Company, 1970), pp. 3–12.

21. Minutes, 9 May 1917.

22. Extracts from minutes of "Special Meeting" of the board of governors, held on Jekyl Island, 9 March 1918, JPMP.

23. F. G. Bourne to J. P. Morgan, 15, 18, 21 March 1918, Robert S. Brewster to Morgan, 25, 30 April 1918, JPMP; Bourne to shareholders of Jekyl Island Club, 13 April 1918, CMP.

10. The Golden Years of Dr. James

1. *NYT*, 10, 16 March 1919; Minutes, 10 March 1919.

2. Biographical details in "Obituary notices, Dr. Walter B. James," *Bulletin*, New York Academy of Medicine, 3 (1927):443–45; typed sketch of Walter B. James by his son Oliver B. James in possession of Henry H. Anderson, Jr.; *National Cyclopaedia* 21:25–27; *NYT*, 7, 9 April 1927.

3. Minutes, 10 March, 6 May 1919.

4. Almira Rockefeller to Emma McAlpin, 14 January 1920, McAlpin Correspondence, WRP; James to Charles Maurice, 12 April 1920, MP.

5. Krech to Aldrich, 10 April 1920, WAP.

6. James to Maurice, 3 November 1920, Maurice to Claflin, 7 November 1920, MP; James to McCormick, 6 October 1920, CMP.

7. McCormick to Grob, 30 January 1923, McCormick to James Simpson, 5 March 1923, CMP.

8. Information on the golf course is in McCormick to James Simpson, 5 March 1923, Alice Hoit to Simpson, 11 April 1923, CMP; Connie Lee to Winthrop W. Aldrich, 29 February, 10 March 1928, WAP; *BN*, 8 November 1926, 18 January 1928.

9. Walter Jennings and H. J. Fisher to Jekyl Island Club Members (printed circular), 1 March 1928, WAP.

10. Anna to Emma McAlpin, 5 September 1922, McAlpin Correspondence, WRP. See Allen Nevins, *John D. Rockefeller: The Heroic Age of American Enterprise*, 2 vols. (New York: Charles Scribner's Sons, 1940), 1:110, 288–94, 2:431–43, 526–29; Ingham, ed. *Biographical Directory* 2:1182–96; *Dictionary of American Biography*, s.v. "Rockefeller, William."

11. Almira Rockefeller to Emma McAlpin, 14 January 1920, McAlpin Correspondence, WRP.

12. Ibid.; Anna to Emma McAlpin, 5 September 1920, Almira Rockefeller to Emma McAlpin, [?] January 1920, WRP.

13. Almira Rockefeller to Emma McAlpin, 14 January 1920, WRP.

14. *BN*, 18 January 1920; Emma Rockefeller McAlpin Diary, 1916–20, entries 17, 19 January 1920, WRP (hereafter cited as McAlpin Diary).

15. McAlpin Diary, 11–28 February, 1–7 March 1921.

16. Lydia French to Marian Maurice, 16 February 1924, MP.

17. Susan Randall to Emily Randall, 4 February 1921, BRP.

18. Blanchard Randall to Emily Randall, 9 February 1921, Susan Randall to Emily Randall, [?] February 1921, BRP.

19. Randall to Evelyn Randall, [?] February 1921, BRP.

20. Randall to Susan Randall, 11 February 1922, BRP.

21. Randall to Susan Randall, 11, 12, 13, 18 February 1922, BRP.

22. Randall to Susan Randall, 13 February 1922, BRP.

23. Ibid.

24. Randall to Susan Randall, 12, 14 February 1922, BRP.

25. William Lawrence, *Memories of a Happy Life* (New York: Houghton Mifflin Company, 1926), p. 411.

26. Randall to Susan Randall, 16 February 1922, BRP; William Lawrence to Charles Slattery, 10 February 1924, William Lawrence Papers, Diocesan Library and Archives, The Episcopal Diocese of Massachusetts, Boston, Mass. (hereafter cited as Lawrence Papers).

27. Lawrence to Slattery, 30 January [?], Lawrence Papers; Randall to Susan Randall, 16 February 1922, BRP.

28. Randall to Susan Randall, 14 February 1922, Susan Randall to Bessie Randall, [?] March 1926, Randall to Emily Randall, 28 February 1922, BRP.

29. Susan Randall to Bessie Randall, [?] March 1926, Emily Randall to Bess Randall, 6 February 1926, Randall to Susan Randall, 18 February 1922, Randall to Emily Randall, 28 February 1923, BRP.

30. Randall to Susan Randall, 18 February 1922, BRP. "Scotch stories" mentioned in [?] to Dr. Frederick Shattuck, 12 March 1926, BRP. A copy of James's recollection is in the Albright file, JIM. For a slightly different version of this remark, see Amory, *Last Resorts*, p. 160. Lawrence to Slattery, 27 February 1923, Lawrence Papers.

31. Bessie Randall Slack to Harry Slack, Saturday night, 1926, BRP.

32. Ray Marshall Etter Diary, 20 February, 13 March 1926, in possession of Howard Etter.

33. Howard Elliott to Miss Maurice, 5 March 1924, MP.

34. J. P. Morgan to Ellen Vaughan, 16 March 1926, Ellen Vaughan to J. P. Morgan, 18 March 1926, JPMP.

35. McCormick to Berthet, 4 June 1927, CMP.

11. "They Doubled the L . . ."

1. H. J. Fisher to Members of the Board of Governors, 22 November 1927, CMP; Printed circular, 1 March 1928, WAP.

2. Voucher, office of John Russell Pope, 4 October 1927, GCP.

3. Mogens Tvede to George Cowman, 30 April 1928, Cowman to Grob, 31 October 1928, GCP; *BN*, 14 October 1928.

4. For a copy of the resolution see the Jekyll Island Club constitution, by-laws, charter, 1933, p. 15, CMP.

5. McCormick's contributions are discussed in F. C. Riley to E. Geyer, 19 February 1930, Riley to W. C. Cummins, 13 March 1930, Cyrus McCormick to H. E. Morelock, 14 March 1930, McCormick to Walter Jennings, 15 March 1930, CMP. The infirmary is mentioned in the report of the executive committee to annual meeting of stockholders, February 1930, JIM (hereafter cited as Report of the Executive Committee, February 1930).

6. Crane to Winthrop W. Aldrich, 8 March 1929, WAP; Report of the Executive Committee, February 1930; *BN*, 16 February, 18 June 1930.

7. Quoted in Forbes, *J. P. Morgan*, p. 171.

8. Brewster to Members, 30 July 1931, M. L. De Zutter to Members, 15 December 1931, WAP.

9. *BN*, 20 March 1930.

10. Printed announcement, 22 October 1930, Brewster to Members, 30 July 1931, WAP.

11. Marian Maurice Diary, 2 January 1931, MP.

12. Jekyll Island Club, report of the annual meeting of the members, February 1933, JIM.

13. Marian Maurice Diary, 4–9 January 1933, MP; *NYT*, 10 January 1933.

14. Brewster to Holders of Thirty-year 5% Gold Debenture Bonds of the Jekyll Island Club, 5 April 1933, JPMP.

15. *NYT*, 12, 21 October 1933; J. P. Morgan to Members of the Jekyll Island Club, 3 November 1933, WAP.

16. Morgan to Members, 3 November 1933, Henry J. Fisher to Members, 3 November 1933, WAP.

17. Lee to Aldrich, 16 November 1933, WAP.

18. Morgan to Members, 13 December 1933, WAP; George Brewster to Cyrus McCormick, 19 March 1934, CMP.

19. Brewster to McCormick, 19 March 1934, CMP.

20. Ibid.; transcribed interview with Mrs. Edward W. Fay, formerly Mrs. Reginald Huidekoper, by Richard A. Everett, 25 March 1965, Everett Collection.

21. M. L. De Zutter to Jones, 20 January 1936, Jekyll Island file, SICR.

22. Cornelius S. Lee to Members, 25 January 1936, WAP.

23. Jones to De Zutter, 5 November 1936, SICR. See also Edwin S. S. Sunderland to Jones, 8 February 1936, De Zutter to Jones, 16 October 1936, ibid.

24. De Zutter to Jones, 17 March 1936, SICR; Bartow to J. P. Morgan, 1 July 1937, Morgan to Bartow, 8 July 1937, JPMP.

25. Ellen Vaughan to J. P. Morgan, 11 March 1927, Morgan to Vaughan, 16 March 1927, JPMP; Welfare Committee to Winthrop Aldrich, 31 March 1937, WAP.

26. Forbes, *J. P. Morgan*, p. 85.

27. Morgan to Francis Bartow, 8 July 1937, JPMP; *NYT*, 31 March, 1938.

28. Prentice to Members, 14 May 1938, WAP.

29. Jones to Prentice, 6 June 1938, Prentice to Jones, 9 June 1938, SICR.

30. Prentice to Morgan, 5 May, 25 June 1939, Morgan to Prentice, 27 June 1939, JPMP.

31. Marian Maurice Diary, 4–5 January 1941, MP.

32. Elizabeth Austin Ford, *Jekyll Island* (Decatur, Ga.: Womack Printing Company, 1960), p. 51; Mary Givens Bryan, "Historic Jekyll Island," *Georgia Magazine* (August–September 1958), p. 23. Patton's official itinerary for April 1942 was outlined by Maj. Gen. Kenneth G. Wickham, adjutant general, in a letter to Richard A. Everett, May 23, 1967, Everett Collection. The accuracy of this information was verified in Grace M. Tullock, chief, Special Actions Branch, Department of the Army, to William B. McCash, 4 February 1987.

33. Marian Maurice Diary, 3 March 1942, MP; Prentice to Jones, 6 April 1942, SICR.

34. Marian Maurice Diary, 29 March 1942, MP.

12. End of the Club Era

1. Prentice to Jones, 9 June 1942, Jones to Prentice, 15 June 1942, Prentice to Jones, 23 September 1942, SICR.

2. Prentice to Jones, 18, 25 January 1943, SICR.

3. T. M. Baumgardner to Michael Gavin, 14 August 1942, Baumgardner to Jones, 31 October 1944, transcribed telephone conversation between J. D. Compton and M. L. De Zutter, 2 July 1946, SICR; AC, 13 January 1946.

4. Prentice to Jones, 25 January, 28 July, 5 August 1943, SICR.

5. Jones to Prentice, 26 November 1943, SICR.

6. Minutes of the adjourned special meeting of the stockholders of the Sans Souci Association, 4 April 1944, SICR; Tax Digest, 1942.

7. Arthur Young & Company to Board of Governors (audit), 30 April 1944, SICR.

8. A. M. Harris to Jekyll Island Bondholders, 8 June, 1 August 1944, SICR.

9. Frank M. Gould to Jones (copy to Prentice), 11 July, 1 August 1944, SICR.

10. Marion Fisher Memorandum, 16 January 1945, Edwin S. S. Sunderland to Jones, 17 January 1945, Fisher to Jones, 30 January 1945, J. D. Compton to Jones, 29 March 1946 (with attachments), SICR.

11. Prentice to Jones, 5 August 1946, Jones to Prentice, 5 August 1946, SICR.

12. J. D. Compton to Jones, 20 August 1946, SICR, reporting a telephone conversation with Charles Gowen on 19 August 1946.

13. Ibid.

14. *AC*, 20 September 1946.

15. Transcribed telephone conversation between M. E. Thompson and J. D. Compton, 5 September 1946, SICR.

16. *BN*, 26 September 1946; *AC*, 27 September 1946; Jones to Prentice, 26 September 1946, Ellis Arnall to Prentice, 30 September 1946, SICR.

17. Prentice to Arnall, 3 October 1946, De Zutter to Prentice, 4 October 1946, Jones to E. H. Messick, 1–2 October 1946, SICR.

18. Prentice Memorandum, circumstances leading up to the condemnation . . . of Jekyll Island, 14 November 1947, SICR.

19. M. E. Thompson, J. Eugene Cook, and B. E. Thrasher, Jr., to Gentlemen, 4 February 1947, Charles Gowen to Lawrence Condon, 20 May 1947, Jones to Prentice, 8 April 1947, SICR.

20. M. E. Thompson to Prentice, 19 May 1947, Prentice to Thompson, 26 May 1947, SICR.

21. *NYT*, 4, 22 June 1947; unidentified newspaper clippings, 4, 19 June 1947, Everett Collection; *Savannah News*, 6 June 1947; *Atlanta Journal*, 6 June 1947; *AC*, 20, 22 June 1947.

22. John Gilbert to Edwin Sunderland, 27 October 1947, SICR.

23. Lawrence R. Condon to Gilbert, 23 June 1947, Margaret Maurice to Jones, 21 June 1947, Jones to Margaret Maurice, 25 June 1947, SICR.

24. *BN*, 9 July 1947; Gilbert to George W. Palmer, 27 June 1947; transcribed telephone conversation between Gilbert and Jones, 11 July 1947, SICR.

25. Final decree and judgment, Superior Court, Glynn County, Georgia, 4 October 1947, SICR; *Citizen and Georgian*, 18 October 1947; Jones to Prentice, 5 June 1948, SICR.

26. Margaret Maurice to J. D. Compton, 18 October 1947, Marian Maurice to Compton, 19 November 1947, SICR; Marian Maurice Diary, 14 February–7 March 1947, passim, MP.

27. Minutes of a special meeting of the stockholders of the Jekyll Island Club, 5 November 1947, transcribed telephone conversations between Prentice and Compton, 14, 22 October 1947, SICR.

28. Minnie Clark to Prentice, 8 December 1947, SICR.

29. Catherine Clark to Nancy Albright Hurd, 26 December 1978, Albright file, JIM. The article to which Clark was responding had appeared in the *Florida Times-Union*, 24 December 1978.

30. Ernest Van R. Stires to Richard Everett [ca. 1966], Everett Collection.

Index